Expansion and Reform, 1815-1850

SOURCES IN AMERICAN HISTORY

GENERAL EDITOR: *George H. Knoles*

Professor of History and Director of
the Institute of American History,
Stanford University

1. PROVINCIAL AMERICA, 1600-1763
   BRADLEY CHAPIN, *State University of New York at Buffalo*

2. THE REVOLUTIONARY GENERATION, 1763-1789

3. THE YOUNG REPUBLIC, 1789-1815
   JOHN C. MILLER, *Stanford University*

4. EXPANSION AND REFORM, 1815-1850
   CHARLES M. WILTSE
   Chief Historian, United States Army Medical Service

5. THE UNION IN CRISIS, 1850-1865
   ROBERT W. JOHANNSEN, *University of Illinois*

6. THE UNION IN CRISIS, 1865-1877
   ROBERT W. JOHANNSEN, *University of Illinois*

7. THE NATIONALIZING OF AMERICAN LIFE, 1877-1900
   RAY GINGER, *Brandeis University*

8. THE RESPONSIBILITIES OF POWER, 1900-1929
   GEORGE H. KNOLES, *Stanford University*

9. THE NEW DEAL AT HOME AND ABROAD, 1929-1945
   CLARKE A. CHAMBERS, *University of Minnesota*

10. THE UNITED STATES IN THE CONTEMPORARY WORLD,
    1945-1962
    RICHARD L. WATSON, JR., *Duke University*

Expansion and Reform
1815-1850

Edited by Charles M. Wiltse

Chief Historian
United States Army
Medical Service

The Free Press, New York
Collier-Macmillan Limited, London

Preface

THE CHARGE IS SOMETIMES MADE THAT AMERICAN history lacks the color and drama that characterize the histories of most of the nations of Europe. The United States possesses no Italian Renaissance, no Protestant Reformation, no French Revolution, no Napoleon Bonaparte in its immediate historical heritage. If such experiences provide the sole measure of color and drama, the allegation, of course, has merit. If, on the other hand, the processes of creating a new nation from remnants of a powerful eighteenth-century European empire; expanding across 3,000 miles of land on a 1,000-mile front to provide a continental domain and bringing European civilization to a howling wilderness; and, withal, developing a political framework and practice based on, and dedicated to, democratic principles afford a different species of color and drama, then the statement needs qualification.

Dr. Charles M. Wiltse, who has a thorough understanding and an accomplished grasp of that period of our past from the close of the Napoleonic wars to the beginning of the American Civil War, has selected materials for this volume of our series that reflect the many aspects of this ebullient era of American history. Problems engendered by geographical, economic, social, and political expansion and proposals offering solutions to those problems receive attention here. Moreover, in his introductory essay, Dr. Wiltse has with consummate skill provided the student a theoretical structure useful in helping him to come to terms with these thirty-five years so significant in the growth of the new nation. Emerging from the War of 1812 somewhat the worse for wear, the American people, with a remarkable burst of energy, embarked upon a variety of programs—not all of them well con-

ceived or ably led—that brought them by mid-century a degree
of economic prosperity, political power and stability, cultural
maturity, and social cohesiveness sufficient to provide the material and psychological resources for weathering the crises of the
ensuing two decades.

Stanford University   GEORGE HARMON KNOLES

Contents

Preface by George H. Knoles   v

Introduction   1

1. Inland Commerce   23
    DeWitt Clinton: Memorial in Favor of a Canal

2. Indian Policy   37
    Jedediah Morse: Report to the Secretary of War
    on Indian Affairs

3. Foreign Relations   46
    Documents Relating to the Origins of the
    Monroe Doctrine

4. Protection of Industry   62
    Hezekiah Niles: Address of the Harrisburg
    Convention

5. The Slavery Controversy   81
    David Walker: An Appeal to the Coloured Citizens
    of the World

6. The Constitutional Debate   93
    Joseph Story: Commentaries on the Constitution

7. The Bank Controversy   107
    Andrew Jackson: Removal of Government Deposits
    from the U.S. Bank

8. Texas   127
    Stephen F. Austin: Address on Texas

9. The Democratic Principle   143
    The Democratic Review: A Confession of Faith

10. **Education**   162
    Horace Mann: First Annual Report of the Secretary
    of the Massachusetts Board of Education

11. **The Eastern States, 1841-42**   173
    Sir Charles Lyell: Travels in North America

12. **Oregon, 1843**   185
    John Charles Fremont: Report of the
    Expedition to Oregon

13. **Literature and Criticism**   201
    Ralph Waldo Emerson: New England Reformers

14. **Manners and Customs**   221
    Alexander Mackay: The Western World

15. **California, 1849**   237
    Bayard Taylor: Eldorado

16. **The Compromise of 1850**   245
    Daniel Webster: Seventh of March Speech

Expansion and Reform, 1815-1850

Introduction

OUT OF THE AMERICAN REVOLUTION CAME POLITICAL independence, but the onetime colonies, now semi-autonomous "states," remained more dependent upon Europe than they were upon each other. They were still far from achieving that "more perfect union" that had been one of the primary reasons for adopting the Constitution. The rise of Napoleon Bonaparte and the extension of the all-encompassing struggle between Great Britain and France offered new ways for some Americans to become rich, but it also showed that the states of the American Union, collectively and severally, were neither self-sufficient nor strong enough to resist determined aggression.

The War of 1812, almost accidental in its inception, incredibly bungled in its execution, and indecisive in its termination, was the turning point for American nationalism. In the flush of pride over Andrew Jackson's spectacular victory at New Orleans, the near-treasonable opposition of New England to the war was forgotten. The localism of the Hartford Convention was quickly submerged in a new spirit of self-reliance, a new awareness of the vast resources that were the heritage of all Americans, and a brash confidence in a future no longer dictated by the old world.

That future was bound up with the settlement and exploitation of the North American continent. The term "manifest destiny" would not be coined for another generation, but the concept was there, and the beginning had been made. Lewis and Clark had planted the flag at the mouth of the Columbia almost a decade earlier, and their journals, first published in 1814, were firing imaginations in the more prosaic East. Moreover, the return of peace brought a return of commerce. The British textile industry, long starved for cotton and stimulated by improved machinery, promised limitless wealth to the southern planter if only he could get enough land and enough slaves to cultivate it. The rolling country beyond the Ohio produced quantities of grain and other exportable crops, and was capable of producing still more as soon as new land could be cleared and a new wave of settlers established. Expansion would certainly be followed by prosperity, which would stimulate further expansion in endless cycles.

To be sure, there were still a few chinks in the armor of American self-sufficiency. Roads were miserable and rivers navigable by cargo vessels were both limited and long. The Atlantic cities—Boston, New York, Philadelphia, Baltimore, and Charleston—were easily accessible to Europe and to each other by sea, but the only links with the rich, boisterous, exuberant western country were the Mississippi River system, with its outlet at remote New Orleans, the Great Lakes, restricted by the falls of Niagara whose outlet was the foreign and, until very recently, enemy port of Montreal, and the National Road which by 1817 linked Baltimore and Philadelphia with the navigable waters of the Ohio, but which was slow, relatively expensive, and of meager capacity.

There was also a scarcity of manufactured products, despite significant industrial growth during the years that British goods were unavailable. To make good these deficiencies would require money—"capital" was the word coming into common use—but money, too, was lacking even for investment in a future as bright as that of young America except as the ancient enemy and new competitor seated in London might deign to lend it.

Led by men as youthful as the Union itself, America set out to provide for her own needs, cutting once and for all the umbilical cord that joined her to the mother country. In 1816 Congress voted to impose a tariff on the importation of a variety of manufactured goods, including cotton textiles, to equalize production costs and so enable American manufacturers to compete with their European rivals. At the same time the Second Bank of the United States was chartered to finance the impending expansion. Certain revenues accruing to the government from the Bank were set aside for improving internal transportation by a system of east-west roads and canals similar to the scheme Albert Gallatin had urged upon Jefferson in 1808. Collectively the tariff, the Bank, and internal improvements—called the American System in the language of Henry Clay, one of its chief architects—comprised a blueprint for national development. Tariff revenues would provide money for internal improvements, which would in turn promote markets: western and southern markets for manufactured products of the New England and middle states, eastern markets for western grain and southern cotton. The Bank would finance manufacturer and farmer, and provide a stable currency, so that neither would be cheated by inflation.

It was not important that President Madison vetoed the internal transportation measure. The states and private investors quickly supplied the needed capital in a surge of nationalism, confidence, and ebullience that was not to be denied. In all sections of the country, the order of the day was a challenge to improve, to grow, to change, to move, and to compete with one another and with a Europe that Americans were already beginning to regard with tolerant contempt. Between 1815 when the second war for national independence ended, and 1850 when that independence came close to being destroyed by internal stresses, growth in all directions was without parallel. It was the first American Age of Enterprise, when nothing seemed impossible and very little was, except perhaps self-discipline and self-restraint. In that single generation the national territory almost doubled, sweeping from the Mississippi Valley to the Pacific Ocean. Population tripled and the national wealth increased five fold. Science and technology advanced, and with them education, agriculture, industry. An identifiably American literature took root, and out of the welter of remorseless struggle for wealth and power, an American conscience emerged. It was a generation of excitement, of aggrandizement, of peril; a generation that carried the young nation to the very brink of civil war, yet left that nation powerful enough and firm enough of moral purpose to survive the holocaust when it came a decade later, and to be the stronger for it.

The mill towns of New England were already booming when the Tariff of 1816 ratified their prosperity and promised similar gain to other manufacturing areas. Only cheap transportation to market the abundance that surely lay ahead was lacking, and that was soon to be provided. On July 4, 1817, Governor DeWitt

Clinton of New York turned the first spadeful of earth for the
Erie Canal [1].* Extending more than 350 miles between Albany
and Buffalo when it was completed in 1825, the canal joined
Lake Erie with the navigable waters of the Hudson River. An
increasing volume of commerce that would have gone to New
Orleans or overland to Philadelphia and Baltimore began to
travel from Ohio and the new states of Indiana and Illinois to
the port of New York.

As New York outstripped her rival ports in size and in wealth,
Pennsylvania and Maryland chartered canal systems of their
own. In Pennsylvania the mountains were too steep and the
supply of water too meager for operation of the conventional
type of lock. Inclined planes, or ramps, were therefore substituted, over which the canal boats were hauled on rollers with
stationary steam engines furnishing the power. The system flourished for a short period, but was soon superseded by the railroad.
For similar reasons the Chesapeake and Ohio Canal, that was to
have joined the waters of the Potomac and Ohio Rivers, never
got beyond Cumberland.

Lending urgency to the development of cheap transportation
was the rapid settlement of the lands from which the Creeks and
Shawnees had been driven as a consequence of the War of
1812 [2]. The Indians themselves were eventually resettled beyond the Mississippi in what is now Oklahoma. The generation
of Americans who drove the perimeter of settlement to and beyond the Mississippi River were concerned little with morality
but much with profit, and the Indians were now too weak to bar
the way. So cotton lands replaced Creek hunting grounds in
Alabama, Mississippi, and Arkansas, while a more varied agriculture moved out onto the northwestern plains on the heels of
the Shawnees.

Meanwhile the Second Bank of the United States had opened
its doors in Philadelphia, still the financial capital of the United
States, and had begun through its branch banks an expansion
compatible with American prospects but not at all in keeping
with accepted lending practices. The Bank's officials had not
been wisely chosen, and some of the branches, notably that in
Baltimore, were soon being managed for the primary profit of

---

*Numerals in brackets refer to sections of the text.

their officers and directors. The jealousy of local banks led some of the states to impose excessive taxes upon the branches of the United States Bank, and, in the leading case of *McCulloch vs. Maryland,* to a classic dictum by Chief Justice John Marshall: the federal government is supreme over the states; the states, therefore, have no power to impede, by taxation or in any other manner, the operations of any instrumentality established by Congress within the framework of the Constitution.

The Supreme Court, however, has never had power to put hostility to rest. The Bank survived only by drastic reorganization, and the nation sagged into a depression aggravated if not actually precipitated by a policy of financial stringency. The effectiveness of the Tariff of 1816 in bringing prosperity to the protected industries made inevitable a widespread demand for still higher duties, on an extended list of imports. This agitation for more thoroughgoing protection culminated in the Tariff of 1824, which coincided in time with the selection of Nicholas Biddle to head the reorganized Bank of the United States and with the completion of the Erie Canal.

During the decade following the War of 1812 the whole face of America changed. James Monroe, last of the "Virginia Dynasty," had succeeded Madison in 1817 and now thought of himself as above party. For a time his uncompromising fairness led to the characterization of his administration as the "Era of Good Feelings." But Monroe belonged to the past—the world of Washington, whose aide he had once been, and of his friends and neighbors, Thomas Jefferson and James Madison. It was an eighteenth-century world, more European than American, concerned with philosophical concepts like the rights of man, and the historically demonstrable tendency of governments to become tyrannical in proportion to their strength. Those who spoke for the coming age of expansion and reform were young men, to whom the prerevolutionary past was no more than hearsay. For them government would be a useful instrument but never a master.

Among those who would dominate the national scene for a generation were Henry Clay, Virginia-born Kentuckian who had done more than any other to establish the American System, and through sheer force of personality exercised unprecedented power as speaker of the House; John Quincy Adams, son of the second President, seasoned diplomat, chief draftsman of the Treaty of Ghent ending the War of 1812, and secretary of state in Monroe's Cabinet; and Martin Van Buren, who had learned machine politics in the tough New York school and entered the Senate in 1821 as spokesman for the city whose interests were already distinct from those of the state.

Other major figures, best remembered for their careers in the Senate, were John C. Calhoun, New England-trained South Carolinian, who as Congressman had been a pillar of strength to the nation in the darkest days of the recent conflict, had earned his place as Monroe's secretary of war, and would soon be self-appointed spokesman for the South; Daniel Webster, who would forsake the particularism of the Hartford Convention to become the authentic voice of American nationalism; and Thomas Hart Benton who reached Missouri by way of North Carolina and Tennessee but identified himself completely with the West.

Towering over them all was the lean, austere, indomitable Andrew Jackson, at once brawler and diplomat, gambler and businessman, partisan and executive, but above all a consummate leader of men.

As the Era of Good Feelings crumbled into sectional quarrels and personal rivalries, these were the men who would pick up the pieces, and under new party labels would move the nation forward toward world power. It fell to Adams to define once and for all the American position vis-a-vis the rest of the world. The revolt of her American colonies against Spain began about the time that Monroe entered the White House. Clay urged recognition, for after all were not these fellow inhabitants of the western hemisphere simply following our own example and guiding their actions by our precepts? Adams believed them not yet ready for self-government, and refused to advise the President to intervene in their behalf. When in 1818 Jackson violated Spanish sovereignty in Florida while pursuing a band of marauding Seminole Indians, however, Adams backed him up and turned the incident into a lever that would leave Spain no alternative but to sell the Floridas, which she clearly could no longer protect, to the United States.

Adams was fresh from this diplomatic triumph when the Holy

Alliance showed signs of willingness to restore the new Latin American republics to their former colonial status. Russia simultaneously asserted a jurisdiction over the western coast of North America as far south as Vancouver Island. The Secretary repudiated both gestures as hostile to the United States, and formulated the doctrine set forth by President Monroe in his annual message to Congress in December, 1823 [3]. The western hemisphere was declared to be no longer open to colonization by any European power. Europe was warned not to interfere in American affairs, and the United States pledged herself to take no part in any war of strictly European concern. In this memorable message the United States gave public expression to the self-sufficiency that had in fact been her policy for a decade.

By 1824 the direction of national development was fairly clear. In physical terms, settlers were moving out onto the plains of Iowa, and along the lake routes into Michigan and Wisconsin. Missouri, with its old French heritage, had become a state in 1821. St. Louis, center of the fur trade long before the Louisiana Purchase, was now the jumping-off point for the Western adventurer and the settler who followed. Still other restless Americans were moving into Texas under a special grant from the Mexican government, and Arkansas, lying west of the Mississippi but with soil and climate well suited to the cultivation of cotton, was filling up with planters. Even the distant Oregon country, whose sovereignty remained undecided, was open to settlers under the terms of a treaty with Great Britain (1818) providing for joint occupation by British and American citizens.

The very nature of the expansion, however, tended to emphasize differences in economy and in social situation between the principal sections of the nation. Those moving into the northwest area, where slavery had been forbidden even before the Constitution was adopted, were predominantly from New England stock. They were farmers, artisans, merchants; they brought with them a deeply ingrained Calvinist heritage, no less persistent for being diluted by liberal congregationalism. Those who pushed into the cotton lands, on the other hand, were planters from the older South, born to a belief in slavery and convinced beyond any rational argument that their staple crop could not be profitably grown without the labor of African slaves.

Friction between North and South went back to colonial days, but its basic cause—a sharp moral divergence on the question of slavery—had been swept under the rug by those who drafted the Constitution. It came out into the open in full force when Missouri applied for admission to the Union late in 1819. A New York congressman proposed as a condition of admission that slavery in the new state be abolished, and the debate was on. This particular clash of ideologies was resolved the following year by the famous compromise under which Missouri entered the Union as a slave state and Maine, detached from Massachusetts, came in simultaneously as a free state to maintain the existing balance. The compromise then further provided that in the future slavery should not exist in any state to be thereafter carved from territory lying north of 36°30′—the parallel of latitude between Missouri and Arkansas.

The heightened sectional antagonisms brought into the open by the Missouri Compromise were still in evidence when Monroe's term as president drew to a close. Of the four leading candidates for the succession, three—Andrew Jackson of Tennessee, Secretary of the Treasury William H. Crawford of Georgia, and Henry Clay of Kentucky—were slaveholders. Only John Quincy Adams represented free soil. Jackson polled the largest number of votes, but no candidate had a majority, and so the election went to the House of Representatives where each state delegation cast one vote. There, supported by northern and northwestern votes and with the aid of Clay's following, Adams won the presidency, and again the depth of the sectional rift was revealed.

Sectional issues were already sharply in the forefront. A move led by manufacturing interests in New England and the middle states to raise the tariff duties was strongly opposed by southern senators and representatives in Congress, who argued, with some plausibility, that every increase in duties on goods imported from abroad cut down to the same extent the foreign market for their cotton. The Tariff of 1824, raising the average duty from 20 to 33 per cent, was nevertheless enacted, and the South moved closer to the unity in opposition that would in another generation lead her to renounce the Union.

It was the tariff issue, once more raised in 1827, that put

Calhoun, elected vice-president in 1824 with the support of both Adams and Jackson factions, into opposition. With the Senate deadlocked over a bill to increase the tariff on woolens, Calhoun cast his vote as presiding officer against the bill. The protective policy, however, was too profitable to northern and western manufacturers to be abandoned [4]. The "Tariff of Abominations" in 1828 put the average level of duties at 45 per cent and threw the South into near revolt. The southern position was rationalized by Calhoun in a closely reasoned paper that came to be called the *South Carolina Exposition*. It was at once a constitutional brief, an abstract treatise on political theory, and a defense of the class structure of southern society.

Paralleling these economic and social developments was the growth of a political party structure that has not changed materially from Jackson's day to our own. Jefferson's original "Republican" party had been based on an alliance between his own Virginia following and Aaron Burr's New York City machine. Expanded and refined, it became a combination of southern conservatives who wanted above all to maintain the status quo and a radical northern urban electorate growing rapidly in importance as cities grew and the franchise was extended downward. With Monroe's reelection in 1820 the old Federalist party of Hamilton and Adams passed out of existence. Over the next eight years the dominant Republican party broke into factions, out of which new parties formed. All candidates in 1824 claimed Jeffersonian descent—even Adams, the son of Jefferson's ancient rival—but the differences were just below the surface. Control of the Republican machine passed during Monroe's administration to shrewd, politically minded William H. Crawford, whose position as secretary of the treasury put at his disposal the most important elements of patronage at the national level. When illness forced Crawford into retirement after the election of 1824, Martin Van Buren took over the machine, and midway of Adams' administration turned it to the service of Andrew Jackson, in whom he recognized a sure winner.

By this date divergences of policy were so clear as to make the old Republican label meaningless. Adams and Clay, his secretary of state and political heir, began calling their faction, in terms of its emphasis, "National Republican," while the Van Buren-Jackson party, appealing as it did to people rather than to property, soon became known as "The Democracy," or simply, the Democratic party. Its success in 1828 was the measure both of its principles and of its methods. The candidate was presented in many guises to appeal to varied and even mutually antagonistic interests. In protectionist Pennsylvania, for example, Jackson had called for a judicious tariff without details; but to keep the anti-tariff South in line, Calhoun was retained on the ticket to succeed himself as vice-president. When victory was achieved, such controversial issues were avoided altogether until Van Buren, in his new role as secretary of state, had appointed to available government jobs those democrats who were most likely to appease all elements of the party.

Andrew Jackson was the last of the revolutionary generation to achieve the White House, and the first president to be elected by a vote that was truly popular in its basis of suffrage. But he was molded by, not the molder of, the age to which we give his name; its symbol rather than its moving force. The secret of his success was his uncanny knack of judging correctly the reaction of a majority of the people to any specific policy issue. He led the people where they wanted to go, and so they followed him and gave him more personal power than any previous president had ever wielded. His contributions were only two in number but they were vast in their consequences, even though they had little direct bearing on social, economic, or even political reform. He gave power, prestige, and influence to the presidency, and in an era dominated by sectional strife he never once deviated from an uncompromising nationalism, realized in the supremacy of the nation over the states.

Although Jackson's victory in 1828 was the product, as Jefferson's had been, of political strength in both northern and southern states, it did nothing to resolve the basic sectional differences. The Missouri Compromise had shown that the localism of the Hartford Convention was by no means dead. It had simply moved south where states' rights soon became the vehicle for opposition to the tariff, still believed by southern economists to be the cause of declining cotton prices in England. States' rights also proved a convenient handle for the defense of slavery, which in northern eyes increasingly was becoming a moral blight upon the nation.

Ever since the formation of the Union, and even earlier, the institution of slavery had been intermittently under attack by the Society of Friends and other religious groups. But it was never doubted by any man of good will, North or South, that slavery would eventually be given up in the South just as it had been in the North. The question argued was not "if" but "when." The Missouri Compromise changed the whole direction of the contest. In rallying to the defense of slavery in Missouri southerners admitted for the first time out loud that they did not intend to part with their "peculiar institution," then or at any time in the foreseeable future. Northerners realized with something of a shock that the institution they had considered moribund was not only alive but growing. The slave revolt of 1822 in Charleston, South Carolina, led by Denmark Vesey, a free Negro, served only to convince each group of its own essential rightness, and to make a reconciliation of differences the more difficult.

At about the same time that Vice-President Calhoun's tie-breaking vote defeated the woolens bill in 1827, opposition to slavery took a new twist. A Negro periodical, *Freedom's Journal*, appeared in New York, dedicated to the abolition of slavery. Its Boston correspondent was David Walker, whose *Appeal to the Coloured Citizens of the World* [5], published in September 1829, turned the passive resistance of the Quakers into a militant crusade. Southern reaction was immediate and harsh. State legislatures imposed curbs upon the freedom of speech and press, and established exaggerated penalties for inciting slaves. William Lloyd Garrison's *Liberator* began publication in January 1831, further to incense the South. Nat Turner's rebellion in August of that year was quickly linked with Walker and Garrison by the now thoroughly aroused South. Two years later the American Antislavery Society was formed, and the lines of cleavage were all but irrevocably fixed.

The southern defense of slavery was based on a constitutional doctrine that necessarily gave primacy to the states rather than to the federal government; but the legal principles were fought out, not over the real point of difference but in terms of a secondary or perhaps even a fictitious issue—the right of the federal government to subsidize domestic industry by means of high customs duties on competing products. In opposition to the tariff, Calhoun developed his heretical doctrine of "nullification" which held that a state, by virtue of her original sovereignty, could refuse to enforce a federal law she deemed unconstitutional until that law had been validated by three-fourths of the states— the number required to amend the Constitution.

Calhoun first propounded the doctrine in the *South Carolina Exposition* of 1828, deriving it in seemingly logical steps from the Constitution by way of the Viriginia and Kentucky Resolutions of 1798-9. It received its first full scale debate early in 1830 when it was expounded on the floor of the Senate by Robert Y. Hayne of South Carolina, challenged and eloquently repudiated by Webster in one of the most celebrated debates in American history. That might have been the end of it then and there had not the price of cotton continued to decline. The planters saw no escape from economic ruin except in a reduction of the tariff, which they had convinced themselves would in fact almost automatically restore their profits. Hard pressed by extremists who talked openly of secession, and fearful of losing power in his own state, Calhoun in the fall of 1832 led South Carolina—or was pushed by her—into invoking the remedy he had devised. A convention elected for that purpose declared the tariffs of 1828 and 1832 to be null and void and forbade their enforcement within the state.

Jackson, who had just been reelected, did not hesitate. By proclamation of December 10, 1832, he repudiated the doctrine, called upon the citizens of South Carolina to stay clear of treason, and announced his intention to enforce the law. Calhoun resigned the vice-presidency to speak for his state on the Senate floor, and again the Constitutional issue was thrashed out. The protagonists, Calhoun and Webster, argued for days with skill, learning, and eloquence; but Jackson's proclamation had already said it all. There was background and precedent in Chief Justice John Marshall's assertion of national sovereignty in a dozen leading decisions, and the theme would soon be amplified and documented by Associate Justice Joseph Story in his immensely influential *Commentaries on the Constitution* [6], but none of these expositions matched the simple logic of the President. The national government, not the states, was sovereign, and had the power to prove it if any doubt existed. The immediate issue, the tariff, was compromised, but the supremacy of the nation was not thereafter seriously challenged except in arms.

While lawyers, politicians, and editors split hairs over constitutional doctrine, a steady expansion had taken place. Manufacturing in New England and the middle states, stimulated and encouraged by the tariff and too generously financed by the Bank of the United States, had outgrown its markets. An endless stream of settlers moving into the western country produced an abundance that could not be sold, and yet continued to borrow from branches of the Bank for speculation in more land to produce more surplus. For a dozen years after its reorganization in 1822, the Bank played a major role in American expansion. Under Nicholas Biddle's expert guidance, it became the strongest and most efficient central bank in the world. But the seeds of suspicion planted by the collapse of 1819 had taken deep root. In the West, where it fell to Biddle's lot to put a curb on speculation by forcing a contraction of paper money, the Bank became an enemy. President Jackson shared this not quite rational hostility, and when he was told that Biddle had worked against his election, he responded in kind.

Although the Bank's charter would not expire until 1836, Henry Clay, then in the Senate, engineered a bill rechartering the institution in 1832. He was seeking a campaign issue in his own second bid for the presidency, but Jackson vetoed the recharter and won a triumphant reelection, materially aided by New York, whose growing business community resented the financial dominance the Bank of the United States gave to Philadelphia. In Jackson's eyes the vote was a mandate to destroy the Bank, even before its charter expired.

So in the fall of 1833, with the nullification crisis settled, Congress not in session, and all relatively quiet on the political front, the President curtly discontinued use of the Bank as a government depository. Since the institution had been established in part for this very purpose, the legality of the act was quickly challenged, and Jackson explained his economic philosophy in making public his reasons for the removal [7]. Biddle fought back; congressmen took sides, and the opposition coalesced under the party name of Whig. In the circumstances, the substitute scheme of using selected local banks as government depositories probably never had a fair chance, but it is doubtful if it ever could have curbed the over-expansion that precipitated the Panic of 1837, and the new nation's second major depression.

Although the old crosscurrents of antagonism between North and South persisted and were to a degree intensified by the hard times, the depression served to emphasize the increasing power and influence of the West as a factor in American life. Only two new states, Arkansas and Michigan, had come into the Union since the Missouri Compromise, but the rate of growth had been greatest west of the Ohio, with tentacles of settlement reaching out into the Rocky mountains and even to the Pacific. The restlessness that seemed to characterize the American from the beginning was making itself felt in many ways. Those who had begun to settle in Texas in 1821, on lands granted for that purpose to Stephen F. Austin, had shown themselves too independent of the Mexican government. In 1836 they revolted and, led by Sam Houston, a protege of Jackson from Tennessee, they won their independence [8]. Texas offered herself to the United States shortly after Van Buren had succeeded Jackson in 1837, but the President, all too aware that annexation of slaveholding Texas would destroy the Missouri Compromise and set off a new wave of antislavery agitation, chose not to act.

Texas, Oregon, the depression, persistent American interference on the side of the rebels in an incipient rebellion in Canada—all these were symptoms and concomitants of growth. Movements for social and political reform tend to emerge out of hard times. The year 1837 was another turning point. The national salvation lay in the development of a truly democratic society in the North and West, transcending the limited eighteenth-century concept of the founding fathers as completely as the territorial confines of the United States eclipsed those of 1789.

As the processes of democracy took hold, extending outward geographically and downward within the social group, a new democratic philosophy was born—new, yet so old in its roots that those who read the popular expressions of it [9] saw no departure from their own traditional faith—was evident in almost every aspect of American life. For at bottom the new democracy of the 1830's and 1840's reflected a shift of emphasis from property to the worth and dignity of man, backed up by votes no longer dependent upon the ownership of land.

The newly enfranchised citizens, for the most part, were too

close to the abuses of the past to forget their heritage. The ballot
and social reform went hand in hand. In cities like Philadelphia
and New York, workingmen's parties arose, exerting through
organization powerful pressures for improvement. Imprisonment
for debt, after long agitation, was abolished, and bankruptcy
laws were altered to favor the common man against what the
eighteenth century had called wealth and privilege. Penal institutions were gradually made less brutal. The mentally ill came
to be treated as sick people rather than as animals, thanks largely
to a frail little lady whose spirit was as tough as the New
England oak, Dorothea Dix.

An intellectual atmosphere was growing also. The liberal uni-
tarian faith gained new converts, and other denominations modified their theological dogmas on the side of charity. Men
experimented with socialism imported from France, and with
home-grown utopian communities. Inevitably the educational system, which was—and remains—the firm foundation of a democratic society, was extended [10], for no nation could hope to
survive universal suffrage without something approaching universal public education. The lecture platform vied with the pul-
pit for the adult mind. A new, self-searching literature, of which
Ralph Waldo Emerson was most representative [13], challenged
the romantic school patterned on Sir Walter Scott. First Irving,
then Cooper, Hawthorne, Melville, and Simms, used American
themes and settings, but with a new depth of meaning. This was
the golden age of American letters in all forms—an age that
included poets like Poe, Whittier, Longfellow, and Whitman;
historians like Bancroft, Prescott, and Parkman; and essayists,
novelists, and journalists by the score. It was an age of oratory,
of showmanship, of fads and fetishes, but above all of self-
expression, self-improvement, self-aggrandizement, and the iden-
tification of each with his own version of the American dream.

Only in the South, where the presence of slavery precluded
recognition of human rights, discouraged universal education,
and would soon lead to a denial of the whole concept of democracy, were the new forces of reform steadily and for a time
successfully resisted. Uneasy of conscience, living in constant
fear of servile revolt, the South moved in an orbit all its own,
pulling farther and farther away from the main stream of

American development. Only in a completely authoritarian world could slavery exist at all; so one by one the southern intellectuals renounced the democratic idea, denied or perverted their Jeffersonian heritage, and turned to a "leader" type of society. By the 1840's sectional differences in manners, customs, ways of life, and even in habits of speech were clearly discernible to the outside observer [11, 14].

Just as cultural divergences between the older sections were emphasized by the depression, so too was interest stimulated in the far West, whence came furs, buffalo hides, and the tall tales that were a recognized byproduct of the frontier. Where Lewis and Clark a generation earlier had been authentic explorers of uncharted lands, young Lieutenant John Charles Fremont, sent by the Army to survey the route to Oregon and California, would mark the trail for one of the great migrations of history. Fremont's expedition to the mouth of the Columbia in 1843 [12] helped to open the lush Oregon country to a wave of settlers and started a westward movement that would within a decade shift the balance of political power in the nation. Among the early western pioneers were the Mormons, themselves an offshoot of the "great awakening" of the early 1830's, who were driven by religious intolerance from the older, more settled regions.

Back in Washington, Martin Van Buren, who had easily defeated Clay for the presidency in 1836, was the first and most prominent victim of Jackson's erratic financial policy. The "flying Dutchman," as he was sometimes derisively called by his political foes, had been in office hardly two months when the failure of a New Orleans cotton broker touched off the Panic of 1837. Van Buren probably did as much as any president in the same situation could have done. He called a special session of Congress, and sought with indifferent success to rectify the mistakes of the past.

In the last year of Jackson's administration, with the national debt paid in full, legislation had been enacted distributing among the states the surplus revenue in the treasury. It would have made more sense to reduce taxes, or to spend the surplus at the federal level in any number of constructive ways; but both alternatives were unthinkable. An age that still gave lip service to state sovereignty could not accept increased Federal spending, while to reduce taxes would be to lower import duties and so to jeopardize the prosperity of the populous manufacturing states. Van Buren promptly halted this drain on the treasury, even as he proposed interim measures to relieve debtors and to provide immediate revenue. The most important feature of Van Buren's recovery program, however, was what came to be known as the Independent Treasury. In effect, the United States Treasury, with branches or subtreasuries in major cities, was to do its own banking, without reliance on any commercial financial institution. The scheme was inferior to the central bank Jackson had destroyed, and to the Federal Reserve System that replaced it, but it served the country adequately for three quarters of a century.[1]

Van Buren's program for economic recovery was hamstrung from the beginning by Whig opposition bent upon reestablishing a national bank, and by a growing split within his own party. The liberal wing of the Democratic party, now incorporating the powerful New York labor movement, backed the President; but these "locofocos" as they came to be called, had little in common with conservative southerners who clung to the party label but rejected its egalitarian base. The major steps that would bring about recovery had nevertheless been taken by 1840, when the next presidential election rolled around.

It was no contest. The average voter blamed Van Buren for the hard times, but gave him no credit for the already discernible improvement in the situation. In a campaign of ballyhoo and baloney, General William Henry Harrison, hero of the Battle of Tippecanoe in which the Shawnees under Tecumseh had been crushed late in 1811, easily defeated one of the most accomplished politicians in our history. Symbols of the campaign were log cabins of all sizes and hard cider by the barrel, which must have amused Harrison if he gave it any thought at all. The aristocratic son of a signer of the Declaration of Independence, he had been born in a Virginia mansion, and his preference in drink was certainly not hard cider.

---

[1] Enacted in 1840, the statute creating the Independent Treasury was repealed by the Whigs in 1841, but reenacted under Polk in 1846. It was supplanted by the Federal Reserve System in 1921.

It was enough that Harrison, like Jackson, was a military hero, though he shared none of Jackson's color, personal charm, or gift of leadership. Elected with him on the slogan "Tippecanoe and Tyler, too" was John Tyler of Virginia, a Calhoun nullifier turned Whig who was supposed to bring with him the southern splinter of the Democratic party. Whether he did or not was immaterial. In one month's time Harrison was dead and Tyler was president of the United States.

Almost at once Tyler clashed with Clay, still Whig leader in the Senate, still the most influential man in the party, and understandably hurt that he had been passed over for the nomination in a year in which victory was certain. Clay wanted to recharter a United States Bank, but Tyler had voted against recharter in the Senate in 1832, and would not now change his mind. He was soon at odds also with his former Democratic colleagues by allowing himself to be maneuvered into supporting a revival of the protective tariff. Of the Cabinet appointed by Harrison, only Daniel Webster in the state department remained after six months. Webster stayed long enough to settle most of the outstanding differences with Great Britain in the Webster-Ashburton Treaty of 1842; then he too deserted Tyler, who was now neither Whig nor Democrat but a president without a party.

It was at this point that Tyler revived the Texas question. A treaty of annexation was negotiated, awaiting only the arrival of the Texan commissioners for signature, when Secretary of State Abel P. Upshur was killed by the explosion of the great gun "Peacemaker" being demonstrated aboard the battleship *Princeton*. Calhoun came out of retirement to take the Cabinet post, but too frankly admitted the southern interest in annexation as a means of extending slavery. The reaction was immediate and sweeping. The treaty was rejected by the Senate, with even Benton, who had beaten the drums for Texas since the 1820's, voting nay. Under public pressure both Clay and Van Buren, each of them in his own party again seeking a presidential nomination, came out against annexation. Tyler persisted, however, and only days before his term expired southern slaveholders and western expansionists joined forces to pass a joint resolution embodying the provisions of the rejected treaty. Thus Tyler accomplished by a simple majority vote of both houses what he could not persuade two-thirds of the Senate to do.

James K. Polk of Tennessee, former speaker of the House and long-time Jackson protege, succeeded Tyler and deserves at least a measure of the credit for annexation of Texas, since his partisans supported it and it had been one of his campaign pledges. So, too, had been the occupation of Oregon clear to the southern limit of Russian Alaska: "Fifty-four forty or fight!" It was not Polk's expansionist views, however, that enabled him to defeat by a narrow margin Clay, who was again the Whig candidate. He won the presidency because the first avowed antislavery candidate, James G. Birney, representing the four-year-old Liberty Party—the political action wing of the antislavery movement—took enough Whig votes away from Clay in New York to give that decisive state to Polk. Ironically, both Polk and Clay were slaveholders; but Birney opened wide a gate that would not again be closed.

Polk's pretensions to Oregon were soon compromised at the forty-ninth parallel, the present boundary between the United States and Canada west of the Great Lakes. Texas posed a more difficult and potentially more dangerous problem, for Tyler had annexed that controversial land clear to the Rio Grande, although Mexico had never conceded that Texas extended south of the Nueces River. Between the two streams lay 150 miles of largely uninhabited but suddenly very desirable country. Under orders from the President, General Zachary Taylor marched south from Corpus Christi at the mouth of the Nueces, early in March 1846. On the northern side of the Rio Grande, opposite the Mexican city of Matamoros, he established a base which he called Fort Brown—the present Brownsville. A Mexican raid across the river cost some American lives and touched off the war that had been inevitable from the day Taylor moved an American army into the disputed territory.

The war with Mexico lasted a little over two years, adding more than half a million square miles to the United States, exclusive of Texas. It gave full scope to the military genius of Taylor and of Winfield Scott, and gave the first combat experience to those like Grant and Lee who would in another fifteen years fight against each other in one of the most destructive wars in history. But the significance of the Mexican War went far beyond the military exploits of its leaders or its territorial gains. Politically and morally it was a point of no return that brought old conflicts to a head, but at the same time renewed the nationalistic forces that would in the end resolve the sectional differences.

In the decade before the Mexican war, major technological advances had been introduced: Samuel Colt's revolver, McCormick's reaper that was destined to revolutionize agriculture, Morse's telegraph, Howe's sewing machine, Hoe's rotary press, capable of printing 8,000 newspapers an hour, and Goodyear's process for vulcanizing rubber. The canal was rapidly being superseded by the railroad, which already linked Boston, New York, Philadelphia, Baltimore, and Washington and was pushing west along the river valleys. Steam vessels and graceful Clipper ships had cut the time of the Atlantic crossing, and brought America once again close to her European heritage. Trade with England was immeasurably improved to the advantage of both countries by the simultaneous reduction of the American tariff and repeal of the British Corn Laws. Metropolitan newspapers, selling for a penny a copy, were becoming rich on advertising and were spending some of their newfound wealth to build reader interest through more sensational if not always more accurate reporting. People, goods, and ideas were on the move as they had never been before.

The Mexican War met with bitter opposition in states dominated by antislavery sentiment. Abraham Lincoln, serving his single term in the House of Representatives, voted consistently against the war measures; and in New England, Henry David Thoreau went to jail rather than pay taxes to support a war he found abhorrent. The same convictions were expressed in more pointed terms when the war was over and the boundaries of the United States extended from the Gulf of Mexico to the Pacific Ocean. Before the war was six weeks old, the basis of the opposition was made a matter of record when Pennsylvania congressman David Wilmot moved to amend a military appropriation bill by providing that slavery should be forever banned in any territory acquired as a result of the conflict.

The Wilmot Proviso did not pass, but over and over again it found its way into the debates in Congress. Northern legislatures passed resolutions of approval; southern partisans grew increasingly bitter at what they felt to be an affront to their homeland. But the North-South balance in the Senate, tacitly established by the

Missouri Compromise, held firm. Wisconsin was admitted to the Union in 1846 to counter Texas. Oregon was organized as a Territory in 1848, but only because two southern senators voted "aye." There the matter rested.

The question of admitting slavery to the territories became a major political issue in 1848, when a new third party, calling for "free soil, free speech, free labor, and free men" merged the Liberty party with the antislavery factions of both Whigs and Democrats on a platform explicitly opposing any extension of the iniquitous system. The Free Soil party nominated Van Buren for president with Charles Francis Adams, son of John Quincy Adams, as his running mate, and polled nearly 300,000 votes or about 10 per cent of all votes cast. After one more presidential election the Free Soilers would be absorbed by the new breed of Republicans, but the slavery question would never again be out of national politics until the institution was abolished.

So determined was the opposition to the spread of slavery that California, New Mexico, and Utah were still unorganized when Polk was succeeded by Zachary Taylor on March 4, 1849. About this time rumors of the discovery of gold in California were confirmed, and gold fever swept over the populous eastern states. By sea around South America; by ship to Panama, across the isthmus, and by ship again to San Francisco [15]; and by horseback, covered wagon, or afoot, adventurers poured into the new Eldorado, where most of them would remain. Almost overnight the population of the still unorganized territory grew from a handful, largely Mexicans and Indians, to almost 100,000 persons, restless, hardened by the life of mining camp and exploding seaport, and quite prepared to set up shop for themselves.

First they declared themselves a Republic; then with the blessing of President Taylor through the military governor who was still nominally in control, they met in convention, drafted a constitution that forbade slavery, and submitted it to the electorate where it was overwhelmingly ratified. An elected state legislature, as one of its first acts, chose Fremont and Tennessee-born Dr. William M. Gwin as United States senators. Permission of Congress to apply for statehood had not been sought nor given, but Fremont and Gwin were in Washington when Congress met in December 1849, ready to take their seats.

Southern fire-eaters responded with a call for a convention to meet in Nashville in the summer of 1850, perhaps to declare the South out of the Union, perhaps like the Hartford Convention only to talk and to pass resolutions. Whatever might impend, the crisis was too real and too immediate to evade. Henry Clay, now past seventy and the acknowledged elder statesman of the day, proposed what came to be known as the Compromise of 1850. The proposal called for the immediate admission of California to the Union as the free state she had declared herself to be; the establishment of territorial governments in New Mexico and Utah, without reference to slavery; the abolition of the slave trade in the District of Columbia, where the jurisdiction of Congress was not in dispute; and for the South a new, more rigorous fugitive slave law to supplant that of 1796.

In a moment of rare drama, the dying Calhoun, already too weak to stand on the Senate floor, listened tensely while Senator Mason of Virginia read his final speech—in opposition to the compromise. Three days later, on March 7, 1850, Daniel Webster replied with a mighty appeal for sectional peace that cost him much of his popularity at home but probably passed the compromise [16].

When the Nashville Convention met in August 1850, both Calhoun and Taylor were dead, Millard Fillmore was president of the United States, and the Compromise of 1850 was an accomplished fact. For the moment both slavery and antislavery forces accepted it, but neither was satisfied. All secondary issues were dead. The cleavage between North and South—or better, between those who reprobated slavery and those who defended it—was not again to be glossed over or covered up or talked away.

The Compromise postponed the Civil War, but had no bearing on the outcome of the conflict. The triumph of the Union was determined when a separation of the states was averted in the 1830's. Thereafter, although the slave states under Calhoun's tutelage gained strength through unity, the free states by virtue of their very freedom grew stronger still. In spite of the still persisting anachronism of slavery, the United States by 1850 had passed psychologically as well as in chronology the midpoint between the eighteenth and the twentieth centuries.

1

Inland Commerce

DeWitt Clinton: Memorial in Favor of a Canal*

As late as 1815 grain, hides, textile fibers, minerals, and other raw materials could be shipped from the Ohio valley by riverboat to New Orleans and thence by sailing vessel to Europe more cheaply than they could be carried overland to Philadelphia or New York. Even the National Road, which penetrated the Appalachian barrier to reach the Ohio at Wheeling in 1817, did not solve the problem because the cost of hauling freight by wagon was high and the volume limited. Water transportation remained the only feasible answer.

No one understood this better than DeWitt Clinton (1769-1828) whose early and vigorous sponsorship of the Erie Canal is now better remembered than his ten years as governor of New York or his bipartisan presidential campaign that almost upset Madison in 1812. Begun in 1817 and completed in 1825, "Clinton's Ditch" was 363 miles long, with a net rise of 568 feet from Albany to Buffalo. Although the federal government paid no part of the $7-million cost, the Erie Canal was nonetheless a major element in the combination of internal improvements, protection of domestic manufactures, and national bank that came to be known as the "American System." The *Memorial* reproduced here embodies the arguments that convinced the New York state legislature. It is written with earnestness and an almost passionate conviction that this great opportunity could not— must not—be lost or the nation itself would perish.

The standard biography is Dorothie Bobbé, *DeWitt Clinton* (New ed., Port Washington, N. Y.: Ira J. Freedman, 1962). Carter Goodrich, ed., *Canals and American Economic Development* (New York: Columbia, 1961) puts a well-worked subject into fresh perspective. In the selection contained here note (1) the analysis of benefits expected to accrue to New York City; (2) the anticipated list of commodities to be carried as freight on the canal; (3) Clinton's frank appeal to

---

*DeWitt Clinton, *Memorial of the Citizens of New York, in favour of a Canal Navigation between the Great Western Lakes and the tide-waters of the Hudson* (New York, Samuel Wood & Son, 1816), pamphlet.

patriotism against the commercial rivalry of Montreal; (4) his acute awareness of sectionalism as a potentially disruptive force; and (5) his understanding of the role of communications in overcoming sectionalism.

To the Legislature of the State of New-York,

The memorial of the subscribers, in favour of a canal navigation between the great western lakes and the tide-waters of the Hudson, most respectfully represents:

That they approach the legislature with a solicitude proportioned to the importance of this great undertaking, and with a confidence founded on the enlightened public spirit of the constituted authorities. If, in presenting the various considerations, which have induced them to make this appeal, they should occupy more time than is usual on common occasions, they must stand justified by the importance of the object. Connected as it is with the essential interests of our country, and calculated in its commencement to reflect honour on the state, and in its completion, to exalt it to an elevation of unparalleled prosperity; your memorialists are fully persuaded, that centuries may pass away before a subject is again presented so worthy of all your attention, and so deserving of all your patronage and support.

The improvement of the means of intercourse between different parts of the same country, has always been considered the first duty and the most noble employment of government. If it be important that the inhabitants of the same country should be bound together by a community of interests, and a reciprocation of benefits; that agriculture should find a sale for its productions; manufacturers a vent for their fabrics; and commerce a market for its commodities; it is your incumbent duty, to open, facilitate, and improve internal navigation. The pre-eminent advantages of canals have been established by the unerring test of experience. They unite cheapness, celerity, certainty, and safety, in the transportation of commodities. It is calculated that the expense of transporting on a canal, amounts to one cent a ton per mile, or one dollar a ton for one hundred miles; while the usual cost by land conveyance, is one dollar and sixty cents per hundred weight, or thirty-two dollars a ton for the same distance. The celerity and certainty of this mode of transportation are evident. A loaded boat can be towed by one or two horses at the rate of thirty miles a day. Hence, the seller or buyer can calculate with sufficient precision on his sales or purchases, the period of their arrival, the amount of their avails, and the extent of their value. A vessel on a canal is independent of winds, tides, and currents, and is not exposed to the delays attending conveyances by land; and with regard to safety, there can be no competition. The injuries to which commodities are exposed when transported by land, and the dangers to which they are liable when conveyed by natural waters, are rarely experienced on canals. In the latter way, comparatively speaking, no waste is incurred, no risk is encountered, and no insurance is required. Hence, it follows, that canals operate upon the general interests of society, in the same way that machines for saving labour do in manufactures; they enable the farmer, the mechanic, and the merchant, to convey their commodities to market, and to receive a return, at least thirty times cheaper than by roads. As to all the purposes of beneficial communication, they diminish the distance between places, and therefore encourage the cultivation of the most extensive and remote parts of the country. They create new sources of internal trade, and augment the old channels, for the more cheap the transportation, the more expanded will be its operation, and the greater the mass of the products of the country for sale, the greater will be the commercial exchange of returning merchandize, and the greater the encouragement to manufacturers, by the increased economy and comfort of living, together with the cheapness and abundance of raw materials; and canals are consequently advantageous to towns and villages, by destroying the monopoly of the adjacent country, and advantageous to the whole country; for though some rival commodities may be introduced into the old markets, yet many new markets will be opened by increasing population, enlarging old and erecting new towns, augmenting individual and aggregate wealth, and extending foreign commerce.

The prosperity of ancient Egypt, and China, may in a great degree be attributed to their inland navigation.—With little foreign commerce, the former of those countries, by these means attained, and the latter possesses, a population and opulence in proportion to their extent, unequalled in any other. And England and Holland, the most commercial nations of modern times, deprived of their canals, would lose the most prolific source of their prosperity and greatness. Inland navigation is in fact to the same community what exterior navigation is to the great family of mankind. As the ocean connects the nations of the earth, by the ties of commerce, and the benefits of communication, so do lakes, rivers, and canals operate upon the inhabitants of the same country; and it has been well observed, that "were we to make the supposition of two states, the one having all its cities, towns, and villages upon navigable rivers and canals, and having an easy communication with each other; the other possessing the common conveyance of land carriage, and supposing both states to be equal as to soil, climate, and industry: commodities and manufactures in the former state might be furnished thirty per cent cheaper than in the latter; or, in other words, the first state would be a third richer, and more affluent than the other."

The general arguments in favour of inland navigation, apply with peculiar force to the United States, and most emphatically to this state. A geographical view of the country, will at once demonstrate the unexampled prosperity that will arise from our cultivating the advantages which nature has dispensed with so liberal a hand. A great chain of mountains passes through the United States, and divides them into eastern and western America. In various places, rivers break through those mountains, and are finally discharged into the ocean. To the west there is a collection of inland lakes exceeding in its aggregate extent, some of the most celebrated seas of the old world. Atlantic America, on account of the priority of its settlement, its vicinity to the ocean, and its favourable position for commerce, has many advantages. The western country, however, has a decided superiority in the fertility of its soil, the benignity of its climate, and the extent of its territory. To connect these great sections by inland navigation, to unite our Mediterranean seas with the ocean, is evidently an object of the first importance to the general prosperity. Nature has effected this in some measure; the St. Lawrence emanates from the lakes, and discharges itself into the ocean in a foreign territory. Some of the streams which flow into the Mississippi, originate near the great lakes, and pass round the chain of mountains. Some of the waters of this state which pass into Lake Ontario, approach the Mohawk; but our Hudson has decided advantages. It affords a tide navigation for vessels of eighty tons to Albany and Troy, 160 miles above New-York, and this peculiarity distinguishes it from all the other bays and rivers in the United States, etc.

The tide in no other ascends higher than the Granite Ridge, or within thirty miles of the Blue Ridge, or eastern chain of mountains. In the Hudson it breaks through the Blue Ridge, and ascends above the eastern termination of the Catskill, or great western chain; and there are no interposing mountains to prevent a communication between it and the great western lakes.

The importance of the Hudson river to the old settled parts of the state, may be observed in the immense wealth with is daily borne on its waters, in the flourishing villages and cities on its banks, and in the opulence and prosperity of all the country connected with it, either remotely or immediately. It may also be readily conceived, if we only suppose that by some awful physical calamity, some overwhelming convulsion of nature, this great river was exhausted of its waters; where then would be the abundance of our markets, the prosperity of our farmers, the wealth of our merchants? Our villages would become deserted; our flourishing cities would be converted in masses of mouldering ruins, and this state would be precipitated into poverty and insignificance. If a river or natural canal, navigable about 170 miles, has been productive of such signal benefits, what blessings might not be expected if it were extended 300 miles through the most fertile country in the universe, and united with the great seas of the west! The contemplated canal would be this extension, and viewed in reference only to the productions and consumptions of the state, would perhaps convey more riches on its waters, than any other canal in the world. Connected with the Hudson, it might be considered as a navigable stream that extends 450 miles through a fruitful country, embracing a great population, and abounding with all the productions of industry; if we were to suppose all the rivers and canals in England and Wales, combined into one, and discharged into the ocean at a great city, after passing through the heart of that country, then we can form a distinct idea of the importance of the projected canal; but it indeed comprehends within its influence a greater extent of territory, which will in time embrace a greater population. If this work be so important, when we confine our views to this state alone, how unspeakably beneficial must it appear, when we extend our contemplations to the great lakes, and the country affiliated with them? Waters extending two thousand miles from the beginning of the canal, and a country containing more territory than all Great Britain and Ireland, and at least as much as France.

While we do not pretend that all the trade of our western world will centre in any given place (nor indeed would it be desirable, if it were practicable, because we sincerely wish the prosperity of all the states) yet we contend that our natural advantages are so transcendant, that it is in our power to obtain the greater part, and put successful competition at defiance. As all the other communications are impeded by mountains; the only formidable rivals of New-York, for this great prize, are New-Orleans and Montreal; the former relying on the Mississippi, and the latter on the St. Lawrence.

In considering this subject, we will suppose the commencement of the canal somewhere near the outlet of Lake Erie.

The inducements for preferring one market to another, involve a variety of considerations; the principal are the cheapness and facility of transportation, and the goodness of the market. If a cultivator or manufacturer can convey his commodities with the same ease and expedition to New-York, and obtain a higher price for them than at Montreal or New-Orleans, and at the same time supply himself at a cheaper rate with such articles as he may want in return, he will undoubtedly prefer New-York. It ought also to be distinctly understood, that a difference in price may be equalized by a difference in the expense of conveyance, and that the vicinity of the market is at all times a consideration of great importance.

From Buffalo, at or near the supposed commencement of the canal, it is 450 miles to the city of New-York, and from that city to the ocean, 20 miles. From Buffalo to Montreal, 350 miles; from Montreal to the chops of the St. Lawrence, 450. From Buffalo to New-Orleans, by the great lakes, and the Illinois river, 2,250 miles; from New-Orleans to the Gulf of Mexico, 100. Hence the distance from Buffalo to the ocean, by the way of New-York, is 470 miles; by Montreal, 800; and by New-Orleans, 2,350.

As the upper lakes have no important outlet but into Lake Erie, we are warranted in saying that all their trade must be auxiliary to its trade, and that a favourable communication by water from Buffalo, will render New-York the great depot and warehouse of the western world.

In order, however, to obviate all objections that may be raised against the place of comparison, let us take three other positions —*Chicago,* near the southwest end of Lake Michigan, and a creek of that name, which sometimes communicates with the Illinois, the nearest river from the lakes to the Mississippi; *Detroit,* on the river of that name, between Lakes St. Clair and Erie; and *Pittsburgh,* at the confluence of the Allegany and Monongahela rivers, forming the head of the Ohio, and communicating with Le Beuf[1] by water, which is distant fifteen miles from Lake Erie.

The distance from Chicago to the ocean, by New-York, is about 1,200 miles. To the mouth of the Mississippi, by New-Orleans, near 1,600 miles, and to the mouth of the St. Lawrence, by Montreal, near 1,600 miles.

The distance from Detroit to the ocean, by New-York, is near 700 miles. From Detroit to the ocean, by Montreal, is 1,050 miles. From Detroit to the ocean, pursuing the nearest route, by Cleveland, down the Muskingum, 2,400 miles. The distance from Pittsburgh to the ocean, by Le Beuf, Lake Erie, Buffalo, and New-York, is 700 miles. The same to the ocean by Buffalo and Montreal 1,050 miles. The same to the ocean by the Ohio and Mississippi, 2,150.

These different comparative views shew that New-York has, in every instance, a decided advantage over her great rivals. In other essential respects, the scale preponderates equally in her favour. Supposing a perfect equality of advantages as to the navigation of the lakes, yet from Buffalo, as the point of departure, there is no comparison of benefits. From that place the voyager to Montreal, has to encounter the inconveniences of a

---

1. Fort Le Boeuf on the headwaters of the Allegheny River, now Waterford, just south of Erie, Pa.

portage at the cataract of Niagara, to load and unload at least three times, to brave the tempests of Lake Ontario, and the rapids of the St. Lawrence.

In like manner the voyager to New-Orleans, has a portage between the Chicago and Illinois, an inconvenient navigation on the latter stream, besides the well known obstacles and hazards of the Mississippi. And until the invention of steam boats, an ascending navigation was considered almost impracticable. This inconvenience is, however, still forcibly experienced on that river, as well as on the St. Lawrence between Montreal and Lake Ontario.

The navigation from Lake Erie to Albany, can be completed in ten days with perfect safety on the canal, and from Albany to New-York, there is the best sloop navigation in the world.

From Buffalo to Albany, a ton of commodities could be conveyed on the intended canal for three dollars, and from Albany to New-York, according to the present prices of sloop transportation, for $2.80, and the return cargoes would be the same.

We have not sufficient data upon which to predicate very accurate estimates with regard to Montreal and New-Orleans, but we have no hesitation in saying, that the descending conveyance to the former, would be four times the expense, and to the latter at least ten times, and that the cost of the ascending transportation would be greatly enchanced.

It has been stated by several of the most respectable citizens of Ohio, that the present expense of transportation by water, from the city of New-York to Sandusky, including the carrying places, is $4.50 per hundred, and allowing it to cost two dollars per hundred for transportation to Clinton, the geographical centre of the state, the whole expense would be $6.50, which is only fifty cents more than the transportation from Philadelphia to Pittsburgh, and at least $2.50 less than the transportation by land and water from these places, and that, in their opinion, New-York is the natural emporium of that trade, and that the whole commercial intercourse of the western country north of the Ohio, will be secured to her by the contemplated canal.

In addition to this, it may be stated that the St. Lawrence is generally locked up by ice seven months in the year, during which time produce lies a dead weight on the hands of the owner; that the navigation from New-York to the ocean, is at all times easy, and seldom obstructed by ice; and that the passage from the Balize to New-Orleans is tedious; that perhaps one out of five of the western boatmen, who descend the Mississippi, become victims to disease; and that many important articles of western production are injured or destroyed by the climate. New-York is, therefore, placed in a happy medium between the insalubrious heat of the Mississippi, and the severe cold of the St. Lawrence. She has also pre-eminent advantages, as to the goodness and extensiveness of her market. All the productions of the soil, and the fabrics of art, can command an adequate price, and foreign commodities can generally be procured at a lower rate. The trade of the Mississippi is already in the hands of her merchants, and although accidental and transient causes may have concurred to give Montreal an ascendancy in some points, yet the superiority of New-York is founded in nature, and if improved by the wisdom of government, must always soar above competition.

Granting, however, that the rivals of New-York will command a considerable portion of the western trade, yet it must be obvious from these united considerations, that she will engross more than sufficient to render her the greatest commercial city in the world. The whole line of canal will exhibit boats loaded with flour, pork, beef, pot and pearl ashes, flaxseed, wheat, barley, corn, hemp, wool, flax, iron, lead, copper, salt, gypsum, coal, tar, fur, peltry, ginseng, bees-wax, cheese, butter, lard, staves, lumber, and the other valuable productions of our country; and, also, with merchandize from all parts of the world. Great manufacturing establishments will spring up; agriculture will establish its granaries, and commerce its warehouses, in all directions. Villages, towns, and cities, will line the banks of the canal, and the shores of the Hudson, from Erie to New-York.—"The wilderness and the solitary place will become glad, and the desert will rejoice and blossom as the rose.". . .

It is, however, alleged, that it is not practicable to make this canal; and that if practicable, the expense will be enormous, and will far transcend the faculties of the state.

Lake Erie is elevated 541 feet above the tide waters at Troy. The only higher ground between it and the Hudson is but a few miles from the lake; and this difficulty can be easily surmounted by deep cutting; of course no tunnel will be required. The rivers which cross the line of the canal, can be easily passed by aqueducts; on every summit level, plenty of water can be obtained, whenever there is a great rise or descent, locks can be erected, and the whole line will not require more than sixty-two; perhaps there is not an equal extent of country in the world, which presents fewer obstacles to the establishment of a canal. The liberality of nature has created the great ducts and arteries, and the ingenuity of art can easily provide the connecting veins. The general physiognomy of the country is champaign, and exhibits abundance of water; a gentle rising from the Hudson to the lake; a soil well adapted for such operations; no impassable hills, and no insurmountable waters. As to distance, it is not to be considered in relation to practicability. If a canal can be made for fifty miles, it can be made for three hundred, provided there is no essential variance in the face of the country; the only difference will be, that in the latter case, it will take more time, and consume more money.

But this opinion does not rest for its support upon mere speculation. Canals have been successfully cut through more embarrassing ground, in various parts of the United States; and even in part of the intended route from Schenectady to Rome locks have been erected at the Little Falls, and at other places; and short canals have been made, and all these operations have taken place in the most difficult parts of the whole course of the contemplated Erie navigation. Mr. William Weston, one of the most celebrated civil engineers in Europe, who has superintended canals in this state and Pennsylvania, and who is perfectly well acquainted with the country, has thus expressed his opinion on this subject: "Should your noble but stupendous plan of uniting Lake Erie with the Hudson, be carried into effect, you have to fear no rivalry. The commerce of the immense extent of country, bordering on the upper lakes, is yours for ever, and to such an incalculable amount as would baffle all conjecture to conceive. Its execution would confer immortal honour on the projectors and supporters, and would in its eventual consequences, render New-York the greatest commercial emporium in the world, with, perhaps, the exception, at some distant day, of New-

Orleans, or some other depot at the mouth of the majestic Mississippi. From your perspicuous topographical description, and neat plan and profile of the route of the contemplated canal, I entertain little doubt of the practicability of the measure."

With regard to the expense of this work, different estimates will be formed. The commissioners appointed for that purpose, were of opinion that it would not cost more than five millions of dollars. On this subject we must be guided by the light which experience affords in analogous cases. . . .

From a deliberate consideration of these different estimates and actual expenditures, we are fully persuaded that this great work will not cost more than 20,000 dollars a mile, or six millions of dollars in the whole; but willing to make every possible allowance, and even conceding that it will cost double that sum, yet still we contend that there is nothing which ought to retard its execution. This canal cannot be made in a short time. It will be the work perhaps of ten or fifteen years.

The money will not be wanted at once. The expenditure, in order to be beneficial, ought not to exceed 500,000 dollars a year, and the work may be accomplished in two ways; either by companies incorporated for particular sections of the route, or by the state. If the first is resorted to, pecuniary sacrifices will still be necessary on the part of the public, and great care ought to be taken to guard against high tolls, which will certainly injure, if not ruin the whole enterprise.

If the state shall see fit to achieve this great work, there can be no difficulty in providing funds. Stock can be created and sold at an advanced price. The ways and means of paying the interest will be only required. After the first year, supposing an annual expenditure of 500,000 dollars, 30,000 dollars must be raised to pay an interest of six per cent; after the second year, 60,000, and so on. At this rate the interest will regularly increase with beneficial appropriation, and will be so little in amount that it may be raised in many shapes without being burdensome to the community. In all human probability, the augmented revenue proceeding from the public salt works, and the increased price of the state lands in consequence of this undertaking, will more than extinguish the interest of the debt contracted for that purpose. We should also take into view, the land already subscribed by individuals for this work, amounting to 105,632 acres. These donations, together with those which may be confidently anticipated, will exceed in value a million of dollars, and it will be at all times in the power of the state to raise a revenue from the imposition of transit duties which may be so light as scarcely to be felt, and yet the income may be so great as in a short time to extinguish the debt, and this might take effect on the completion of every important section of the work.

If the legislature shall consider this important project in the same point of view, and shall unite with us in opinion, that the general prosperity is intimately and essentially involved in its prosecution, we are fully persuaded that *now* is the proper time for its commencement. Delays are the refuge of weak minds, and to procrastinate on this occasion is to shew a culpable inattention to the bounties of nature; a total insensibility to the blessings of Providence, and an inexcusable neglect of the interests of society. If it were intended to advance the views of individuals, or to foment the divisions of party; if it promoted the interests of a few, at the expense of the prosperity of the many; if its benefits were limited as to place, or fugitive as to duration, then indeed it might be received with cold indifference, or treated with stern neglect; but the overflowing blessings from this great fountain of public good and national abundance, will be as extensive as our country, and as durable as time.

The considerations which now demand an immediate, and an undivided attention to this great object, are so obvious, so various, and so weighty, that we shall only attempt to glance at some of the most prominent.

In the first place, it must be evident, that no period could be adopted in which the work can be prosecuted with less expense. Every day augments the value of the land through which the canal will pass; and when we consider the surplus hands which have been recently dismissed from the army into the walks of private industry, and the facility with which an addition can be procured to the mass of our active labour, in consequence of the convulsions of Europe, it must be obvious that this is now the time to make those indispensable acquisitions.

2. The longer this work is delayed, the greater will be the difficulty in surmounting the interests that will rise up in opposi-

tion to it. Expedients on a contracted scale have already been adopted for the facilitation of intercourse. Turnpikes, locks, and short canals have been resorted to, and in consequence of those establishments, villages have been laid out, and towns have been contemplated. To prevent injurious speculation, to avert violent opposition, and to exhibit dignified impartiality and paternal affection to your fellow citizens, it is proper that they should be notified at once of your intentions.

3. The experience of the late war has impressed every thinking man in the community, with the importance of this communication. The expenses of transportation frequently exceeded the original value of the article, and at all times operated with injurious pressure upon the finances of the nation. The money thus lost for the want of this communication, would perhaps have defrayed more than one half of its expense.

4. Events which are daily occurring on our frontiers, demonstrate the necessity of this work. Is it of importance that our honourable merchants should not be robbed of their legitimate profits; that the public revenues should not be seriously impaired by dishonest smuggling, and that the commerce of our cities should not be supplanted by the mercantile estabishments of foreign countries? Then it is essential that this sovereign remedy for maladies so destructive and ruinous, should be applied. It is with inconceivable regret we record the well known fact, that merchandize from Montreal, has been sold to an alarming extent on our borders for fifteen per cent. below the New-York prices.

5. A measure of this kind will have a benign tendency in raising the value of the national domains, in expediting the sale, and enabling the payment. Our national debt may thus, in a short time, be extinguished. Our taxes of course will be diminished, and a considerable portion of revenue may then be expended in great public improvements; in encouraging the arts and sciences; in patronizing the operations of industry; in fostering the inventions of genius, and in diffusing the blessings of knowledge.

6. However serious the fears which have been entertained of a dismemberment of the Union by collisions between the north and the south, it is to be apprehended that the most imminent danger lies in another direction, and that a line of separation

may be eventually drawn between the Atlantic and the western states, unless they are cemented by a common, an ever acting and a powerful interest. The commerce of the ocean, and the trade of the lakes, passing through one channel, supplying the wants, increasing the wealth, and reciprocating the benefits of each great section of the empire, will form an imperishable cement of connexion, and an indissoluble bond of union. New-York is both Atlantic and western, and the only state in which this union of interests can be formed and perpetuated, and in which this great centripetal power can be energetically applied. Standing on this exalted eminence, with power to prevent a train of the most extensive and afflicting calamities that ever visited the world, (for such a train will inevitably follow a dissolution of the Union,) she will justly be considered an enemy to the human race, if she does not exert for this purpose the high faculties which the Almighty has put into her hands.

Lastly, it may be confidently asserted, that this canal, as to the extent of its route, as to the countries which it connects, and as to the consequences which it will produce, is without a parallel in the history of mankind. The union of the Baltic and the Euxine; of the Red Sea and the Mediterranean; of the Euxine and the Caspian, and of the Mediterranean and the Atlantic, has been projected or executed by the chiefs of powerful monarchies, and the splendour of the design, has always attracted the admiration of the world. It remains for a free state to create a new era in history, and to erect a work more stupendous, more magnificent, and more beneficial than has hitherto been achieved by the human race. Character is as important to nations, as to individuals, and the glory of a republic, founded on the promotion of the general good, is the common property of all its citizens.

We have thus discharged with frankness and plainness, and with every sentiment of respect, a great duty to ourselves, to our fellow citizens, and to posterity, in presenting this subject to the fathers of the commonwealth. And may that Almighty Being in whose hands are the destinies of states and nations, enlighten your councils and invigorate your exertions in favour of the best interests of our beloved country.

2

Indian Policy

Jedediah Morse: Report to the Secretary of War on Indian Affairs*

American policy toward the Indians was anticipated when the first white man bartered a handful of beads for a piece of land. The eastern tribes had already been absorbed or isolated when the War of 1812 sent the Creeks on the warpath from Tennessee to the Gulf of Mexico and the powerful Shawnees, under Tecumseh, north and west of the Ohio. The inevitable defeat of both tribes was only a beginning. What was to become of the Indians, now that their hunting grounds were open to land-hungry settlers?

For help in answering that question, the Secretary of War called upon the Reverend Jedediah Morse (1751-1826), who was as favorably known for his sympathetic interest in Indian affairs as for his immensely popular *American Universal Geography*. In the summer of 1820, in response to the war department's invitation, Morse visited the distant outpost of Green Bay in Michigan Territory. There and en route he talked with missionaries, army officers, factors, and fur-traders, each of whom had some special knowledge bearing on the problem.

Morse's *Report*, excerpts from which appear here, was published in 1822 and its major recommendations were placed before Congress. Although they reflect a spirit of reform that would eventually give character to an age, his proposals ran counter to much of the common thinking of the frontier and were disregarded. The policy actually adopted, and substantially carried out between 1825 and 1840, was that of removing the tribes bodily to new lands west of the Mississippi. Grant Foreman, *Indian Removal: the Emigration of the Five Civilized Tribes* (Norman, Okla.: U. of Oklahoma Press, 1953) follows the migration of specific tribes. The Indian as a person is graphically portrayed in Alvin M. Josephy, *The Patriot Chiefs* (New York: Viking, 1961). In reading Morse's *Report*, note (1) what kind of an attitude

---

*Jedediah Morse, *Report to the Secretary of War of the United States on Indian Affairs, Comprising a Narrative of a Tour Performed in the Summer of 1820* (New Haven: S. Converse, 1822), pp. 79-87.

he displayed toward the Indians; (2) what uses he thought education could serve; (3) his views concerning the moral issues involved;
(4) what changes Indian leaders thought appropriate; and (5) what
role he thought government should play in dealing with the Indians.

The claims of the Indians on the government and people of the United States, and the way to satisfy these claims

IN THE EXISTING STATE OF THE INDIANS, AND OF OUR
connections with them, what de we owe them?
What are the duties, in reference to them, of the civil, and of the
religious community? The duties of each are different, but connected. Neither, alone, can do all that seems necessary to be
done. There is enough for both to do; and a necessity that there
should be mutual co-operation.

The Government, according to the law of nations, having jurisdiction over the Indian territory, and the exclusive right to dispose of its soil, the whole Indian population is reduced, of
necessary consequence, to a *dependent* situation. They are without the privileges of self-government, except in a limited degree;
and without any *transferable* property. They are ignorant of
nearly all the useful branches of human knowledge, of the Bible,
and of the only Savior of men, therein revealed. They are weak,
and ready to perish; we are strong, and with the help of God,
able to support, to comfort and to save them. In these circumstances, the Indians have claims on us of high importance to
them, and to our own character and reputation, as an enlightened, just and christian nation. In return for what they *virtually*
yield, they are undoubtedly entitled to expect from our honor
and justice, protection in all the rights which they are permitted
to retain. They are entitled, as *"children"* of the government, for
so we call them, *peculiarly* related to it, to kind, paternal treatment, to justice in all our dealings with them, to education in the
useful arts and sciences, and in the principles and duties of our
religion. In a word, they have a right to expect and to receive
from our civil and religious communities combined, that sort of
education, in all its branches, which we are accustomed to give

to the *minority* of our own population, and thus to be raised gradually and ultimately, to the rank, and to the enjoyment of all the rights and privileges of freemen, and citizens of the United States. This I conceive to be the precise object of the Government. If we fulfil not these duties, which grow naturally out of our relation to Indians, we cannot avoid the imputation of injustice, unkindness, and unfaithfulness to them,—our national character must suffer in the estimation of all good men. If we refuse to do the things we have mentioned for the Indians, let us be consistent, and cease to call them *"children"*—and let them cease to address our President, as their "great Father." Let us leave to them the unmolested enjoyment of the territories they now possess, and give back to them those which we have taken away from them.

But the Government, and it is honorable to their character, have not forgotten their obligations. In fulfilment of them, in part, the Congress of the United States have placed at the disposal of their President, the annual sum of ten thousand dollars, which will doubtless be increased, as the plans of the government shall be extended, and require it, to be expended by him in ways which he may judge the most suitable, for the civilization and happiness of the Indians. The regulations adopted to guide in the expenditure of this fund, and the account rendered by the Secretary of War, of the manner in which it has been expended, will exhibit this paternal and benevolent effort of the Government, both in principle and operation.

Objections to civilizing the Indians

When we look back in the pages of history four or five hundred years, and see what then was the state of our own Ancestors, and whence sprung the most polished and scientific nations of Europe, we should scarcely have supposed, that any man, acquainted with history, or making any pretensions to candor, would be found among the objectors to attempts to civilize our Indians, and thus to save them from perishing. Yet, painful as is the fact, objections have been made to the present course of procedure with Indians, and from men too, whose standing and office in society are such, as it would be deemed disrespectful to pass unnoticed. "The project," it has been said, "is visionary and impracticable. Indians can never be tamed; they are incapable of receiving, or of enjoying, the blessings proposed to be offered to them." Some, I will hope, for the honor of our country, that the number is small, have proceeded farther, and said, "Indians are not worth saving. They are perishing—let them perish. The sooner they are gone, the better." And to hasten such a catastrophe, *a formal project has been actually devised, and put on paper,* and the projector has had the effrontery to offer his infernal project for adoption of the government! ! !

A sufficient answer to such of these objections, as require notice (for truly some of them are so shocking, that one can hardly *think* of them, much less undertake to *answer* them) will be found, I conceive, in the *facts* collected into the Appendix of this work. It is too late to say that Indians cannot be civilized. The facts referred to, beyond all question, prove the contrary. The evidence of actual experiment in every case, is paramount to all objections founded in mere *theory,* or, as in the present case, in naked and unsupported *assertions.* The specimens of composition, and the account given, on unquestionable authority, of the acquisitions of Indian youths, of other kinds of knowledge, in the Cornwall, and other Indian schools, can hardly fail to convince all, who are willing to be convinced, that it *is* practicable to civilize, educate and save Indians. Without fear of contradiction, then, we assume this point as established. Indians are of the same nature and original, and of one blood, with ourselves; of intellectual powers as strong, and capable of cultivation, as ours. They, as well as ourselves, are made to be immortal. To look down upon them, therefore, as an inferior race, as untameable, and to profit by their ignorance and weakness; to take their property from them for a small part of its real value, and in other ways to oppress them; is undoubtedly wrong, and highly displeasing to our common Creator, Lawgiver and final Judge.

Plan for civilizing the Indians

The *general* plan, embracing all its ramifications, which I would respectfully submit to the consideration and adoption of the government, with the improvements hereafter mentioned, is that, *substantially,* which has been devised by the American Board of Commissioners for Foreign Missions, and is now in successful operation under the direction of this Board, and of other similar associations of different denominations, and has already received the sanction and patronage of the Government. This plan, "in the full tide of successful experiment," is now in a course of exhibition before the public, and is looked at with joy and admiration, by philanthropists on both sides of the Atlantic.

Removal and colonization of the Indians, now living within the settlements of the white people

On the subject of the removal of the Indians, who now dwell within our settlements, there are different opinions among wise and good men. The point on which they divide is, whether it be best to let these Indians quietly remain on their present Reservations, and to use our endeavors to civilize them where they are, or for the Goverment to take their Reservations, and give them an equivalent in lands to be purchased of other tribes beyond our present settlements. The Indians themselves too, are divided in opinion on this subject; a part are for removing, and a part for remaining, as in the case of the Cherokees, Delawares, Senecas, Oneidas, Shawnees, and indeed most of the other tribes living among us. Difficulties in deciding this question present themselves, on which side soever it be viewed. To remove these Indians far away from their present homes, from "the bones of their fathers," into a wilderness, among strangers, possibly hostile, to live as their new neighbors live, by hunting, a state to which they have not lately been accustomed, and which is incompatible with civilization, can hardly be reconciled with the professed views and objects of the Government in civilizing them. This would not be deemed by the world a wise course, nor one which would very probably lead to the desired end. Should that part of the tribes only, remove, who are willing to go, and the remainder be permitted to stay—this division of already enfeebled *remnants* of tribes, would but still more weaken their strength, diminish their influence, and hasten their destruction. Nor would this partial removal satisfy those who are for removing the whole; nor those either, who are for retaining the whole. The latter wish them to remain for the benevolent purpose of educating them all where they now are, urging, that they are now among us, in view of examples of civilized life; and where necessary instruction can be conveniently, and with little expense, imparted to them. On the other hand there is much to be said in favor of the removal of the *smaller* tribes, and remnants of tribes—not, however, into the wilderness, to return again to the savage life, but to some suitable, *prepared* portion of our country, where, collected in one body, they may be made comfortable, and with advantage be educated together, as has already been mentioned, in the manner in which we educate our own children. Some such course as this, I apprehend, will satisfy a great majority of the reflecting part of those who interest themselves at all in this subject, and is, in my belief, the only practicable course which can be pursued, consistently with the professed object of the Government.

Revolution now in operation among the Indians

There is evidently a great and important revolution in the state of our Indian population already commenced, and now rapidly going forward, affecting immediately the tribes among us and on our borders, and which will ultimately and speedily be felt by those at the remotest distance. The evidence of this revolution exists in the *peculiar* interest which is felt and manifested for the general improvement and welfare of Indians, and in the peculiar corresponding feelings and movements among the Indians themselves. The civil and religious communities are remarkably awake on this subject, and are making joint efforts for the improvement and happiness of Indians, such as were never made in any former period of our history. The Chiefs and sensible men among these tribes, to a great extent, feel that a change in their situation has become necessary, that they must quit the hunter, and adopt the agricultural state, or perish. Of this fact I myself am a witness. There is an increasing willingness, which in some instances rises to strong desire, on the part of the Indians, to accept the benevolent offers of instruction held out to them by the Government and by Christian Associations. There is a most remarkable reciprocity of feelings on this subject, which plainly indicates, that the hand of heaven is in it; as no power short of this could ever have produced such a state of things. This is for our encouragement and it is encouragement enough, to persevere. In such circumstances we cannot go back. Honor, justice, humanity, all that makes man respectable in the sight of God and men, imperiously require us to go forward, in full faith, till this work, so auspiciously commenced, shall be accomplished.

Obligations of the government to meet this new state of things, and the manner of fulfilling these obligations

This new state of things requires corresponding measures on the part of the government, to whom we look to take the lead in carrying on this revolution, which, if rightly directed and conducted, will save the Indians from ruin, and raise them to respectability and happiness, and reflect high and lasting honor on the Administration which shall accomplish it.

As the government assumes the guardianship of the Indians, and in this relation provides for their proper education, provision also should be made for the exercise of a suitable government and control over them. This government, unquestionably, should be in its nature *parental—absolute, kind* and *mild,* such as may be created by a wise union of a well-selected military establishment, and an Education Family: The one possessing the power, the other the softening and qualifying influence; both combined would constitute, to all the purposes requisite, the parental or guardian authority. A code of laws and regulations must also be formed, to meet the new state of the Indians, which should remove the unjust, mortifying, and provoking differences which are now made between them and white people, in the administration of justice; a code, which shall provide effectually against the introduction of spirituous liquors among them, which are the source and immediate occasion of most of the difficulties, quarrels and wars, which take place among themselves, and between them and us. This is an evil, which, if not effectually cured, will hinder and render abortive, all efforts which may be made for their benefit. No good can be done to the Indians, while this evil remains.

Another evil equally destructive of the Indians, and equally necessary to be provided against by proper laws and regulations, is, intercourse with *unprincipled* white people. Indians complain, and justly too, that their "morals are corrupted by *bad white men.*" This is well known to be the fact, and the cause of incalculable injury to the Indians, as well as of national disgrace. As we would hope to promote their welfare, this evil must, in some way, by the wisdom and arm of the government, be removed. It can be done effectually in one way, and but one way; and that is, by the appointment, *exclusively,* of good men to fill all public offices relating to Indians; men of principle, who, in the discharge of their official duties, will honestly, faithfully and disinterestedly promote the welfare of Indians. Such men, of competent abilities and qualifications, can undoubtedly be found, and in sufficient numbers, to carry on the whole trade, and other intercourse with the Indians, on the plan suggested in another part of this Report; and to fill all the offices pertaining to the superintendancy and agency of Indian affairs, as well as to negotiate treaties for various objects, with the Indian tribes.

I am fully aware of the delicacy of this subject, in the view of it I am now taking; but its importance in order to the attainment of the object of the government, forbids that I should pass it unnoticed. I dare not be unfaithful to my government—to my conscience—nor to my GOD. Example, in the case before us, *peculiarly,* as in all other cases, must accompany instruction and precept. We cannot reasonably expect that the latter will have any good effect, where the first is wanting. Let, then, the plan of Indian trade, the selection of officers and soldiers for the military establishments, which are connected with Indians, the appointment of Indian superintendants and agents, and treaty commissioners, all be made, in future, in reference to the influence which these establishments and officers, respectively, are expected to exert over the Indians. Let this whole combined influence be uniform in its character, and wholly good, and be made to bear upon every measure put in operation for the civil, moral, and intellectual improvement of the Indians.

In other words, and to come to the very *pivot* of this business. Let the whole existing system of operations in regard to Indians, embracing trade, and all other kinds of intercourse with them by

Indian Agencies, Treaties for their lands, and all laws relating to them, be annulled, and all things removed out of the way, preparatory to the laying of *new foundations,* and the erection of a new and more commodious and sightly fabric. I pass no censure on the present system. It was formed by our wise men. But it was formed for other times, and for a state of things among ourselves, and among the Indians, widely different from the present. The alterations in this system, which have been made at different periods, to meet the changes which have taken place, have deformed it. It is now an unsightly, and, compared with what it might be made, an inefficient mass. In many instances its operations are wasteful and injurious. Many agencies, formerly necessary, from the removal of the Indians, or a change in their circumstances, have become mere *sinecures,* places of emolument, without business, consuming the public money, without contributing any thing to the public good. Several of these agencies combined, would furnish no more business than a single man, of proper qualifications for an agent, could perform. The fault is in the system itself, not in the minister whose office it is to carry this system into effect; nor yet in the officers who occupy these sinecures. Many abuses, many sinks, uselessly swallowing up the public funds exist, which require, and no doubt will receive the pointed eye of the Executive, and remedies, which Congress alone can supply. These remedies will be found in a *new system* throughout, of all Indian affairs, into which is to be incorporated all that is sound and good in the old, leaving out only that which has become obsolete—a system shaped to the new state of things, to the great changes now in operation—a system, that shall combine in it all the results of past experience, all the wisdom of the Government, and command in its execution the energies of the nation—a system, which shall hereafter, when they shall have felt its effects, call forth the thanks of the Indians, and secure for our nation the applauses of the world.

3

Foreign Relations

Documents Relating to the Origins of the Monroe Doctrine

The famous doctrine laid down by President James Monroe (1758-1831) in his annual message to Congress, December 2, 1823, consisted of three separate principles: (1) the Americas were to be considered as no longer open to colonization by any European power; (2) the nations of Europe were not to interfere with any American country that had declared and was in fact maintaining its independence; and (3) the United States would take no part in any war that related only to the affairs of Europe.

The noncolonization principle was formulated by Secretary of State John Quincy Adams (1767-1848) in direct response to a Russian claim to hegemony over the Pacific coast of North America as far south as Vancouver Island. The noninterference principle grew out of a well-founded suspicion that the Holy Alliance meant to restore Spain's lost colonies in the western hemisphere; in modified form, it was first suggested by the British Foreign Minister to the American minister in London, Richard Rush (1780-1859). The principle of American abstention from European wars was no more than a reaffirmation of Washington's farewell warning to his countrymen.

The classic treatment of the subject is that of Dexter Perkins, summarized in his *History of the Monroe Doctrine* (Boston: Little, Brown, 1955). The most recent and most readable study is Frank Donovan, *Mr. Monroe's Message* (New York: Dodd-Mead, 1963). For more general discussion the reader should consult Ruhl Bartlett, *Policy and Power* (New York: Hill and Wang, 1963); and Samuel Flagg Bemis, *John Quincy Adams and the Foundations of American Foreign Policy* (New York: Knopf, 1949). In the various excerpts assembled here, note (1) the character and nature of the relationships sustained by the United States and other countries on both sides of the world; (2) the tone of the Russian edict; (3) the manner in which Adams summarizes developments for Rush; (4) evidences of the tendency on the part of the protagonists to go behind words in search of motives; (5) the way in which this most important of all American foreign policy statements was delivered to the world.

The Russian Minister to the Secretary of State,
February 11, 1822*

THE UNDERSIGNED ENVOY EXTRAORDINARY AND minister plenipotentiary of his majesty the emperor of all the Russias, in consequence of orders which have lately reached him, hastens herewith to transmit to Mr. Adams, Secretary of State in the Department of Foreign Affairs, a printed copy of the regulation adopted by the Russian American Company, and sanctioned by his imperial majesty, relative to foreign commerce in the waters bordering the establishments of the said company, on the northwest coast of America.

The undersigned conceives it to be moreover his duty to inform Mr. Adams, that the imperial government, in adopting the regulation, supposes that a foreign ship, which shall have sailed from a European port after the 1st of March, 1822, or from one of the ports of the United States after the 1st of July of the same year, cannot lawfully pretend ignorance of these new measures.

Edict Of His Imperial Majesty, Autocrat of all the Russias.

The Directing Senate maketh known unto all men: Whereas, in an Edict of His Imperial Majesty, issued to the Directing Senate on the 4th day of September, and signed by his Imperial Majesty's own hand, it is thus expressed:

"Observing, from reports submitted to us, that the trade of our subjects on the Aleutian Islands and on the northwest coast of America appertaining unto Russia, is subjected, because of secret and illicit traffic, to oppression and impediments; and finding that the principal cause of these difficulties is the want of rules establishing the boundaries for navigation along these coasts, and the order of naval communication, as well in these places as on the whole of the eastern coast of Siberia and the Kurile Islands, we have deemed it necessary to determine these communications by specific regulations, which are hereto attached.

"In forwarding these regulations to the Directing Senate, we command that the same be published for universal information, and that the proper measures be taken to carry them into execution."

---

* Message of the President . . . transmitting . . . information in relation to claims set up by Foreign Governments to Territory of the United States upon the Pacific Ocean. 17th Congress, 1st Session, House Document 112.

Rules established for the limits of navigation and order of communication along the coast of the Eastern Siberia, the northwestern coast of America, and the Aleutian, Kurile, and other islands.

SEC. 1. The pursuits of commerce, whaling, and fishery, and of all other industry, on all islands, ports, and gulfs, including the whole of the northwest coast of America, beginning from Behring's Straits, to the 51° of northern latitude, also from the Aleutian islands to the eastern coast of Siberia, as well as along the Kurile islands from Behring's Straits to the south cape of the island of Urup, viz: to the 45°50′ northern latitude, is exclusively granted to Russian subjects.

SEC. 2. It is therefore prohibited to all foreign vessels, not only to land on the coasts and islands belonging to Russia, as stated above, but also to approach them within less than an hundred Italian miles. The transgressor's vessel is subject to confiscation, along with the whole cargo. . . .

The Secretary of State to the Russian Minister, February 25, 1822

SIR: I have had the honor of receiving your note of the 11th inst. enclosing a printed copy of the regulations adopted by the Russian American Company, and sanctioned by His Imperial Majesty, relating to the commerce of foreigners in the waters bordering on the establishments of that company upon the northwest coast of America.

I am directed by the President of the United States to inform you, that he has seen with surprize in this edict the assertion of a territorial claim on the part of Russia, extending to the 51st degree of north latitude on this continent; and a regulation interdicting to all commercial vessels, other than Russian, upon the penalty of seizure and confiscation, the approach, upon the high seas, within one hundred Italian miles of the shores to which that claim is made to apply. The relations of the United States with His Imperial Majesty have always been of the most friendly character; and it is the earnest desire of this government to preserve them in that state. It was expected, before any act which should define the boundary between the territories of the United States and Russia, on this continent, that the same would have been arranged, by treaty, between the parties. To exclude the vessels of our citizens from the shore, beyond the ordinary distance to which the territorial jurisdiction extends, has excited still greater surprize.

This ordinance affects so deeply the rights of the United States and of their citizens, that I am instructed to inquire whether you are authorized to give explanations of the grounds of right, upon principles generally recognized by the laws and usages of nations, which can warrant the claims and regulations contained in it.

The Russian reply argued that the Pacific coast of North America, "from Behring's Strait to the 51° of north latitude," was Russian by right of discovery. The southern limits were vague, but the 51st parallel represented the approximate midpoint between the Russian outpost of New Archangel (Sitka) and the American settlement of Astoria at the mouth of the Columbia.

The Secretary of State to the Russian Minister, March 30, 1822

SIR: I have had the honor of receiving your letter of the 28th ult. which has been submitted to the consideration of the President of the United States.

From the deduction which it contains of the grounds upon which articles of regulation of the Russian American Company have now, for the first time, extended the claim of Russia, on the northwest coast of America, to the 51st degree of north latitude, its only foundation appears to be the existence of the small settlement of Novo Archangelsk, situated not on the American continent, but upon a small island in latitude 57; and the principle upon which you state that this claim is now advanced, is, that the 51st degree is equi-distant from that settlement of Nov Archangelsk and the establishment of the United States at the mouth of Columbia river. But, from the same statement, it appears that, in the year 1799, the limits prescribed by the Emperor Paul to the Russian American Company were fixed at the 55th degree of latitude, and that, in assuming now the latitude of 51, a new pretension is asserted, to which no settlement, made since the year 1799, has given the color of a sanction.

This pretension is to be considered not only with reference to the question of territorial right, but also to that prohibition to the vessels of other nations, including those of the United States, to approach within one hundred Italian miles of the coasts. From the period of the existence of the United States as an independent nation, their vessels have freely navigated those seas, and the right to navigate them is a part of that independence. . . . The right of the citizens of the United States to hold commerce with the aboriginal natives of the northwest coast of America, without the territorial jurisdiction of other nations, even in arms and ammunitions of war, is as clear and indisputable as that of navigating the seas. That right has never been exercised in a spirit unfriendly to Russia, and, although general complaints have occasionally been made on the subject of this commerce by some of your predecessors, no specific ground of charge has ever been alleged by them of any transaction in it which the United States were, by the ordinary laws and usages of nations, bound either to restrain or to punish. Had any such charge been made, it would have received the most pointed attention of this government, with the sincerest and firmest disposition to perform every act and obligation of justice to yours, which could have been required. I am commanded by the President of the United States to assure you that this disposition will continue to be entertained, together with the earnest desire that the most harmonious relations between the two countries may be preserved.

Relying upon the assurance, in your note, of similar dispositions reciprocally entertained by his Imperial Majesty towards the United States, the President is persuaded that the citizens of this Union will remain unmolested in the prosecution of their lawful commerce, and that no effect will be given to an interdiction manifestly incompatible with their rights.

The Russians continued to argue their case, but the edict was not enforced, pending negotiations that resulted in a treaty in 1824. The agreement fixed the southern boundary of Russian influence on the North American continent at 54°40′ north latitude, the present southern boundary of Alaska. In the meantime American views so far crystallized that Adams was able to lay down for the benefit of the Russian Minister the principle that the western hemisphere was no longer subject to European colonization. He repeated the principle, with amplifications, a few days later for the United States Minister in London, Richard Rush.

Adams' Diary, July 17, 1823*

. . . Baron Tuyl came, enquired if he might inform his government that instructions would be forwarded by Mr. Hughes to Mr. Middleton for negotiating on the Northwest Coast question. I said he might. He then manifested a desire to know as much as I was disposed to tell him as to the purport of those instructions. I told him as much as I thought prudent, as he observed that it was personally somewhat important to him to be so far confided in here as to know the general purport of what we intended to propose. I told him specially that we should contest the right of Russia to any territorial establishment on this continent, and that we should assume distinctly the principle that the American continents are no longer subjects for any new European colonial establishments.

Adams to Rush, July 22, 1823**

. . . The principles settled by the Nootka Sound Convention of Oct. 28, 1790, were:

1. That the rights of fishery in the South Seas; of trading with the Natives of the Northwest Coast of America, and of making settlements on the Coast itself for the purposes of that trade, north of the *actual* settlements of Spain were common to all the European Nations and of course to the United States.

2. That so far as the actual settlements of Spain had extended, she possessed the exclusive rights, territorial and of navigation and fishery, extending to the distance of ten miles from the Coasts so *actually occupied.*

---

*C. F. Adams, ed., *Memoirs of John Quincy Adams* (Boston, 1877), VI, p. 163. Baron de Tuyll was the Russian minister in Washington, while Henry Middleton represented the United States at the Russian court. Christopher Hughes, a career diplomat, was *charge d'affaires* in Stockholm.

**S. Hamilton, ed., *Writings of James Monroe* (New York: G. P. Putnam's Sons, 1902), VI, pp. 356-7.

3. That on the coasts of *South America,* and the adjacent Island, *South* of the parts already occupied by Spain, no settlement shall hereafter be made either by British or Spanish subjects, but on both sides should be retained the liberty of landing and of erecting temporary buildings for the purposes of the fishery. These rights were also of course enjoyed by the people of the United States.

The exclusive rights of Spain to any part of the American Continents have ceased. That portion of the Convention which recognizes the exclusive Colonial rights of Spain on these Continents, though confirmed as between Great Britain and Spain by the first additional Article to the Treaty of the 5th of July 1814 has been extinguished by the fact of the Independence of the South American Nations and of Mexico. These Independent Nations will possess the rights incident to that condition and their territories will of course be subject to no *exclusive* right of navigation in their vicinity or of access to them by any Foreign Nation.

A necessary consequence of this state of things will be that the American Continents henceforth will no longer be subjects of *colonization.* Occupied by civilized Independent Nations, they will be accessible to Europeans and to each other on that footing alone, and the Pacific Ocean in every part of it will remain open to the Navigation of all nations in like manner with the Atlantic.

Incidental to the condition of National Independence and Sovereignty, the rights of interior navigation of their Rivers will belong to each of the American Nations within its own Territories.

The application of Colonial principles of exclusion therefore cannot be admitted by the United States as lawful upon any part of the North West Coast of America, or as belonging to any European nation. Their own settlements there, when organized as Territorial Governments, will be adapted to the freedom of their own Institutions, and as constituent parts of the Union be subject to the principles and provisions of their Constitution. . . .

Before he received Adams' despatch, Rush had been approached unofficially by the British Foreign Minister, George Canning, with a query as to whether the United States would join Britain in a declaration of policy toward the former Spanish colonies in Latin America, whose reconquest by Spain, with French assistance, then seemed possible.

Canning to Rush (private and confidential), August 20, 1823*

Before leaving Town, I am desirous of bringing before you in a more distinct, but still in an unofficial and confidential, shape, the Question which we shortly discussed, the last time that I had the pleasure of seeing you.

Is not the moment come when our Governments might understand each other as to the Spanish American Colonies? And if we can arrive at such an understanding, would it not be expedient for ourselves, and beneficial for all the world, that the principles of it should be clearly settled and plainly avowed?

For ourselves we have no disguise.

1. We conceive the recovery of the Colonies by Spain to be hopeless.
2. We conceive the question of the Recognition of them, as Independent States, to be one of time and circumstances.
3. We are, however, by no means disposed to throw any impediment in the way of an arrangement between them and the mother country by amicable negotiation.
4. We aim not at the possession of any portion of them ourselves.
5. We could not see any portion of them transferred to any other Power with indifference.

If these opinions and feelings are, as I firmly believe them to be, common to your government with ours, why should we hesitate mutually to confide them to each other; and to declare them in the face of the world?

If there be any European Power which cherishes other projects, which looks to a forcible enterprize for reducing the colonies to subjugation, on the behalf or in the name of Spain; or which meditates the acquisition of any part of them to itself, by cession or by conquest; such a declaration on the part of your government and ours would be at once the most effectual and the least offensive mode of intimating our joint disapprobation of such projects.

It would at the same time put an end to all the jealousies of

---

Ibid., pp. 365-6.

Spain with respect to her remaining colonies—and to the agitation which prevails in those colonies, an agitation which it would be but humane to allay; being determined (as we are) not to profit by encouraging it.

Do you conceive that under the power which you have recently received, you are authorized to enter into negotiation, and to sign any Convention upon this subject? Do you conceive, if that be not within your competence, you could exchange with me ministerial notes upon it?

Nothing could be more gratifying to me than to join with you in such a work, and, I am persuaded, there has seldom, in the history of the world, occurred an opportunity, when so small an effort, of two friendly Governments, might produce so unequivocal a good and prevent such extensive calamities.

I shall be absent from London but three weeks at the utmost; but never so far distant, but that I can receive and reply to any communication, within three or four days.

Rush to Adams (No. 325), August 23, 1823*

I yesterday received from Mr. Canning a note headed "private and confidential" setting before me in a more distinct form the proposition respecting South American affairs, which he communicated to me in conversation, on the 16th, as already reported in my number 323. Of his note I lose no time in transmitting a copy for your information, as well as a copy of my answer to it written and sent this day.

In shaping the answer on my own judgment alone, I feel that I have had a task of some embarrassment to perform, and shall be happy if it receives the President's approbation.

I believe that this government has the subject of Mr. Canning's proposition much at heart, and certainly his note bears, upon the face of it, a character of cordiality towards the government of the United States which cannot escape notice.

I have therefore thought it proper to impart to my note a like character, and to meet the points laid down in his, as far as I could, consistently with other and paramount considerations.

These I conceived to be chiefly twofold; first, the danger of

*Ibid., pp. 368-9.

pledging my government to any measure or course of policy which might in any degree, now or hereafter, implicate it in the federated system of Europe; and, secondly, I have felt myself alike without warrant to take a step which might prove exceptionable in the eyes of France, with whom our pacifick and friendly relations remain I presume undisturbed, whatever may be our speculative abhorrence of her attack upon the liberties of Spain.

In framing my answer I had also to consider what was due to Spain herself, and I hope that I have not overlooked what was due to the colonies.

The whole subject is open to views on which my mind has deliberated anxiously.

If the matter of my answer shall be thought to bear properly upon motives and considerations which belong most materially to the occasion, it will be a source of great satisfaction to me.

The tone of earnestness in Mr. Canning's note and the force of some of his expressions naturally start the inference that the British Cabinet cannot be without its serious apprehensions that ambitious enterprizes are meditated against the independence of the South American States, whether by France alone, I cannot say, on any authentick grounds.

British apprehensions were soon put at rest by French assurances that no hostile move toward Latin America was contemplated, and the discussions between Canning and Rush petered out in late September. The very existence of the Latin American republics, however, posed a challenge to the Holy Alliance; one that had to be met directly when Columbia appointed diplomatic representatives to the European states. The Russian Minister in Washington informed the State Department on October 16—just a week after Canning's proposal had reached Washington—that no minister would be reecived from Columbia, "or any of the other Governments *de facto*, which owe their existence to events, of which the new world has been for some years the theatre." In Cabinet discussions during the month of November 1823, both the Russian note and the Canning proposal merged with the broader question of relations between the western hemisphere and Europe. The resolution of the question was promulgated in Monroe's annual message to Congress, December 2, 1823, and came ultimately to be called the Monroe Doctrine.

Adams' Diary, November 7, 1823*

Cabinet meeting at the President's from half-past one till four. Mr. Calhoun, Secretary of War, and Mr. Southard, Secretary of the Navy, present. The subject for consideration was, the confidential proposals of the British Secretary of State, George Canning, to R. Rush, and the correspondence between them relating to the projects of the Holy Alliance upon South America. There was much conversation, without coming to any definite point. The object of Canning appears to have been to obtain some public pledge from the Government of the United States, ostensibly against the forcible interference of the Holy Alliance between Spain and South America; but really or especially against the acquisition to the United States themselves of any part of the Spanish-American possessions. . . .

I remarked that the communications recently received from the Russian Minister, Baron Tuyl, afforded, as I thought, a very suitable and convenient opportunity for us to take our stand against the Holy Alliance, and at the same time to decline the overture of Great Britain. It would be more candid, as well as more dignified, to avow our principles explicitly to Russia and France, than to come in as a cock-boat in the wake of the British man-of-war.

Adams' Diary, November 15, 1823**

I received a note . . . saying that the President wished to see me at the office at noon. I went, and found him there. He asked for the correspondence relating to the intercourse with the British American Colonies, with a view to the particular notice which he intends to take of it in the message; which I thought should have been only in general terms. He also showed me two letters which he had received—one from Mr. Jefferson, 23d Octo-

---

*Adams, *op. cit.*, pp. 177-9.

**Ibid.*, pp. 185-6.

ber, and one from Mr. Madison of 30th October, giving their opinions on the proposals of Mr. Canning. The President had sent them the two dispatches from Richard Rush of 23d August, enclosing the correspondence between Canning and him, and requested their opinions on the proposals. Mr. Jeflerson thinks them more important than anything that has happened since our Revolution. He is for acceding to the proposals, with a view to pledging Great Britain against the Holy Allies: though he thinks the island of Cuba would be a valuable and important acquisition to our Union. Mr. Madison's opinions are less decisively pronounced, and he thinks, as I do, that this movement on the part of Great Britain is impelled more by her interest than by a principle of general liberty.

Adams' Diary, November 21, 1823*

I had received a note from the President requesting me to attend a meeting of the members of the Administration at one. The meeting lasted till five. I took with me the draft of my dispatch to R. Rush in answer to Canning's proposals. . . .

I mentioned my wish to prepare a paper to be delivered confidentially to Baron Tuyl, and the substance of which I would in the first instance express to him in a verbal conference. It would refer to the verbal communications recently made by him, and to the sentiments and dispositions manifested in the extract of a dispatch relating to Spanish affairs which he lately put into my hands. My purpose would be in a moderate and conciliatory manner, but with a firm and determined spirit, to declare our dissent from the principles avowed in those communications, to assert those upon which our own Government is founded, and, while disclaiming all intention of attempting to propagate them by force, and all interference with the political affairs of Europe, to declare our expectation and hope that the European powers will equally abstain from the attempt to spread their principles in the American hemisphere, or to subjugate by force any part of these continents to their will.

The President approved of this idea; and then taking up the sketches that he had prepared for his message, read them to us.

---

*Ibid., pp. 193-5.

Its introduction was in a tone of deep solemnity and of high alarm, intimating that this country is menaced by imminent and formidable dangers, such as would probably soon call for their most vigorous energies and the closest union. It then proceeded to speak of the foreign affairs, chiefly according to the sketch I had given him some days since, but with occasional variations. It then alluded to the recent events in Spain and Portugal, speaking in terms of the most pointed reprobation of the late invasion of Spain by France, and of the principles upon which it was undertaken by the open avowal of the King of France. It also contained a broad acknowledgment to the Greeks as an independent nation, and a recommendation to Congress to make an appropriation for sending a Minister to them.

Of all this Mr. Calhoun declared his approbation. I expressed as freely my wish that the President would reconsider the whole subject before he should determine to take that course. I said the tone of the introduction I apprehended would take the nation by surprise and greatly alarm them. It would come upon them like a clap of thunder. There had never been in the history of this nation a period of so deep calm and tranquillity as we now enjoyed. We never were, upon the whole, in a state of peace so profound and secure with all foreign nations as at this time. This message would be a summons to arms—to arms against all Europe, and for objects of policy exclusively European—Greece and Spain. It would be as new, too, in our policy as it would be surprising.

Adams' Diary, November 26, 1823*

I attended the adjourned Cabinet meeting at the President's, from half-past twelve—four hours. At the President's request, I read the statement of what has passed between Baron Tuyl and me since the 16th of last month, and then my proposed draft of observations upon the communications recently received from him. The President then read the draft of the corresponding paragraph for his message to Congress, and asked whether it should form part of the message. I took a review of the preceding

Ibid., pp. 204-5, 208.

transactions of the Cabinet meetings; remarking that the present questions had originated in a draft which he had presented merely for consideration, of an introduction to the message, of unusual solemnity, indicating extraordinary concern, and even alarm, at the existing state of things, coupled with two paragraphs, one containing strong and pointed censure upon France and the Holy Allies for the invasion of Spain, and the other recommending an appropriation for a Minister to send to the Greeks, and in substance recognizing them as independent; that the course now proposed is a substitute for that, and that it is founded upon the idea that if an issue must be made up between us and the Holy Alliance it ought to be upon grounds exclusively American; that we should separate it from all European concerns, disclaim all intention of interfering with these, and make the stand altogether for an American cause; that at the same time the answer to be given to the Russian communications should be used as the means of answering also the proposals of Mr. George Canning, and of assuming the attitude to be maintained by the United States with reference to the designs of the Holy Alliance upon South America. This being premised, I observed that the whole of the papers now drawn up were but various parts of one system under consideration, and the only really important question to be determined, as it appeared to me, was that yesterday made by Mr. Wirt, and which had been incidentally discussed before, namely, whether we ought at all to take this attitude as regards South America; whether we get any advantage by committing ourselves to a course of opposition against the Holy Alliance. . . .

Suppose the Holy Allies should attack South America, and Great Britain should resist them alone and without our co-operation. I thought this not an improbable contingency, and I believed in such a struggle the allies would be defeated and Great Britain would be victorious, by her command of the sea. But, as the independence of the South Americans would then be only protected by the guarantee of Great Britain, it would throw them completely into her arms, and in the result make them her Colonies instead of those of Spain. My opinion was, therefore, that we must act promptly and decisively. . . .

Excerpts from Monroe's annual Message to Congress,
December 2, 1823*

At the proposal of the Russian Imperial Government, made through the minister of the Emperor residing here, a full power and instructions have been transmitted to the minister of the United States at St. Petersburg to arrange by amicable negotiation the respective rights and interests of the two nations on the northwest coast of this continent. A similar proposal had been made by His Imperial Majesty to the Government of Great Britain, which has likewise been acceded to. The Government of the United States has been desirous by this friendly proceeding of manifesting the great value which they have invariably attached to the friendship of the Emperor and their solicitude to cultivate the best understanding with his Government. In the discussions to which this interest has given rise and in the arrangements by which they may terminate the occasion has been judged proper for asserting, as a principle in which the rights and interests of the United States are involved, that the American continents, by the free and independent condition which they have assumed and maintain, are henceforth not to be considered as subjects for future colonization by any European powers. . . .

In the wars of the European powers in matters relating to themselves we have never taken any part, nor does it comport with our policy so to do. It is only when our rights are invaded or seriously menaced that we resent injuries or make preparation for our defense. With the movements in this hemisphere we are of necessity more immediately connected, and by causes which must be obvious to all enlightened and impartial observers. The political system of the allied powers is essentially different in this respect from that of America. This difference proceeds from that which exists in their respective Governments; and to the defense of our own, which has been achieved by the loss of so much blood and treasure, and matured by the wisdom of their most enlightened citizens, and under which we have enjoyed unexampled felicity, this whole nation is devoted. We owe it,

---

Annals of Congress, 18th Congress, 1st Session.

therefore, to candor and to the amicable relations existing between the United States and those powers to declare that we should consider any attempt on their part to extend their system to any portion of this hemisphere as dangerous to our peace and safety. With the existing colonies or dependencies of any European power we have not interfered and shall not interfere. But with the Governments who have declared their independence and maintained it, and whose independence we have, on great consideration and on just principles, acknowledged, we could not view any interposition for the purpose of oppressing them, or controlling in any other manner their destiny, by any European power in any other light than as the manifestation of an unfriendly disposition toward the United States. In the war between those new Governments and Spain we declared our neutrality at the time of their recognition, and to this we have adhered, and shall continue to adhere, provided no change shall occur which, in the judgment of the competent authorities of this Government, shall make a corresponding change on the part of the United States indispensable to their security.

4

Protection of Industry

Hezekiah Niles: Address of the Harrisburg Convention on Behalf of Domestic Industry*

Alexander Hamilton demonstrated in 1791 that newly established industries could not compete with those already long in operation. His solution was an import duty, or tariff, so adjusted as to raise the price of articles manufactured abroad to the level imposed by the higher manufacturing costs at home. The Tariff of 1816, designed primarily to subsidize a cotton textile industry that had grown to significant proportions during the War of 1812, was the first of a long series of protective tariffs. By 1824 the protective policy was in sharp dispute, with southern cotton planters, whose market was largely in England, most articulate in opposition.

The case for an upward revision of the duties was nevertheless presented by a "General Convention of Agriculturists and Manufacturers" which met in Harrisburg, Pennsylvania in the summer of 1827. The moving spirit of the convention was Hezekiah Niles (1777-1839), a Baltimore editor whose *Weekly Register* was probably the most widely read periodical in the country. As chairman of a committee to draft an "address" or report, Niles prepared the document reproduced in part here, summarizing not only the recommendations of the convention but the whole protectionist doctrine. The "Tariff of Abominations" in 1828, which added to the growing rift between North and South, was largely based on the Harrisburg proposals.

The successive tariff debates have been discussed in their political context in Charles M. Wiltse, *John C. Calhoun* (3 vols.; Indianapolis: Bobbs-Merrill, 1944-51). Good general economic histories of the period are George R. Taylor, *The Transportation Revolution, 1815-1860* (New York: Holt, 1951); and C. Douglas North, *The Economic*

*Hezekiah Niles, "Address of the Committee on behalf of the General Convention of Agriculturists and Manufacturers, and others friendly to the Encouragement of the Domestic Industry of the United States, assembled at Harrisburg, 30th July, 1827," *Niles' Weekly Register*, October 13, 1827.

Growth of the United States, 1790-1860 (Englewood Cliffs, N. J.: Prentice-Hall, 1961). Note in the excerpts reproduced here (1) to what extent Niles was aware of the sectional nature of the opposition to the tariff; (2) what answer he gave to sectional opponents of the tariff; (3) the extent of his understanding of the worldwide setting of the problem; (4) evidences of the extent of his understanding of the American economy; and (5) how realistic his approach was to the practical problems of getting a bill through Congress.

. . . It was the great united and allied interest of agriculture and manufactures, in their *actual* effect upon the state of society, that the convention was charged to consider—with more immediate regard, however, to the growth and manufacture of wool; and for the purpose of really obtaining that degree of protection which is seemingly extended by existing laws, but actually denied, or rendered only partially effective, by the counteraction of foreigners, and in the ingenuity and ability with which they violate the principle supposed to be established, for the protection of American farmers, manufacturers and merchants. It is believed that more than eighty millions of dollars are embarked in the wool business, at the present time—and many millions more would have been invested, but for the rapid and ruinous depreciation of value in the capital so employed. We think that there is no other country in which so great an interest as this would have been so much neglected. But this neglect arises in part from an ill-founded spirit of jealousy, built upon sectional feelings, and in part from peculiar opinions; some of which are antiquated, some very new, and others having more regard to things as they should be than to things as they exist. Great mistakes have been caused by the last, and they are defended, because that European writers on political economy, like other manufacturers, have sent forth their products for *foreign* use. Adam Smith, for example, presents many sound propositions and matters of deep interest, though not, perhaps, always defensible; and his countrymen, with the peculiar adroitness of merchants, recommend his doctrines for *our* adoption, but will not permit them to influence *their own* actions. They restrict trade in every way that it will bear—their whole legislation is directed to their own peculiar advantage, and we do not blame them for that; but they desire others to open their ports unreservedly, and practice the principle of 'free trade,' alleging that commerce is best left to its own regulation!—and supplies of foreign *bread* are refused to their own people, though often half-starved *because of the unnatural price of provisions.* The chapter on British restrictions and prohibitions in the appendix will, no doubt, receive the attentive consideration of the reader, and sustain all that we have said—and more.

But the principle of protecting the domestic industry has been adopted in most nations, *and exists wherever a prosperous people are found.* Without it, misery must prevail, and no more than a grade of happiness beyond that which pertains to savage life can be expected—men being clothed in skins and having their homes as if in dens and caverns.—There are *natural* causes of soil, climate and condition, why these things should be, as well as many accidental or artificial circumstances that bear upon them; and also something which may be called *a value in human life that must be respected.* This is the cost of subsistence, and *forbids* "freedom of trade." There is no speculation in the proposition. It is a fact, that a man in France may be as well subsisted for one half less than a man in England, that a Spaniard does live on food upon which an Englishman would nearly perish, and that an East Indian would starve out a Spaniard on the same supplies. We speak of persons performing labor, or, in other words, producing value. It is impossible then, that these parties can freely exchange commodities.—The operation of natural causes or determinate habits, would enrich the one and beggar the other; both these are beyond the ordinary powers of legislation—and hence restrictive laws. Further, if the annual taxes or rents and rates on a parcel of land in England, capable of yielding one hundred bushels of wheat, be as much in amount as the cost of the fee of a like parcel of land in America, but equally adapted to the growth of barley, the first cannot supply the last with bread and receive beer in full exchange. He must make some substitute for himself, or use water only; for, while the highly taxed Englishman, by a certain number of days' work, could do no more than make a bare living, the lightly taxed American would become rich by like applications of his industry. A free laborer may be hired in the East Indiies for less money than it often costs an American laborer for his drinks and tobacco—and the clothing of persons in the United States costs, many times as much per head as in the south of Italy.

Such are among the values of human life—and they cannot be suddenly changed without fearful revolutions or dangerous exertions of power, unless through an alteration of the laws of nature. It is also certain that nations which have nothing to sell, cannot purchase; or that the fewer their commodities, the greater must be a real and distressing "balance of trade" against them, if they indulge their propensities or gratify their fancy. The miserable Indian barters his robes of fur for whiskey and looking glasses— and perishes in the snow-storm. The British, by the aid of *scientific power,* gathered to themselves, as it were, a command over the labour and the wealth of the world. The bowels of the towering Andes, or the bleak summits of Caucasus, were searched to find whatever might minister to their navigation and commerce, in the purchase of their manufactures; and the profits made enabled them to obtain mighty herds of Russian, Prussian and German slaves to fight for them—to suffer death for them; and a girl at Manchester, by the application of her little strength, could buy the carcases of half a dozen of these degraded human beings. The moral and political degradation which has long existed in Spain and Portugal, was caused by the "freedom of trade," which ruined the manufacturers. The plenty that prevails in France, rests upon the Napoleon system, forbidding as other nations forbid, restricting as other nations restrict, and yielding to no other what the other will not yield unto France. This is all equitable. But Britain, less liberal, presses the sale of her goods upon those of whom she will not buy. She will not accept bread and meat, though offered at half the price of her own, in exchange for her calicoes!—yet Britons talk about "free trade," and advise *us* to "let commerce alone!"

However common it is at the present time, (and we exceedingly regret it,) to draw "geographical lines," we would avoid them; but it is difficult, if not impossible, to render due force to certain important facts without them; parts of this Union being very differently circumstanced, though not possessed of opposing interests, if rightly understood. The grain growing, manufacturing and commercial states contain 5,836,700 of the people—the other, the planting states, only 2,028,000. The whole exports of the products of the U. States, last year, to Great Britain, was $20,413,216—of which $18,604,094 was in cotton and tobacco; leaving for all the rest only $1,809,112. In the same time, the imports from Great Britain were valued at $26,131,969; the proportion of which consumed in the first named class of states, according to *gross* population in both parts, was $17,000,000, and in the other class, $9,000,000. No argument is required to shew, that, of itself and in itself, this trade CANNOT be supported by the northern and western states; and that, if it were not for their manufactures and navigation, by which they are enabled to obtain some of the cotton and tobacco of the southern, to exchange with Great Britain, assisted by their enterprize and industry in trading with other nations, they would have been *compelled* to relinquish it years ago, when the British ports were closed against their bread-stuffs and meats, lumber, fish, and nearly every thing else which they have to sell, or become as Indians, who kill deer, which should supply them with food, merely to obtain skins, that they may get beads, which they can do very well without, or might themselves make substitutes for, if they needs must have ornaments in their noses and ears!

We hope to be excused for this brief and mild reference to parts of the United States, or any other that necessity shall impose upon us for the demonstration of facts which ought to be known and understood—though we might quote high precedents to justify direct appeals to sectional interests and feelings, fatal to the harmony, and detrimental to the welfare of *all* the people of this republic. We are not aware that such interests or feelings have influence over our minds, nor can we discover any need of them to either party in determining the merits of the great questions at issue. It is evident to us, and we trust it will be made appear so to others, that prejudice has had more to do in these things than reason, and that there is as much of a community of interest between the cotton and sugar planters of the south and the manufacturers of the east, as there is between the growers of grain and the makers of iron *within* the state of Pennsylvania— supplying, subsisting and supporting one another, through the medium of many thousand channels, diffusing substantial benefits, and perpetually adding to the common stock of the national prosperity and individual wealth. . . .

It is exceedingly to be regretted that, from circumstances, local or temporary, matters of a sectional character should have been introduced into discussions on the principle of protection, and that some appear disposed to deny unto others what may not only not be injurious, but what shall not be manifestly advantageous to themselves. This is repugnant to the first rules of the constitution, in which compromises and concessions abound—and these must exist in every society, *in every family,* if peace and prosperity are expected to endure in them. We shall not do more than allude to these things—being indisposed to rally to our support any aid not to be derived from the justice of our cause, or bring into this contest other disputed questions of right. There is no disagreeing interest in the people of the United States involved in this matter.—We defy the evidence of those injuries, to any other branch of industry, which prejudice and passion have imputed to the encouragement of domestic manufactures; and the people are happily getting into a frame of mind to reject declamation and ask for proof. We offer experience in opposition to theory—practice against speculation. A large majority of the people of this country, are as if they had no foreign market for their productions, and must have a home one. Without it, the farmer must make his clothes, the taylor his shoes, the blacksmith turn carpenter, and the mason make watches, or do without the things respectively desired.—But, by different pursuits, not only a greater degree of perfection is obtained, but the profits of all parties are enhanced, by the interchange of commodities. The agricultural commodities of the middle and western states, such as grain and its manufactures, have their chief market, for the surplusses raised, in the eastern states, and some of their mineral productions, partly manufactured, pass east and south. The south supplies all with cotton, sugar, tobacco and rice, and receives manufactures in payment for these articles—and thus an internal commerce is carried on compared with which the foreign trade is of no great importance, except in cotton only, unless so far as it serves to regulate, as it is regulated by, the internal trade. The statistical tables from the treasury department, in which are collected all the items, great and small, of the foreign trade, exhibit large amounts, and we see and understand them; but were such tables published of the home trade, the aggregate would exceed five hundred, instead of the fifty millions of dollars. Few persons have ever thought upon this subject, much less ventured to calculate it. And yet it is every man's concern—a business that belongs to the heart and home of all persons. On the White mountains of New Hampshire we find the sugar of Louisiana, and in the plains beyond the Mississippi the cotton cloths of Rhode Island are domesticated—the products of the bowels of the land in Pennsylvania and Virginia, supply the workshops or give fuel to the furnaces and factories of New York—wool from Ohio finds a market at Boston—lead from Missouri and Illinois seeks all our cities, and the cotton of South Carolina is met with every where. All these, working together, constitute the prosperity and power of the United States; and we earnestly recommend our readers to the article on "internal trade" in the appendix. There is much in it that will surprise the most of them, as we ourselves confess that we have been, in considering the facts collected.

The diversity of opinion that we have entertained since the expediency of protecting manufactures was first broadly broached, soon after the conclusion of the late war with Great Britain—introduced by the wrongs and violences of the government of that country, and rendered necessary by our own wants displayed during the continuance of the contest by embargo, non-intercourse, and finally, by arms, had its original formation at a distant period. Persons do not shake off the prejudices of education and the force of habit, with a change of the form of their government—with the transfer of allegiance from one power to that of another. These have duration long after the political ties are sundered by which those prejudices or habits were formed. In all old governments, some certain set of notions prevail in ecclesiastical as well as civil affairs, which become constitutional, and acquire the force of determinate principles, the right of them being hardly questioned. Nothing else than some great act of oppression can bring them into doubt, and reformation of abuses proceeds slowly. Europe has been deluged with blood, and the rivers of Asia choked with carcases of the slain, because of *religious* opinions—and secular revolutions have proceeded to the extent of wholly changing the principles of governments—but still the *nations* remained: "the dog returned to his vomit again, and the sow that was washed to her wallowing in the mire"—revolution failing to produce reformation. Hence it is, that great communities of men, enlightened and deeply thinking on many subjects, adopt others, the policy of their *governments*, either in religion or politics, as things not to be enquired into. Thus in many parts of Germany, and even in Switzerland, the birth place of Tell and theatre of his glory, men are hired for soldiers with the same requisitions and under the same circumstances, that Mexican mountaineers hire mules for the bearing of burthens, and without greater discretion in the first than there remains to the last; except that the former assault and murder those who never wronged them or their country, at the command of a master, and the latter are merely *taxed* animals, contributing in proportion to their natural strength—each being equally *machines*. And, though at times, as in Spain, not long ago, liberal ideas may seem to prevail—yet the people of that country regretted the absent despotism of absolute monarchy, and sighed for a restoration of the "holy inquisition." Such is prejudice—the force of habit, and power of education.

Though the point of these remarks applies less to our own country, than to any other that ever was governed by a king, because of the early spread of knowledge and diffusion of correct ideas of the rights of man—still, to a certain extent, it is applicable, though fifty-one years have passed since the declaration of independence; for some feel as though they were not wholly relieved of allegiance to the king of Great Britain. The body is emancipated by a single struggle, but generations appear necessary to emancipate the mind. Witness the slow progress which a practical understanding of the republican system makes in the new governments of the south. Indeed, it may be said of ourselves, that we had not formed a *national character* anterior to the late war. . . .

The combined operations of agriculture and manufactures have invariably caused an increase of population in every nation and state, or part of a nation or state, using commerce as the handmaid of both. And, as population is the origin of national power and wealth, it should be the first consideration of a statesman,

unless the extent of country is small and the people already overflowing. By these operations knowledge is extended, the comforts of life increased, and moral, as well as natural strength, advanced. On the other hand, when a country is purely agricultural,
and especially if possessed by planters, the population must be
sparse, and the want of concentration materially obstructs the
progress of knowledge, and acquisition of physical and moral
power. The first abounds with small freeholds, begetting a spirit
of independence and exalting the character of man, as lord of the
soil. Habits of industry and frugality are encouraged, because
the profits of them are immediately felt by large numbers of the
people in their own persons. Early marriages take place in consequence, for large families are rather desired than feared. Education is of easy access to all, for school-houses abound, and
children become profitable at an early age—idleness, the parent
vice, being disreputable. As wealth accumulates, roads and
bridges and canals are projected and constructed, and new factories established, for capital is plentiful—and one new business
begets another in geometrical proportion, causing a general reduction in the price of commodities, through increased perfection in the arts of producing them. All these things necessarily
take place in lightly taxed and liberally governed nations, being
agricultural, manufacturing and commercial. But in the reverse,
the population must be thinly scattered, wealth is acquired
slowly because of the sluggish circulation of money, schools are
few and far between, social intercourse is difficult and information not easily obtained—internal improvements are not made,
unless partially, because of the want of condensed power in men
and money to make them, these being dissipated by spreading
over a wide surface; and perhaps the most of all is this disadvantage, that a few are very rich and the many very poor—
some well informed persons, and numerous adults, male and
female, who cannot read and write. We ask those who have
knowledge in these matters and are willing to speak of them,
whether or not these things are so. A purely agricultural region
of country, cannot abound in a wholesome, happy and numerous
population; but when joined to and aided by other pursuits,
agriculturalists are, perhaps, at once the best and the happiest

of all classes of society—"the peculiar deposit for substantial and genuine virtue."

The protection of domestic industry has not only built up the commerce and navigation of the United States, but continues to increase both—it adds to the public revenue, by furnishing the means of purchasing taxed commodities—it has reduced the cost of articles, by exciting the domestic competition—it has probably added 50 per cent. to the internal and coasting trade within the last five years—it has opened *new* markets for flour, and grain, equal to the whole foreign export of these articles—it has caused greatly increased supplies of mineral substances and of coal—it has countervailed, in part, the restrictions and prohibitions of Europe, and will place us on an equality with all nations in matters of trade if persevered in and extended—in short, it has subsisted a large part of the people of the United States, given employment to millions on millions of active capital, and become indispensable to the well being of the republic. Without its aids, we should be poor and miserable as the Portuguese, whose work shops are in their ally, Great Britain. It is incorporated with all that we enjoy in the comforts of private life or possess in national reputation or power. These are broad, but, we think not, bold assertions—and capable of fullest demonstration and undeniable proof. . . .

The low condition of the woollen manufactures in this country at the commencement of the late contest at arms with Great Britain, was shewn by the humiliating request preferred by the secretary of war to congress, that existing laws might be repealed so far as to allow the importation of *six thousand blankets* for the Indian department! We believed then, and believe so still, that this suggestion was made that blankets might be obtained from Great Britain for the preservation of our soldiers, when raised and marched to attack the British colony of Canada! But the law was not repealed; and it will not be regarded as a wild speculation to express an opinion, that we lost more men by the want of woollen clothing and other supplies, during the war, than by battle and all other fair exposures to danger that attended the military life. We might dwell long upon this distressing and disgraceful fact—(we call it *disgraceful,* for a wise policy would

have prevented its occurrence), and relate instances of suffering
which happened on the Niagara frontier, that, even at this day,
would chill the blood of every friend of his country and of man;
but we present it, simple and unadorned, to the sober reflection
of the people, that they may determine whether they will permit
the like terrible waste of human life, and cruel dissipation of the
means of our country to support its dear-bought independence,
ever to happen again.

The wants of the nation and of individuals, caused the establishment of some woollen manufactories, and an extended business in
the few which had existed previous to that time; but they could
supply only a small part of the general demand: and something
very much like smuggling, if it did not approach towards *treason,*
was rather countenanced than condemned, that a trade might be
kept up with an enemy employed in the conflagration of our
villages on the maratime frontier, and who had introduced the
tomahawk of the savage into civilized warfare on our northern
and western borders.

And here, perhaps, an opportunity is best presented to speak
of a rude, indiscriminating and vulgar prejudice which had its
origin at this period—the alleged *extortion* of the manufacturers,
such as that they demanded $12 or $14 for a yard of cloth
which they could have afforded to make for 6 or 7; and these
same illiberal or thoughtless persons felt something like pleasure
in the ruin of the manufacturers which followed the close of the
war, because of this alleged "extortion." Admit, for the sake of
the argument, that the facts proclaimed were true, and what
then? Who charged the farmers with *extortion* when flour was at
$13 or $14 per barrel, and whiskey at 65 or 70 cents per gallon,
in 1817? Who is wicked enough to rejoice that flour has since
fallen to less than 5 dollars, when delivered at our sea-ports, and
whiskey been sold at no more than 20 or 22 cents? Who was so
base as to be delighted when farms that cost from $100 to $150
per acre, were knocked down by hundreds under the sheriff's
hammer, at from $20 to $30 per acre, and tens of thousands of
valuable individuals were suddenly cast from an abundance of
all the comforts of life into stinted allowances of the most common food—that worthy men were hired as daily laborers on the

lands which they had owned? We should like to look such a man in the face, if one there is, that we might avoid him as a person infested with the plague, for a liberal intercourse with that man would be the contamination of all just feelings and a sign of the departure of all good principles! Would we not have called the farmers fools—arrant fools, in 1817, if they had sold their flour for five dollars a barrel, (which it *appears* that they can make it for) when they could just as easily obtain fourteen? Indeed, we should suppose that persons acting thus had, by some calamity, been deprived of the use of their reason! And the cotton planters and others are so situated. Cotton is now made by less than ten cents per pound, it was even lately sold at almost thirty cents per pound; but who was stupid enough to prefer a grave charge of "extortion" against the cotton planters? There was not one man so silly to be found in all the country!—nor one who abused the tobacco planters for receiving $185 per hogshead in 1816! How then is it that some have made a law to regulate the prices and profits on woollen goods, and are willing to leave flour, cotton, every thing else, to the *natural effects of supply and demand?* We will suggest the reason why—it is caused by our old prejudices, fanned by the agents of British manufacturers and merchants, and was kept in flame by a horde of domestic venders of British tapes and bobbins, some of whom openly rejoiced at the defeats and disasters that we met with in the last war, that it might terminate, *and they again have British goods to sell.* THEIR BUSINESS WAS WITH GREAT BRITAIN AND SO WERE THEIR HEARTS. These men had much influence on society by their inter-course with all classes of people—and when, charged with de-manding exorbitant profits for themselves, were always ready to throw the odium of it upon the domestic manufacturers. The writer of this address well recollects a person seeking cloth for a coat—a piece of British goods was shewn to him, and 13 dollars a yard demanded for it, which was pronounced too high. "Yes, said the shopkeeper, it is very high—but *we* cannot help it—see, here is a piece of American cloth not nearly so good, for which we are compelled to ask the same price—but take which you please; *our* profits on either are very small." In thousands of cases, American goods were sold as British, that a *wise* public might pay an additional price for them; and, as they were equally as valuable, that operation was not reproved. We know a manufacturing establishment whose proprietor obtained an understanding with a merchant (strongly suspected of receiving supplies of British goods clandestinely) for the sale of his own American woollens, and large quantities of his cloths, put up after the manner of the British, were sold as such without being questioned—at two or three dollars a yard higher than parts of the same parcels of goods brought when frankly sold for what they were! The merchant kept his secret—but the fact was, that most of the cloths which he sold as being British, were really American! So much for public judgment and public clamor about "extortion."

But this is not all. Such wool which now costs 40 or 50 cents, sold for three or four dollars in 1814—the wages of the people employed were twice the present price, and those of the principal workmen three times as high, for experienced persons were few—all the dyestuffs and other foreign materials were four or five times their present average value, and the cost of machinery and implements at the same extravagant terms. Almost all commodities were at great prices—flour in 1811, 1812, 1813, and 1814, averaged about *ten* dollars per barrel, and all other products of the farmers were at like good profits to them; and they could then far better afford to give *one hundred dollars* for a yard of cloth than five dollars now—for if any one had 100 barrels of flour, or wheat enough to make it, to sell, he received 1,000 dollars for it instead of the less than 500 which he now gets; but the labor and the land requred to make a bushel of wheat was just as much then as at the present time. The *difference* in the receipts for flour is $500, in that of three yards of the best cloth, at $14, to make a a suit of clothes, only twenty-seven dollars, all told, making *one* crop and wanting only *one* suit per annum. Or, if he had 100 lbs. of fine wool to dispose of, it brought him $300, instead of only $40 or $50. And on the whole, if the manufacturers could now receive five dollars a yard for such cloth as they sold for thirteen in 1814, they would make a much larger proportional profit on their capital employed and cost of labor. Then the wool only, cost them six or seven dollars for each yard of the cloth, and it now costs them 80 or 100 cents; and the expense of dyeing and dressing, and other costly operations, are reduced as above stated. . . .

It was the square yard duty and establishment of a minimum, that built up the cotton manufactures—and it is these only which can build up those of wool—which can preserve this valuable branch of industry from ruin. And, a little while protected, it will be as able to protect itself as is the domestic manufacture of coarse cotton goods.

The petition to congress asks a square yard duty on certain established valuations, or *minimums*—say 50 cents, $2 and 50 cents, $4 and $6, and a duty of 40 per centum on the thus established cost of cloths in a foreign country, instead of 33⅓, as payable at the present time; on an advance of 6 2-3 *per cent.* on the valuation, and no more.

Frightful calculations, as to duties levied in this manner, and all that was said about the minimum square yard duty on cottons, will be repeated and enlarged; but the *practical* effect of that duty upon cotton goods has overturned all these calculations; and so will such a duty upon woollens, if directed by congress. But let what be said that may, the *operation* of the bill asked for will be after this manner, and we hope that the people will examine what we shall say—

Goods costing 50 cents per square yard, will pay 20 cents per square yard, instead of 16 ⅔ cents, the present rate of duty;

Those costing two dollars and fifty cents, will pay 100 cents, instead of 83⅓;

Those costing four dollars, will pay 160 cents, instead of 133⅓;

Those costing $6 will pay 240 cents, instead of 200.

The advance of duties asked for is not large; but, the request being granted, the duties *intended to be paid will be paid*, or nearly so, except when smuggled; the difference between the minimums, as regulated by the square yard, being so considerable that fraudulent invoices will seldom be offered and more rarely pass though the custom houses—if the appraisers, with moderate industry, perform their office. . . .

We shall now proceed briefly to notice the other items recommended to the consideration of congress by the convention. The duty of this is easy, because that their subject is better understood than that of wool and woollens.

1. To prevent frauds on the revenue. The article on auctions
in the appendix, contains all which we think necessary to urge
on this point.

2. A small increase of duty on hammered bar iron, and a
correspondent increase of duty upon steel. The report of the committee on this subject gives the views of the convention. Of
hammered iron, we imported last year 467,515 cwt. worth
1,590,350 dollars, chiefly from Sweden and Russia, which together received only $118,760 worth of our products. Iron ore,
with the means of its manufacture, and of all qualities, is abundant in the United States, and in every section of the country. It
is an article of primary necessity; and there is no possible reason
why we should depend upon foreign countries for a single pound
of its first manufactures. Some important particulars are given in
the appendix. Various home fabrics of iron have, because of their
superior quality and cheapness of price, already excluded like
foreign articles; and we exported last year the value of $248,960
dollars in manufactures of iron and steel. With a little assistance,
this great interest will be completely established and with reduced prices to the consumers, the market being guarded against
excessive importations, caused by the wants or speculations of
foreigners; which, on the whole, as is known to every person
conversant with the principles of commerce, produce re-actions,
and rather increase than diminish *average* prices. Steel, as immediately dependent on iron, and being an important manufacture, should be supported *pari passu* with iron. Most of our
farming utensils and castings are home-made, with many articles
of iron-mongery, cutlery, etc. with ample supplies of cannon and
small arms.

The *extra* cost of iron during the late war, to the people of the
United States, probably exceeded the whole value of *all* articles
of iron imported since the proclamation of peace, without at all
regarding the disadvantages and losses, delays and discomfitures,
that ensued because of the deficiency of the supply! The trans-
portations alone, cost several hundred thousand dollars more
than they would have done, had the home manufacture been
even in its present state. All who have a recollection of the
"events of the war," will subscribe to this opinion. The tariff of
1824 was of some service to this interest, though only 90 cents

per cwt. was levied upon hammered bar iron. The following brief notice of the various proceedings relative to the duty upon iron, is curious and useful.

Previous to 1824, the duty on hammered bar iron was 75 cents per cwt. In the bill introduced by Mr. Baldwin, as chairman of the committee on manufactures, in 1820, it was proposed that the duty should be 125 cents, which was agreed to by the house of representatives 90 to 60—but the senate defeated the whole bill, and the duty remained as before. In 1822, Mr. Baldwin introduced a new bill to place the duty at 125 cents, which did not prevail; for in March of the same year, Mr. Smith, of Maryland, chairman of the committee of *ways and means*, reported a general *revenue* bill, in which he placed the duty at 100 cents on hammered bar iron and castings. This bill, being a "revenue bill," excited no animation; even the "chambers of commerce" were silent about it—but it defeated Mr. Baldwin's proposition, and then—*went to sleep*. In 1824, Mr. Tod, the chairman of the committee on manufactures, proposed that the duty should be 112 cents—on the final question it was reduced to 90 cents, 120 yeas, 85 nays. Thus it was sent to the senate, and 90 cents were stricken out, but reinstated before the passage of the bill, which, however, was much and injuriously altered in that body; it being understood that the house of representatives would insist upon 90 cents, and obtain it, or lose the whole bill.

3. Flax and hemp and their manufactures. The full and able report of the committee on this subject leaves us nothing to say, except to recommend that report to our readers.

4. The further protection of distilled spirits. This is a very important interest in the grain growing states, and especially to farmers not having a convenient access to market. In 1826 we imported 535,226 gals. distilled from grain, and 3,182,926 gallons distilled from other materials, worth together $1,587,712. Nearly half the quantity was directly or indirectly from the British West Indies. The whole foreign supply may be conveniently dispensed with. The British levy a duty of 8s. 6d. per gallon, or more if of high proof, on spirits imported from their own colonies, to protect the home distillations and breweries, that the excise may be paid for the support of government.

5. Further protection to cotton goods and printed cottons. It is

known to every one that, in consequence of the protection already afforded, the home-made coarse cotton goods consumed in the United States, are cheaper than such goods manufactured and consumed in England. About this there can be no dispute. But if any should arise, the facts stated in the appendix will end it. In like manner, all common calicoes are making cheaper in this country than in that, and rapidly approaching a supply of the whole domestic demand, being preferred to the British. It is confidently believed, that if the minimum valuation on the square yard shall be raised to only 40 cents for duty, instead of 30, as at present, that the finer calicoes and other fine cotton goods will be speedily supplied on the same good terms as the coarse ones are. We have practical knowledge in this matter, and the whole subject is familiar to the people. And, if any small advance on the current cost of fine cottons should take place, which might or might not happen, it cannot possibly last more than a year or two; and the advance will wholly fall upon those most able to bear it, the wealthy. It may be due to candor to observe, that this increase of the minimum is not sought for by the manufacturers *just now*—they more apprehend domestic competition than foreign rivalry; indeed, they defy the latter: but for the reason that, as the convention believed, the effect would be to extend the business of manufactures generally, and furnish the people with better articles at more reduced prices. Such, at least, was the motive which led to this recommendation; and it would much increase the use of our own finer cottons, for which the British substitute that of Brazil, etc.

There will be found in the appendix many brief notices of other interesting branches of industry, which the committee did not feel themselves authorised to bring out in this address. Some of them have strong claims on the public support, especially such as hats and bonnets in imitation of the Leghorn, laces, gloves and artificial flowers. These may afford neat and pleasant and profitable employment to dear, lovely and interesting, but comparatively helpless females—at their own homes, in the bosom of their families, by the side of their little children, in the company of their mothers! From some rough estimates that we have seen, the four articles named would fill up the spare time of 100,000 women and girls, if the home market was insured to them. There is a distressing want of employment for many times that number of such as would gladly labor, in businesses suited to their particular condition and sex—and their several small earnings, amounting to millions in the whole, would be as a clear gain to our country. There is much feeling—much interest to society—much of all the best motives that can influence human actions, in a consideration of these things. We would that the widow's heart might be caused to leap with joy, and that the tears of honest poverty were brushed from the orphan's cheek, in independence gained through patient industry, and a willingness to earn an honest and respectable support—and in keeping families together, aged parents or helpless little ones, whom to separate, might render violence to feelings which even the untutored Indian would respect. Virtue is not an inheritance of the wealthy—nay, it rather resides in the cottage than the palace; but beset with all the ills which dependence inflicts, it is then that virtue is tried, and proved as it were in the furnace of affliction. "Lead us not into temptation, but deliver us from evil," is a prominent part of the wisest petition ever offered up to THE FOUNTAIN OF ALL GOOD, and it operates as a *command* upon all that we should help one another; but it is especially the duty of *man* to exert himself in behalf of *woman,* and yield that protection which "nature and nature's GOD" designed him to bestow; that the venerable matron, when called upon to resign her spirit to HIM who gave it, may have the last, best consolation this world can afford, in a well founded hope that the children of her care, her orphan daughters, may prosper and be happy—and, obtaining an honorable subsistence by the labor of their own hands, cause her own memory to be respected in the manners of their life. Sweet is such consolation to the heart of a parent—but dear, of earthly things most dear, is it to the heart of a departing *mother!*

The committee has thus zealously endeavored to fulfil the directions and explain the views of the convention, with a sincere desire to ascertain truth, and present it in familiar terms to their fellow citizens for action upon it. The result is with them, for the national legislature will receive its impulse from their judgment. If it shall be their good fortune to invigorate the strong, help the weak, and arrest the minds of the wavering; or, by the presentation of authentic facts or well digested opinions, to dissipate prejudices and place principles on the high ground which belongs to them, that they may be seen and understood by the American people—and allay the ardency of party feelings, by shewing the great national interests that are common to all parts of this republic and all parties—the committee will, indeed, be gratified: but if, on the other hand, they shall fail in all these, the consciousness will be left that they have striven to deserve success, and that will console them for time and labor lost in this *first* attempt at a general developement of the resources of our country: and there will be some merit, perhaps, even to fail in such an effort to subserve the public intelligence.

We have only to add, that we have spared no pains to keep out of consideration particular regard for sectional interests, except so far as parts of our country, the most populous, may be more particularly concerned; and not even then in known opposition to the interests of others. The will of the majority ought to prevail; but the minority have also interests and feelings that must be respected by all who respect themselves as they ought. It is our serious belief, that the protection of the vast capital vested in manufactures, and the greater capital involved in the allied pursuits of agriculture, and the property and persons employed in commerce and navigation, interior and exterior, is as much for the benefit of the planting interest of either or any other, in the reduced price of articles for domestic consumption and in an increased demand for the productions of the earth. If we have mistaken these things, we have honestly erred, and ask for information; which we hope will be given with that regard for moderation and justice which should mark the course of honorable men, zealous of good works, and engaged to advance the public and private welfare of *our* beloved country and countrymen.

　　　　　　　　　　　　For the committee,
Oct. 10, 1827.　　　　　　　　　H. NILES, *Chairman.*

5

The Slavery Controversy

David Walker:
An Appeal to the Coloured Citizens of the World*

The comfortable assumption of most Americans in the northern states that slavery was moribund and would soon be allowed to die without mourners was rudely shattered by the Missouri Compromise debates of 1819-21. In opposing restriction of slavery in Missouri, the South made clear her intention not only to retain but to extend the iniquitous system. From this revelation the abolition movement gained new impetus until it became at last a mighty and inexorable tide.

One of the most effective and certainly the most influential of the antislavery documents was *An Appeal to the Coloured Citizens of the World*. David Walker (1785-1830), son of a free Negro mother and a slave father, had traveled widely through the South before settling in Boston. There the *Appeal*, preaching revolt and violence, was first published in 1829. Southern legislatures went to exorbitant lengths to suppress the pamphlet, even to imposing a death penalty for circulating abolition literature among slaves. Southern intellectuals undertook to refute Walker's arguments, and the public defense of slavery as a positive good began. A final, enlarged, edition of the *Appeal* was issued before Walker died under suspicious circumstances in June 1830.

The best and most comprehensive study of the whole slavery controversy is Dwight L. Dumond, *Antislavery: The Crusade for Freedom in America* (Ann Arbor: U. of Michigan, 1962). For slavery as an episode in Negro history, the reader should consult John Hope Franklin, *From Slavery to Freedom: A History of American Negroes* (Rev. ed.; New York: Knopf, 1956). A more detailed discussion of Walker will be found in Charles M. Wiltse's *Introduction* to a recent reprint of the *Appeal* (New York: Hill and Wang, 1965). In the excerpt reprinted here, note (1) evidences suggestive of Walker's educational achievement; (2) Walker's treatment of certain American heroes and

---

*David Walker, *An Appeal to the Coloured Citizens of the World* (3rd ed.; Boston, 1830), 9-21.

his reasons; (3) what implications he drew from the religious convictions professed by the slaveholders; and (4) what characteristics of style mark Walker's writing.

Our wretchedness in consequence of slavery

M Y BELOVED BRETHREN:—THE INDIANS OF NORTH AND of South America—the Greeks—the Irish, subjected under the king of Great Britain—the Jews, that ancient people of the Lord—the inhabitants of the islands of the sea—in fine, all the inhabitants of the earth (except however, the sons of Africa) are called *men,* and of course are, and ought to be free. But we (coloured people) and our children are *brutes!!* and of course are, and *ought to be* SLAVES to the American people and their children forever!! to dig their mines and work their farms; and thus go on enriching them, from one generation to another with our *blood* and our *tears!!!!*

I promised in a preceding page to demonstrate to the satisfaction of the most incredulous, that we (coloured people of these United States of America) are the *most wretched, degraded* and *abject* set of beings that *ever lived* since the world began, and that the white Americans having reduced us to the wretched state of *slavery,* treat us in that condition *more cruel* (they being an enlightened and Christian people) than any heathen nation did any people whom it had reduced to our condition. These affirmations are so well confirmed in the minds of all unprejudiced men, who have taken the trouble to read histories, that they need no elucidation from me. But to put them beyond all doubt, I refer you in the first place to the children of Jacob, or of Israel in Egypt, under Pharaoh and his people. Some of my brethren do not know who Pharaoh and the Egyptians were—I know it to be a fact, that some of them take the Egyptians to have been a gang of *devils,* not knowing any better, and that they (Egyptians) having got possession of the Lord's people, treated them *nearly* as cruel as *Christian Americans* do us, at the present day. For the information of such, I would only mention that the Egyptians, were Africans or coloured people, such as we are—

some of them yellow and others dark—a mixture of Ethiopians and the natives of Egypt—about the same as you see the coloured people of the United States at the present day.—I say, I call your attention then, to the children of Jacob, while I point out particularly to you his son Joseph, among the rest, in Egypt.

"And Pharaoh said unto Joseph, thou shalt be over my house, and according unto thy word shall all my people be ruled: only in the throne will I be greater than thou."

"And Pharaoh said unto Joseph, see, I have set thee over all the land of Egypt."

"And Pharaoh said unto Joseph, I am Pharaoh, and without thee shall no man lift up his hand or foot in all the land of Egypt."

Now I appeal to heaven and to earth, and particularly to the American people themselves, who cease not to declare that our condition is not *hard,* and that we are comparatively satisfied to rest in wretchedness and misery, under them and their children. Not, indeed, to show me a coloured President, a Governor, a Legislator, a Senator, a Mayor, or an Attorney at the Bar.—But to show me a man of colour, who holds the low office of a Constable, or one who sits in a Juror Box, even on a case of one of his wretched brethren, throughout this great Republic!!—But let us pass Joseph the son of Israel a little father in review, as he existed with that heathen nation.

"And Pharaoh called Joseph's name Zaphnathpaaneah; and he gave him to wife Asenath the daughter of Potipherah priest of On. And Joseph went out over all the land of Egypt."

Compare the above, with the American institutions. Do they not institute laws to prohibit us from marrying among the whites? I would wish, candidly, however, before the Lord, to be understood, that I would not give a *pinch of snuff* to be married to any white person I ever saw in all the days of my life. And I do say it, that the black man, or man of colour, who will leave his own colour (provided he can get one, who is good for any thing) and marry a white woman, to be a double slave to her, just because she is *white,* ought to be treated by her as he surely will be, viz: as a NIGER!!!! It is not, indeed, what I care about inter-marriages with the whites, which induced me to pass this subject in review; for the Lord knows, that there is a day coming when they will be glad enough to get into the company of the blacks, notwithstanding, we are, in this generation, levelled by them, almost on a level with the brute creation: and some of us they treat even worse than they do the brutes that perish. I only made this extract to show how much lower we are held, and how much more cruel we are treated by the Americans, than were the children of Jacob, by the Egyptians.—We will notice the sufferings of Israel some further, under *heathen Pharaoh*, compared with ours under the *enlightened Christians of America*.

"And Pharaoh spake unto Joseph, saying, thy father and thy brethren are come unto thee:"

"The land of Egypt is before thee: in the best of the land make thy father and brethren to dwell; in the land of Goshen let them dwell: and if thou knowest any men of activity among them, then make them rulers over my cattle."

I ask those people who treat us so *well*, Oh! I ask them, where is the most barren spot of land which they have given unto us? Israel had the most fertile land in all Egypt. Need I mention the very notorious fact, that I have known a poor man of colour, who laboured night and day, to acquire a little money, and having acquired it, he vested it in a small piece of land, and got him a house erected thereon, and having paid for the whole, he moved his family into it, where he was suffered to remain but nine months, when he was cheated out of his property by a white man, and driven out of door! And is not this the case generally? Can a man of colour buy a piece of land and keep it peaceably? Will not some white man try to get it from him, even if it is in a *mud hole*? I need not comment any farther on a subject, which all, both black and white, will readily admit. But I must, really, observe that in this very city, when a man of colour dies, if he owned any real estate it most generally falls into the hands of some white person. The wife and children of the deceased may weep and lament if they please, but the estate will be kept snug enough by its white possessor.

But to prove farther that the condition of the Israelites was better under the Egyptians than ours is under the whites. I call upon the professing Christians, I call upon the philanthropist, I call upon the very tyrant himself, to show me a page of history, either sacred or profane, on which a verse can be found, which maintains, that the Egyptians heaped the *insupportable insult* upon the children of Israel, by telling them that they were not of the *human family*. Can the whites deny this charge? Have they not, after having reduced us to the deplorable condition of slaves under their feet, held us up as descending originally from the tribes of *Monkeys* or *Orang-Outangs?* O! my God! I appeal to every man of feeling—is not this insupportable? Is it not heaping the most gross insult upon our miseries, because they have got us under their feet and we cannot help ourselves? Oh! pity us we pray thee, Lord Jesus, Master.—Has Mr. Jefferson declared to the world, that we are inferior to the whites, both in the endowments of our bodies and of minds? It is indeed surprising, that a man of such great learning, combined with such excellent natural parts, should speak so of a set of men in chains. I do not know what to compare it to, unless, like putting one wild deer in an iron cage, where it will be secured, and hold another by the side of the same, then let it go, and expect the one in the cage to run as fast as the one at liberty. So far, my brethren, were the Egyptians from heaping these insults upon their slaves, that Pharaoh's daughter took Moses, a son of Israel for her own, as will appear by the following.

"And Pharaoh's daughter said unto her, [Moses' mother] take this child away, and nurse it for me, and I will pay thee thy wages. And the woman took the child [Moses] and nursed it."

"And the child grew, and she brought him unto Pharaoh's daughter and he became her son. And she called his name Moses: and she said because I drew him out of the water."

In all probability, Moses would have become Prince Regent to the throne, and no doubt, in process of time but he would have been seated on the throne of Egypt. But he had rather suffer shame, with the people of God, than to enjoy pleasures with that wicked people for a season. O! that the coloured people were long since of Moses' excellent disposition, instead of courting favour with, and telling news and lies to our *natural enemies,* against each other—aiding them to keep their hellish chains of slavery upon us. Would we not long before this time, have been respectable men, instead of such wretched victims of oppression as we are? Would they be able to drag our mothers, our fathers, our wives, our children and ourselves, around the world in

chains and hand-cuffs as they do, to dig up gold and silver for
them and theirs? This question, my brethren, I leave for you to
digest; and may God Almighty force it home to your hearts.
Remember that unless you are united, keeping your tongues
within your teeth, you will be afraid to trust your secrets to
each other, and thus perpetuate our miseries under the *Christians*!!!!! ADDITION.—Remember, also to lay humble at the feet of
our Lord and Master Jesus Christ, with prayers and fastings.
Let our enemies go on with their butcheries, and at once fill up
their cup. Never make an attempt to gain our freedom or *natural
right*, from under our cruel oppressors and murderers, until you
see your way clear[1]—when that hour arrives and you move, be
not afraid or dismayed; for be you assured that Jesus Christ the
King of heaven and of earth who is the God of justice and of
armies, will surely go before you. And those enemies who have
for hundreds of years stolen our *rights*, and kept us ignorant of
Him and His divine worship, he will remove. Millions of whom,
are this day, so ignorant and avaricious, that they cannot conceive how God can have an attribute of justice, and show mercy
to us because it pleased Him to make us black—which colour,
Mr. Jefferson calls unfortunate!!!!!! As though we are not as
thankful to our God, for having made us as it pleased himself,
as they (the whites) are for having made them white. They
think because they hold us in their infernal chains of slavery,
that we wish to be white, or of their color—but they are dread-
fully deceived—we wish to be just as it pleased our Creator to
have made us, and no avaricious and unmerciful wretches, have
any business to make slaves of, or hold us in slavery. How would
they like for us to make slaves of, and hold them in cruel slavery,
and murder them as they do us?—But is Mr. Jefferson's assertions

----

[1]It is not to be understood here, that I mean for us to wait until God shall
take us by the hair of our heads and drag us out of abject wretchedness and
slavery, nor do I mean to convey the idea for us to wait until our enemies
shall make preparations, and call us to seize those preparations, take it away
from them, and put every thing before us to death, in order to gain our
freedom which God has given us. For you must remember that we are men
as well as they. God has been pleased to give us two eyes, two hands, two
feet, and some sense in our heads as well as they. They have no more right
to hold us in slavery than we have to hold them, we have just as much
right, in the sight of God, to hold them and their children in slavery and
wretchedness, as they have to hold us, and no more.

true? viz. "that it is unfortunate for us that our Creator has been pleased to make us *black.*" We will not take his say so, for the fact. The world will have an opportunity to see whether it is unfortunate for us, that our Creator *has made us* darker than the *whites.*

Fear not the number and education of our *enemies*, against whom we shall have to contend for our lawful right; guaranteed to us by our Maker; for why should we be afraid, when God is, and will continue (if we continue humble) to be on our side?

The man who would not fight under our Lord and Master Jesus Christ, in the glorious and heavenly cause of freedom and of God—to be delivered from the most wretched, abject and servile slavery, that ever a people was afflicted with since the foundation of the world, to the present day—ought to be kept with all of his children or family, in slavery, or in chains, to be butchered by his *cruel enemies.*

I saw a paragraph, a few years since, in a South Carolina paper, which, speaking of the barbarity of the Turks, it said: "The Turks are the most barbarous people in the world—they treat the Greeks more like *brutes* than human beings." And in the same paper was an advertisement, which said: "Eight well built Virginia and Maryland *Negro fellows* and four *wenches* will positively be *sold* this day, *to the highest bidder!*" And what astonished me still more was, to see in this same *humane* paper!! the cuts of three men, with clubs and budgets on their backs, and an advertisement offering a considerable sum of money for their apprehension and delivery. I declare, it is really so amusing to hear the Southerners and Westerners of this country talk about *barbarity*, that it is positively enough to make a man *smile.*

The sufferings of the Helots among the Spartans, were somewhat severe, it is true, but to say that theirs were as severe as ours among the Americans, I do most strenuously deny—for instance, can any man show me an article on a page of ancient history which specifies, that, the Spartans chained, and hand-cuffed the Helots, and dragged them from their wives and children, children from their parents, mothers from their suckling babes, wives from their husbands, driving them from one end of the country to the other? Notice the Spartans were heathens, who lived long before our Divine

Master made his appearance in the flesh. Can Christian Americans deny these barbarous cruelties? Have you not, Americans, having subjected us under you, added to these miseries, by insulting us in telling us to our face, because we are helpless, that we are not of the human family? I ask you, O! Americans, I ask you, in the name of the Lord, can you deny these charges? Some perhaps may deny, by saying, that they never thought or said that we were not men. But do not actions speak louder than words?— have they not made provisions for the Greeks, and Irish? Nations who have never done the least thing for them, while *we,* who have enriched their country with our blood and tears—have dug up gold and silver for them and their children, from generation to generation, and are in more miseries than any other people under heaven, are not seen, but by comparatively, a handful of the American people? There are indeed, more ways to kill a dog, besides choking it to death with butter. Further—The Spartans or Lacedemonians, had some frivolous pretext, for enslaving the Helots, for they (Helots) while being free inhabitants of Sparta, stirred up an intestine commotion, and were, by the Spartans subdued, and made prisoners of war. Consequently they and their children were condemned to perpetual slavery.

I have been for years troubling the pages of historians, to find out what our fathers have done to the *white Christians of America,* to merit such condign punishment as they have inflicted on them, and do continue to inflict on us their children. But I must aver, that my researches have hitherto been to no effect. I have therefore, come to the immoveable conclusion, that they (Americans) have, and do continue to punish us for nothing else, but for enriching them and their country. For I cannot conceive of any thing else. Nor will I ever believe otherwise, until the Lord shall convince me.

The world knows that slavery as it existed among the Romans (which was the primary cause of their destruction) was, comparatively speaking, no more than a *cypher,* when compared with ours under the Americans. Indeed I should not have noticed the Roman slaves, had not the very learned and penetrating Mr. Jefferson said, "when a master was murdered, all his slaves in the same house, or within hearing, were condemned to death."— Here let me ask Mr. Jefferson (but he is gone to answer at the bar of God, for the deeds done in his body while living) I therefore ask the whole American people, had I not rather die, or be put to death, than to be a slave to any tyrant, who takes not only my own, but my wife and children's lives by the inches? Yea, would I meet death with avidity far! far!! in preference to such *servile submission* to the murderous hands of tyrants. Mr. Jefferson's very severe remarks on us have been so extensively argued upon by men whose attainments in literature, I shall never be able to reach, that I would not have meddled with it, were it not to solicit each of my brethren, who has the spirit of a man, to buy a copy of Mr. Jefferson's "Notes on Virginia," and put it in the hand of his son. For let no one of us suppose that the refutations which have been written by our white friends are enough—they are *whites*—we are *blacks*. We, and the world wish to see the charges of Mr. Jefferson refuted by the blacks *themselves,* according to their chance; for we must remember that what the whites have written respecting this subject, is other men's labours, and did not emanate from the blacks. I know well, that there are some talents and learning among the coloured people of this country, which we have not a chance to develope, in consequence of oppression; but our oppression ought not to hinder us from acquiring all we can. For we will have a chance to develope them by and by. God will not suffer us, always to be oppressed. Our sufferings will come to an *end,* in spite of all the Americans this side of *eternity.* Then we will want all the learning and talents among ourselves, and perhaps more, to govern ourselves.—"Every dog must have its day," the American's is coming to an end.

But let us review Mr. Jefferson's remarks respecting us some further. Comparing our miserable fathers, with the learned philosophers of Greece, he says: "Yet notwithstanding these and other discouraging circumstances among the Romans, their slaves were often their rarest artists. They excelled too, in science, insomuch as to be usually employed as tutors to their master's children; Epictetus, Terence and Phædrus, were slaves,—but they were of the race of whites. It is not their *condition* then, but *nature,* which has produced the distinction." See this, my brethren!! Do you believe that this assertion is swallowed by millions of the whites? Do you know that Mr. Jefferson was one of as great characters as ever lived among the whites? See his writings for the world, and public labours for the United States of America. Do you believe that the assertions of such a man, will pass away into oblivion unobserved by this people and the world? If you do you are much mistaken—See how the American people treat us—have we souls in our bodies? Are we men who have any spirits at all? I know that there are many *swell-bellied* fellows among us, whose greatest object is to fill their stomachs. Such I do not mean—I am after those who know and feel, that we are MEN, as well as other people; to them, I say, that unless we try to refute Mr. Jefferson's arguments respecting us, we will only establish them.

But the slaves among the Romans. Every body who has read history, knows, that as soon as a slave among the Romans obtained his freedom, he could rise to the greatest eminence in the State, and there was no law instituted to hinder a slave from buying his freedom. Have not the Americans instituted laws to hinder us from obtaining our freedom? Do any deny this charge? Read the laws of Virginia, North Carolina, etc. Further: have not the Americans instituted laws to prohibit a man of colour from obtaining and holding any office whatever, under the government of the United States of America? Now, Mr. Jefferson tells us, that our condition is not so hard, as the slaves were under the Romans!!!!!!

It is time for me to bring this article to a close. But before I close it, I must observe to my brethren that at the close of the first Revolution in this country, with Great Britain, there were but thirteen States in the Union, now there are twenty-four, most of which are slave-holding States, and the whites are dragging us around in chains and in hand-cuffs, to their new States and Territories to work their mines and farms, to enrich them and their children—and millions of them believing firmly that we being a little darker than they, were made by our Creator to be an inheritance to them and their children for ever—the same as a parcel of *brutes*.

Are we MEN!!—I ask you, O my brethren! are we MEN? Did our Creator make us to be slaves to dust and ashes like ourselves? Are they not dying worms as well as we? Have they not to make their appearance before the tribunal of Heaven, to answer for the deeds done in the body, as well as we? Have we any other Master but Jesus Christ alone? Is he not their Master as well as ours?—What right then, have we to obey and call any other Master, but Himself? How we could be so *submissive* to a gang of men, whom we cannot tell whether they are *as good* as ourselves or not, I never could conceive. However, this is shut up with the Lord, and we cannot precisely tell—but I declare, we judge men by their works.

The whites have always been an unjust, jealous, unmerciful, avaricious and blood-thirsty set of beings, always seeking after power and authority.—We view them all over the confederacy of Greece, where they were first known to be any thing (in consequence of education) we see them there, cutting each other's throats—trying to subject each other to wretchedness and misery —to effect which, they used all kinds of deceitful, unfair, and unmerciful means. We view them next in Rome, where the spirit of tyranny and deceit raged still higher. We view them in Gaul, Spain, and in Britain.—In fine, we view them all over Europe, together with what were scattered about in Asia and Africa, as heathens, and we see them acting more like devils than accountable men. But some may ask, did not the blacks of Africa, and the mulattoes of Asia, go on in the same way as did the whites of Europe. I answer, no—they never were half so avaricious, deceitful and unmerciful as the whites, according to their knowledge.

But we will leave the whites or Europeans as heathens, and take a view of them as Christians, in which capacity we see them as cruel, if not more so than ever. In fact, take them as a body, they are ten times more cruel, avaricious and unmerciful than ever they were; for while they were heathens, they were bad enough it is true, but it is positively a fact that they were not quite so audacious as to go and take vessel loads of men, women and children, and in cold blood, and through devilishness, throw them into the sea, and murder them in all kind of ways. While they were heathens, they were too ignorant for such barbarity. But being Christians, enlightened and sensible, they are completely prepared for such hellish cruelties. Now suppose God were to give them more sense, what would they do? If it were possible, would they not *dethrone* Jehovah and seat themselves

upon his throne? I therefore, in the name and fear of the Lord
God of Heaven and of earth, divested of prejudice either on the
side of my colour or that of the whites, advance my suspicion of
them, whether they are *as good by nature* as we are or not. Their
actions, since they were known as a people, have been the reverse, I do indeed suspect them, but this, as I before observed,
is shut up with the Lord, we cannot exactly tell, it will be proved
in succeeding generations.—The whites have had the essence of
the gospel as it was preached by my master and his apostles—the
Ethiopians have not, who are to have it in its meridian splendor
—the Lord will give it to them to their satisfaction. I hope and
pray my God, that they will make good use of it, that it may
be well with them.[2]

---

[2]It is my solemn belief, that if ever the world becomes Christianized
(which must certainly take place before long) it will be through the means
under God of the *Blacks,* who are now held in wretchedness, and degradation, by the white *Christians* of the world, who before they learn to do justice to us before our Maker—and be reconciled to us, and reconcile us to
them, and by that means have clear consciencies before God and man.—
Send out Missionaries to convert the Heathens, many of whom after they
cease to worship gods, which neither see nor hear, become ten times more
the children of Hell, then ever they were, why what is the reason? Why the
reason is obvious, they must learn to do justice at home, before they go into
distant lands, to display their charity, Christianity, and benevolence; when
they learn to do justice, God will accept their offering (no man may think
that I am against Missionaries for I am not, my object is to see justice done
at home, before we go to convert the Heathens).

6

The Constitutional Debate

Joseph Story: Commentaries on the Constitution*

The appeal to states' rights is almost as old as the Constitution itself. First invoked in 1798 by resolutions of the Kentucky Legislature against the Alien and Sedition Acts, the doctrine was used over and over again to justify opposition to unpopular laws or court decisions, until in 1861 it provided the rationale for secession. Whatever twist was given to the states' rights argument, however, it rested in the end upon the theory that the Constitution was a compact to which the states were parties. In the classic refutation of the doctrine reproduced here, Joseph Story (1779-1845), Associate Justice of the Supreme Court and Professor of Law at Harvard, sets himself to destroy the compact theory on which it rested.

Story's *Commentaries* first appeared in 1833, immediately after the Constitutional controversy had been pushed to the very brink of rebellion. A series of nationalistic Supreme Court decisions, the Missouri Compromise, and disagreement over tariff policy were all factors in a debate that reached its climax late in 1832. In November of that year South Carolina forbade the collection of import duties within the state on the ground that the tariffs of 1828 and 1832 were unconstitutional and therefore void. President Jackson upheld the law and Congress backed him up by authorizing the use of force to collect the duties. The particular episode was compromised before any blood was spilled, but there was one casualty: the doctrine of states' rights. Since that time the supremacy of the national government over the states, though it has been challenged even to the point of armed rebellion and is still, upon occasion, vociferously disputed, remains the cornerstone of our jurisprudence.

The constitutional controversy that climaxed in the 1830's is fully treated in Andrew C. McLaughlin, *Constitutional History of the United States* (New York: Appleton, 1936); and more recently by Bernard Schwartz, *The Reins of Power* (New York: Hill and Wang,

*Joseph Story, *Commentaries on the Constitution of the United States,* (3 vols.; Boston, 1833) I, pp. 318-43.

1963). The reader should note in the selection reprinted here (1) to what extent Story succeeded in using nonlegalistic language; (2) evidence of his awareness of the political aspects of the constitutional controversy; (3) his knowledge of the historical and legal literature bearing on the subject and how effectively he utilized that knowledge in his presentation; and (4) the manner and tone that Story used toward the protagonists in the then current debate.

350. In what light, then, is the constitution of the United States to be regarded? Is it a mere compact, treaty, or confederation of the states composing the Union, or of the people thereof, whereby each of the several states, and the people thereof, have respectively bound themselves to each other? Or is it a form of government, which, having been ratified by a majority of the people in all the states, is obligatory upon them, as the prescribed rule of conduct of the sovereign power, to the extent of its provisions?

351. Let us consider, in the first place, whether it is to be deemed a compact? By this, we do not mean an act of solemn assent by the people to it, as a form of government (of which there is no room for doubt) but a contract imposing mutual obligations, and contemplating the permanent subsistence of parties having an independent right to construe, control, and judge of its obligations. If in this latter sense it is to be deemed a compact, it must be, either because it contains on its face stipulations to that effect, or because it is necessarily implied from the nature and objects of a frame of government.

352. There is nowhere found upon the face of the constitution any clause, intimating it to be a compact, or in anywise providing for its interpretation, as such. On the contrary, the preamble emphatically speaks of it, as a solemn ordinance and establishment of government. The language is, "We, the people of the United States, do *ordain* and *establish* this *constitution* for the United States of America." *The people* do *ordain* and *establish*, not contract and stipulate with each other. The people of the *United States*, not the distinct people of a *particular state* with the people of the other states. The people ordain and establish a "*constitution*," not a "*confederation*." The distinction be-

tween a constitution and a confederation is well known and understood. The latter, or at least a pure confederation, is a mere treaty or league between independent states, and binds no longer, than during the good pleasure of each. It rests forever in articles of compact, where each is, or may be the supreme judge of its own rights and duties. The former is a permanent form of government, where the powers, once given, are irrevocable, and cannot be resumed or withdrawn at pleasure. Whether formed by a single people, or by different societies of people, in their political capacity, a constitution, though originating in consent, becomes, when ratified, obligatory, as a fundamental ordinance or law. The constitution of a confederated republic, that is, of a national republic formed of several states, is, or at least may be, not less an irrevokable form of government, than the constitution of a state formed and ratified by the aggregate of the several counties of the state.

353. If it had been the design of the framers of the constitution or of the people, who ratified it, to consider it a mere confederation, resting on treaty stipulations, it is difficult to conceive, that the appropriate terms should not have been found in it. The United States were no strangers to compacts of this nature. They had subsisted to a limited extent before the revolution. The articles of confederation, though in some few respects national, were mainly of a pure federative character, and were treated as stipulations between states for many purposes independent and sovereign. And yet (as has been already seen) it was deemed a political heresy to maintain, that under it any state had a right to withdraw from it at pleasure, and repeal its operation; and that a party to the compact had a right to revoke that compact. The only places, where the terms, *confederation* or *compact,* are found in the constitution, apply to subjects of an entirely different nature, and manifestly in contradistinction to *constitution.* Thus, in the tenth section of the first article it is declared, that "no state shall enter into any treaty, alliance, or *confederation";* "no state shall, without the consent of congress, etc. enter into any agreement or *compact* with another state, or with a foreign power." Again, in the sixth article it is declared, that "all debts contracted, and engagements entered into, before the adoption of this constitution, shall be as valid against the United States

under this *constitution,* as under the *confederation.*" Again, in
the tenth amendment it is declared, that "the powers not *dele-*
gated by the constitution, nor prohibited by it to the states, are
reserved to the states respectively, or to the people." A contract
can in no just sense be called a delegation of powers.

354. But that, which would seem conclusive on the subject,
(as has been already stated,) is, the very language of the constitution itself, declaring it to be a supreme fundamental law,
and to be of judicial obligation, and recognition in the administration of justice. "This constitution," says the sixth artcle, "and
the laws of the United States, which shall be made in pursuance
thereof, and all treaties made, or which shall be made under the
authority of the United States, *shall be the supreme law of the*
land; and the *judges* in every state shall be bound thereby, *any*
thing in the constitution or laws of any state to the contrary
notwithstanding." If it is the supreme law, how can the people
of any state, either by any form of its own constitution, or
laws, or other proceedings, repeal, or abrogate, or suspend it?

355. But, if the language of the constitution were less explicit
and irresistible, no other inference could be correctly deduced
from a view of the nature and objects of the instrument. The
design is to establish a form of government. This, of itself, imports legal obligation, permanence, and uncontrollability by any,
but the authorities authorized to alter, or abolish it. The object
was to secure the blessings of liberty to the people, and to their
posterity. The avowed intention was to supercede the old confederation, and substitute in its place a new form of government.
We have seen, that the inefficiency of the old confederation
forced the states to surrender the league then existing, and to
establish a national constitution. The convention also, which
framed the constitution, declared this in the letter accompanying
it. "It is obviously impracticable in the federal government of
these states," says that letter, "to secure all rights of independent
sovereignty to each, and yet provide for the interest and safety
of all. Individuals entering into society must give up a share of
liberty to preserve the rest." "In all our deliberations on this subject, we kept steadily in our view that, which appeared to us the
greatest interest of every true American, the *consolidation of our*
Union, in which is involved our prosperity, felicity, safety, per-

haps our national existence." Could this be attained consistently with the notion of an existing treaty or confederacy, which each at its pleasure was at liberty to dissolve?

356. It is also historically known, that one of the objections taken by the opponents of the constitution was, "that it is not a *confederation* of the states, but a *government* of individuals." It was, nevertheless, in the solemn instruments of ratification by the people of the several states, assented to, as a constitution. The language of those instruments uniformly is, "We, etc. do *assent* to, and *ratify* the said *constitution.*" The forms of the convention of Massachusetts and New-Hampshire are somewhat peculiar in their language. "The convention, etc. acknowledging, with grateful hearts, the goodness of the Supreme Ruler of the Universe in affording the people of the United States, in the course of his providence, an opportunity, deliberately and peaceably, without force or surprise, of entering into an *explicit* and *solemn compact* with each other, *by assenting to, and ratifying a new constitution,* etc. do assent to, and ratify the said constitution." And although many declarations of rights, many propositions of amendments, and many protestations of reserved powers are to be found accompanying the ratifications of the various conventions, sufficiently evincive of the extreme caution and jealousy of those bodies, and of the people at large, it is remarkable, that there is nowhere to be found the slightest allusion to the instrument, as a confederation or compact of states in their sovereign capacity, and no reservation of any right, on the part of any state, to dissolve its connexion, or to abrogate its assent, or to suspend the operations of the constitution, as to itself. On the contrary, that of Virginia, which speaks most pointedly to the topic, merely declares, "that the powers granted under the constitution, *being derived from the people of the United States,* may be resumed by *them* [not by any one of the states] whenever the same shall be perverted to their injury or oppression."

357. So that there is very strong negative testimony against the notion of its being a compact or confederation, of the nature of which we have spoken, founded upon the known history of the times, and the acts of ratification, as well as upon the antecedent articles of confederation. The latter purported on their face to

be a mere confederacy. The language of the third article was, "The said states hereby severally enter into a firm *league* of friendship with each other for their common defence, etc. binding themselves to assist each other." And the ratification was by delegates of the state legislatures, who solemnly plighted and engaged the *faith* of their respective constituents, that they should abide by the determination of the United States in congress assembled on all questions, which, by the said confederation, are submitted to them; and that the articles thereof should be inviolably observed by the states they respectively represented.

358. It is not unworthy of observation, that in the debates of the various conventions called to examine and ratify the constitution, this subject did not pass without discussion. The opponents, on many occasions, pressed the objection, that it was a consolidated government, and contrasted it with the confederation. None of its advocates pretended to deny, that its design was to establish a national government, as contradistinguished from a mere league or treaty, however they might oppose the suggestions, that it was a consolidation of the states. In the North Carolina debates, one of the members laid it down, as a fundamental principle of every safe and free government, that "a government is a compact between the rulers and the people." This was most strenuously denied on the other side by gentlemen of great eminence. They said, "A compact cannot be annulled, but by the consent of both parties. Therefore, unless the rulers are guilty of oppression, the people, on the principles of a compact, have no right to new-model their government. This is held to be the principle of some monarchical governments in Europe. Our government is founded on much nobler principles. The people are known with certainty to have originated it themselves. Those in power are their servants and agents. And the people, without their consent, may new-model the government, whenever they think proper, not merely because it is oppressively exercised, but because they think another form will be more conducive to their welfare."

359. Nor should it be omitted, that in the most elaborate expositions of the constitution by its friends, its character, as a permanent form of government, as a fundamental law, as a

supreme rule, which no state was at liberty to disregard, suspend, or annul, was constantly admitted, and insisted on, as one of the strongest reasons, why it should be adopted in lieu of the confederation. It is matter of surprise, therefore, that a learned commentator should have admitted the right of any state, or of the people of any state, without the consent of the rest, to secede from the Union at its own pleasure.[1] The people of the United States have a right to abolish, or alter the constitution of the United States; but that the people of a single state have such a right, is a proposition requiring some reasoning beyond the suggestion, that it is implied in the principles, on which our political systems are founded. It seems, indeed, to have its origin in the notion of all governments being founded in *compact,* and therefore liable to be dissolved by the parties, or either of them; a notion, which it has been our purpose to question, at least in the sense, to which the objection applies.

360. To us the doctrine of Mr. Dane appears far better founded, that "the constitution of the United States is not a compact or contract agreed to by two or more parties, to be construed by each for itself, and here to stop for the want of a common arbiter to revise the construction of each party or state. But that it is, as the people have named and called it, truly a Constitution; and they properly said, 'We, the people of the United States, do ordain and establish this constitution,' and not, we, the people of each state." And this expotion has been sustained by opinions of some of our most eminent statesmen and judges. It was truly remarked by the Federalist, that the constitution was the result neither from the decision of a majority of the people of the union, nor from that of a majority of the states. It resulted from the unanimous assent of the several states that are parties to it, differing no otherwise from their ordinary assent, than its being expressed, not by the legislative authority but by that of the people themselves.

361. But if the constitution could in the sense, to which we have alluded, be deemed a compact, between whom is it to be deemed a contract? We have already seen, that the learned commentator on Blackstone, deems it a compact with several aspects,

---

1. Story's reference is to William Rawle, *View of the Constitution* (Philadelphia, 1825; 2nd ed., 1829).

and first between the *states* (as contradistinguished from the *people* of the states) by which the several states have bound themselves to each other, and to the federal government.[2] The Virginia Resolutions of 1798, assert, that "Virginia views the powers of the federal government, as resulting from the *compact, to which the states are parties.*" This declaration was, at the time, matter of much debate and difference of opinion among the ablest representatives in the legislature. But when it was subsequently expounded by Mr. Madison in the celebrated Report of January, 1800, after admitting, that the term "states" is used in different senses, and among others, that it sometimes means the *people* composing a political society in their highest sovereign capacity, he considers the resolution unobjectionable, at least in this last sense, because in that sense the constitution was submitted to the "states"; in that sense the "states" ratified it; and in that sense the states are consequently parties to the compact, from which the powers of the federal government result. And that is the sense, in which he considers the states parties in his still later and more deliberate examinations.[3]

362. This view of the subject is, however, wholly at variance with that, on which we are commenting; and which, having no foundation in the words of the constitution, is altogether a gratuitous assumption, and therefore inadmissible. It is no more true, that a state is a party to the constitution, as such, because it was framed by delegates chosen by the states, and submitted by the legislatures thereof to the people of the states for ratification, and that the states are necessary agents to give effect to some of its provisions, than that for the same reasons the governor, or senate, or house of representatives, or judges, either of a state or of the United States, are parties thereto. No state, as such, that is the body politic, as it was actually organized, had any power to establish a contract for the establishment of any new government over the people thereof, or to delegate the powers of government in whole, or in part to any other sovereignty. The state governments were framed by the people to administer the

2. St. George Tucker, ed., *Blackstone's Commentaries with Notes to the Constitution of the United States* (Philadelphia, 1803), p. 169.

3. The reference is to Madison's detailed examination of the Constitution in the *North American Review* for October, 1830.

state constitutions, such as they were, and not to transfer the administration thereof to any other persons, or sovereignty. They had no authority to enter into any compact or contract for such a purpose. It is no where given, or implied in the state constitutions; and consequently, if actually entered into (as it was not) would have had no obligatory force. The people, and the people only, in their original sovereign capacity, had a right to change their form of government, to enter into a compact, and to transfer any sovereignty to the national government. And the states never, in fact, did in their political capacity, as contradistinguished from the people thereof, ratify the constitution. They were not called upon to do it by congress; and were not contemplated, as essential to give validity to it.

363. The doctrine, then, that the states are parties is a gratuitous assumption. In the language of a most distinguished statesman, the "the constitution itself in its very front refutes that. It declares, that it is ordained and established *by the* PEOPLE *of the United States.* So far from saying, that it is established by the governments of the several states, it does not even say, that it is established *by the people of the several states.* But it pronounces, that it is established by the people of the United States in the aggregate. Doubtless the people of the several states, taken collectively, constitute the people of the United States. But it is in this their collective capacity, it is as all the people of the United States, that they establish the constitution."[4]

364. But if it were admitted, that the constitution is a compact between the states, "the inferences deduced from it," as has been justly observed by the same statesmen, "are warranted by no just reason. Because, if the constitution be a compact between the states, still that constitution or that compact has established a government with certain powers; and whether it be one of these powers, that it shall construe and interpret for itself the terms of the compact in doubtful cases, can only be decided by looking to the compact, and inquiring, what provisions it contains on that point. Without any inconsistency with natural reason, the government even thus created might be trusted with this

---

4. Story is quoting from Daniel Webster's second reply to Senator Robert Y. Hayne, January 26, 27, 1830, the high point of one of the most famous debates in American history.

power of construction. The extent of its powers must, therefore, be sought in the instrument itself." "If the constitution were the mere creation of the state governments, it might be modified, interpreted, or construed according to their pleasure. But even in that case, it would be necessary, that they should agree. One alone could not interpret it conclusively. One alone could not construe it. One alone could not modify it." "If all the states are parties to it, one alone can have no right to fix upon it her own peculiar construction."

365. Then, is it a compact between the people of the several states, each contracting with all the people of the other states? It may be admitted, as was the early exposition of its advocates, "that the constitution is founded on the assent and ratification of the people of America, given by deputies elected for the special purpose; but that this assent and ratification is to be given by the whole people, not as individuals, composing one entire nation, but as composing the distinct and independent states, to which they respectively belong. It is to be the assent and ratification of the several states, derived from the supreme authority in each state, the authority of the people themselves. The act, therefore, establishing the constitution will not be [is not to be] a national, but a federal act." "It may also be admitted," in the language of one of its most enlightened commentators, that "it was formed, not by the governments of the component states, as the federal government, for which it was substituted, was formed. Nor was it formed by a majority of the people of the United States, as a single community, in manner of a consolidated government. It was formed by the states, that is, by the people in each of the states acting in their highest sovereign capacity; and formed consequently by the same authority, which formed the state constitutions."[5] But this would not necessarily draw after it the conclusion, that it was to be deemed a compact, (in the sense, to which we have so often alluded,) by which each state was still, after the ratification, to act upon it, as a league or treaty, and to withdraw from it at pleasure. A government may originate in the voluntary compact or assent of the people of several states, or of a people never before united, and yet when adopted and ratified by them, be no longer a matter rest-

---

5. *North American Review,* XXXI (October 1830), 537-8.

ing in compact; but become an executed government or constitution, a fundamental law, and not a mere league. But the difficulty in asserting it to be a compact between the people of each state, and all the people of the other states, is that the constitution itself contains no such expression, and no such designation of parties. We, "the people of the United States, etc. do *ordain*, and *establish* this *constitution*," is the language; and not we, the people of each state, do establish this *compact* between ourselves, and the people of all the other states. We are obliged to depart from the words of the instrument, to sustain the other interpretation; an interpretation, which can serve no better purpose, than to confuse the mind in relation to a subject otherwise clear. It is for this reason, that we should prefer an adherence to the words of the constitution, and to the judicial exposition of these words according to their plain and common import.

366. But supposing, that it were to be deemed such a compact among the people of the several states, let us see what the enlightened statesman, who vindicates that opinion, holds as the appropriate deduction from it. "Being thus derived (says he) from the same source, as the constitutions of the states, it has, within each state, the same authority, as the constitution of the state; and is as much a constitution within the strict sense of the term, within its prescribed sphere, as the constitutions of the states are, within their respective spheres. But with this obvious and essential difference, that being a compact among the states in their highest sovereign capacity, and *constituting the people thereof one people for certain* purposes, it cannot be altered, or annulled at the will of the states individually, as the constitution of a state may be at its individual will."[6]

367. The other branch of the proposition, we have been considering, is, that it is not only a compact between the several states, and the people thereof, but also a compact between the states and the *federal government;* and *e converso* between the *federal government*, and the several states, and every citizen of the United States. This seems to be a doctrine far more involved, and extraordinary, and incomprehensible, than any part of the preceding. The difficulties have not escaped the observation of those, by whom it has been advanced. "Although (says the

6. *Ibid.*

learned commentator) the federal government can, in no *possible view*, be considered as a party to a compact made anterior to its existence; yet, as the creature of that compact, it must be bound by it to its creators, the several states in the Union, and the citizens thereof."[7] If by this, no more were meant than to state, that the federal government cannot lawfully exercise any powers, except those conferred on it by the constitution, its truth could not admit of dispute. But it is plain, that something more was in the author's mind. At the same time, that he admits, that the federal government could not be a party to the compact of the constitution "in any possible view," he still seems to insist upon it, as a compact, by which the federal government is bound to the several states, and to every citizen; that is, that it has entered into a contract with them for the due execution of its duties.

368. And a doctrine of a like nature, viz. that the federal government is a party to the compact, seems to have been gravely entertained on other solemn occasions. The difficulty of maintaining it, however, seems absolutely insuperable. The federal government is the result of the constitution, or (if the phrase is deemed by any person more appropriate) the creature of the compact. How, then, can it be a party to that compact, to which it owes its own existence? How can it be said, that it has entered into a contract, when at the time it had no capacity to contract; and was not even *in esse?* If any provision was made for the general government's becoming a party, and entering into a compact, after it was brought into existence, where is that provision to be found? It is not to be found in the constitution itself. Are we at liberty to *imply* such a provision, attaching to no power given in the constitution? This would be to push the doctrine of implication to an extent truly alarming; to draw inferences, not from what is, but from what is not, stated in the instrument. But, if any such implication could exist, when did the general government signify its assent to become such a party? When did the people authorize it to do so? Could the government do so, without the express authority of the people? These are questions, which are more easily asked, than answered.

7. Tucker's *Blackstone,* I, p. 170.

369. In short, the difficulties attendant upon all the various theories under consideration, which treat the constitution of the United States, as a compact, either between the several states, or between the people of the several states, or between the whole people of the United States, and the people of the several states, or between each citizen of all the states, and all other citizens, are, if not absolutely insuperable, so serious, and so wholly founded upon mere implication, that it is a matter of surprise, that they should have been so extensively adopted, and so zealously propagated. These theories, too, seem mainly urged with a view to draw conclusions, which are at war with the known powers, and reasonable objects of the constitution; and which, if successful, would reduce the government to a mere confederation. They are objectionable, then, in every way; first, because they are not justified by the language of the constitution; secondly, because they have a tendency to impair, and indeed to destroy, its express powers and objects; and thirdly, because they involve consequences, which, at the will of a single state, may overthrow the constitution itself. One of the fundamental rules in the exposition of every instrument is, so to construe its terms, if possible, as not to make them the source of their own destruction, or to make them utterly void, and nugatory. And if this be generally true, with how much more force does the rule apply to a constitution of government, framed for the general good, and designed for perpetuity? Surely, if any implications are to be made beyond its terms, they are implications to preserve, and not to destroy it.

370. The cardinal conclusion, for which this doctrine of a compact has been, with so much ingenuity and ability, forced into the language of the constitution (for the language no where alludes to it) is avowedly to establish, that in construing the constitution, there is no common umpire; but that each state, nay each department of the government of each state, is the supreme judge for itself, of the powers, and rights, and duties, arising under that instrument. Thus, it has been solemnly asserted on more than one occasion, by some of the state legislatures, that there is no common arbiter, or tribunal, authorized to decide in the last resort, upon the powers and the interpretation

of the constitution. And the doctrine has been recently revived with extraordinary zeal, and vindicated with uncommon vigour.[8] A majority of the states, however, have never assented to this doctrine; and it has been, at different times, resisted by the legislatures of several of the states, in the most formal declarations.

371. But if it were admitted, that the constitution is a compact, the conclusion, that there is no common arbiter, would neither be a necessary, nor natural conclusion from that fact standing alone. To decide upon the point, it would still behove us to examine the very terms of the constitution, and the delegation of powers under it. It would be perfectly competent even for confederated states to agree upon, and delegate authority to construe the compact to a common arbiter. The people of the United States had an unquestionable right to confide this power to the government of the United States, or to any department thereof, if they chose so to do. The question is, whether they have done it. If they have, it becomes obligatory and binding upon all the states.

372. It is not, then, by artificial reasoning founded upon theory, but upon a careful survey of the language of the constitution itself, that we are to interpret its powers, and its obligations. We are to treat it, as it purports on its face to be, as a CONSTITUTION of government; and we are to reject all other appellations, and definitions of it, such, as that it is a compact, especially as they may mislead us into false constructions and glosses, and can have no tendency to instruct us in its real objects.

---

8. Story is referring specifically to the extended debate in the Senate early in 1830, of which the Webster-Hayne contest was a part; to resolutions of the Virginia, South Carolina, and Georgia legislatures asserting the right of each state to judge for itself whether the Constitution has been violated, because "there is no common arbiter"; and, finally, to Vice-President Calhoun's widely publicized letter to Governor James Hamilton, Jr., of South Carolina, on the eve of the nullification convention.

7

The Bank Controversy

Andrew Jackson:
Removal of Government Deposits from the U.S. Bank*

The Second Bank of the United States, as conceived by those who sponsored its charter in 1816, was to serve two broad functions. It was to supply the capital for a tariff-fostered industrial expansion, and for the roads and canals that would carry a growing internal commerce; and it was to provide the uniform currency so necessary to trade. It would probably have served both purposes adequately but for mismanagement by its own officers, hostility of various competing state banks, and the beginning of a postwar depression. The Bank survived both reorganization and retrenchment and by 1822, under the leadership of dynamic Nicholas Biddle (1786-1844), began truly to fulfill its mission. Many business interests had suffered from the retrenchment, however, especially in the West where abundant land had become the traditional basis for easy credit.

Among those who held the Bank responsible for the hard times was Andrew Jackson (1767-1845), who carried his suspicions with him into the White House. As early as 1829 he questioned the Bank's activities. In 1832 he vetoed a bill to renew the charter, and the following year he directed the Secretary of the Treasury to remove government funds on deposit in the Bank. His reasons for this action are explained in the document reproduced here.

The controversy that culminated in Jackson's removal of the deposits is discussed from the President's point of view in Arthur M. Schlesinger, Jr., *The Age of Jackson* (Boston: Little, Brown, 1945), and from Biddle's point of view in Thomas C. Govan, *Nicholas Biddle, Nationalist and Public Banker, 1786-1844* (Chicago: U. of Chicago Press, 1959). The most impartial analysis is that of Bray Hammond, *Banks and Politics in America from the Revolution to the Civil War* (Princeton: Princeton University Press, 1957). In the accompanying selection the reader should note (1) upon whom Jackson placed the

*"Reasons of the President, Read to the Cabinet on the 18th of September, 1833." *Register of Debates in Congress*, 23rd Congress, 1st Session, X, Appendix, pp. 284-89.

blame for any unfortunate consequences arising out of the Bank controversy; (2) what practices of the Bank elicited Jackson's ire; (3) what mandate Jackson read into the election returns of 1832; (4) how Jackson as president interpreted his own powers and duties respecting the Bank; (5) what substitute system for the Bank Jackson proposed; and (6) the character of the economic beliefs on which the proposed actions rested.

H AVING CAREFULLY AND ANXIOUSLY CONSIDERED ALL the facts and arguments which have been submitted to him relative to a removal of the public deposits from the Bank of the United States, the President deems it his duty to communicate in this manner to his Cabinet the final conclusions of his own mind and the reasons on which they are founded, in order to put them in durable form and to prevent misconceptions.

The President's convictions of the dangerous tendencies of the Bank of the United States, since signally illustrated by its own acts, were so overpowering when he entered on the duties of Chief Magistrate that he felt it his duty, notwithstanding the objections of the friends by whom he was surrounded, to avail himself of the first occasion to call the attention of Congress and the people to the question of its recharter. The opinions expressed in his annual message of December, 1829, were reiterated in those of December, 1830 and 1831, and in that of 1830 he threw out for consideration some suggestions in relation to a substitute. At the session of 1831-'2 an act was passed by a majority of both Houses of Congress rechartering the present bank, upon which the President felt it his duty to put his constitutional veto. In his message returning that act he repeated and enlarged upon the principles and views briefly asserted in his annual message, declaring the bank to be, in his opinion, both inexpedient and unconstitutional, and announcing to his countrymen very unequivocally his firm determination never to sanction by his approval the continuance of that institution or the establishment of any other upon similar principles.

There are strong reasons for believing that the motive of the bank in asking for a recharter at that session of Congress was to make it a leading question in the election of a President of the United States the ensuing November, and all steps deemed necessary were taken to procure from the people a reversal of the President's decision.

Although the charter was approaching its termination, and the bank was aware that it was the intention of the Government to use the public deposit as fast as it has accrued in the payment of the public debt, yet did it extend its loans from January, 1831, to May, 1832, from $42,402,304.24 to $70,428,070.72, being an increase of $28,025,766.48 in sixteen months. It is confidently believed that the leading object of this immense extension of its loans was to bring as large a portion of the people as possible under its power and influence; and it has been disclosed that some of the largest sums were granted on very unusual terms to the conductors of the public press. In some of these cases the motive was made manifest by the nominal or insufficient security taken for the loans, by the large amounts discounted, by the extraordinary time allowed for payment, and especially by the subsequent conduct of those receiving the accommodations.

Having taken these preliminary steps to obtain control over public opinion, the bank came into Congress and asked a new charter. The object avowed by many of the advocates of the bank was to *put the President to the test,* that the country might know his final determination relative to the bank prior to the ensuing election. Many documents and articles were printed and circulated at the expense of the bank to bring the people to a favorable decision upon its pretensions. Those whom the bank appears to have made its debtors for the special occasion were warned of the ruin which awaited them should the President be sustained, and attempts were made to alarm the whole people by painting the depression in the price of property and produce and the general loss, inconvenience, and distress which it was represented would immediately follow the reelection of the President in opposition to the bank.

Can it now be said that the question of a recharter of the bank was not decided at the election which ensued? Had the veto been equivocal, or had it not covered the whole ground—if it had merely taken exceptions to the details of the bill or to the time of its passage—if it had not met the whole ground of constitutionality and expediency, then there might have been some plausibility for the allegation that the question was not decided by the people. It was to compel the President to take his stand that the question was brought forward at that particular time. He met the challenge, willingly took the position into which his adversaries sought to force him, and frankly declared his unalterable opposition to the bank as being both unconstitutional and inexpedient. On that ground the case was argued to the people, and now that the people have sustained the President, notwithstanding the array of influence and power which was brought to bear upon him, it is too late, he confidently thinks, to say that the question has not been decided. Whatever may be the opinions of others, the President considers his reelection as a decision of the people against the bank. In the concluding paragraph of his veto message he said:

I have now done my duty to my country. If sustained by my fellow-citizens, I shall be grateful and happy; if not, I shall find in the motives which impel me ample grounds for contentment and peace.

He was sustained by a just people, and he desires to evince his gratitude by carrying into effect their decision so far as it depends upon him.

Of all the substitutes for the present bank which have been suggested, none seems to have united any considerable portion of the public in its favor. Most of them are liable to the same constitutional objections for which the present bank has been condemned, and perhaps to all there are strong objections on the score of expediency. In ridding the country of an irresponsible power which has attempted to control the Government, care must be taken not to unite the same power with the Executive branch. To give a President the control over the currency and the power over individuals now possessed by the Bank of the United States, even with the material difference that he is responsible to the people, would be as objectionable and as dangerous as to leave it as it is. Neither one nor the other is necessary, and therefore ought not to be resorted to.

On the whole, the President considers it as conclusively settled that the charter of the Bank of the United States will not be renewed, and he has no reasonable ground to believe that any substitute will be established. Being bound to regulate his course by the laws as they exist, and not to anticipate the interference of the legislative power for the purpose of framing new systems, it is proper for him seasonably to consider the means by which the services rendered by the Bank of the United States are to be performed after its charter shall expire.

The existing laws declare that the deposits of the money of the United States in places in which the said bank and branches thereof may be established shall be made in said bank or branches thereof unless the Secretary of the Treasury shall at any time otherwise order and direct, in which case the Secretary of the Treasury shall immediately lay before Congress, if in session, and, if not, immediately after the commencement of the next session, the reasons of such order or direction.

The power of the Secretary of the Treasury over the deposits is *unqualified*. The provision that he shall report his reasons to Congress is no limitation. Had it not been inserted he would have been responsible to Congress had he made a removal for any other than good reasons, and his responsibility now ceases upon the rendition of sufficient ones to Congress. The only object of the provision is to make his reasons accessible to Congress and enable that body the more readily to judge of their soundness and purity, and thereupon to make such further provision by law as the legislative power may think proper in relation to the deposit of the public money. Those reasons may be very diversified. It was asserted by the Secretary of the Treasury, without contradiction, as early as 1817, that he had power "to control the proceedings" of the Bank of the United States at any moment "by changing the deposits to the State banks" should it pursue an illiberal course toward those institutions; that "the Secretary of the Treasury will always be disposed to support the credit of the State banks, and will invariably direct transfers from the deposits of the public money in aid of their legitimate exertions to maintain their credit'"; and he asserted a right to employ the State banks when the Bank of the United States should refuse to receive on deposit the notes of such State banks as the public interest required should be received in payment of the public dues. In several instances he did transfer the public deposits to State banks in the immediate vicinity of branches, for reasons connected only with the safety of those banks, the public convenience, and the interests of the Treasury.

If it was lawful for Mr. Crawford, the Secretary of the Treasury at that time, to act on these principles, it will be difficult to discover any sound reason against the application of similar principles in still stronger cases. And it is a matter of surprise that a power which in the infancy of the bank was freely asserted as one of the ordinary and familiar duties of the Secretary of the Treasury should now be gravely questioned, and attempts made to excite and alarm the public mind as if some new and unheard-of power was about to be usurped by the executive branch of the Government.

It is but a little more than two and a half years to the termination of the charter of the present bank. It is considered as the decision of the country that it shall then cease to exist, and no man, the President believes, has reasonable ground for expectation that any other Bank of the United States will be created by Congress. To the Treasury Department is intrusted the safe keeping and faithful application of the public moneys. A plan of collection different from the present must therefore be introduced and put in complete operation before the dissolution of the present bank. When shall it be commenced? Shall no step be taken in this essential concern until the charter expires and the Treasury finds itself without an agent, its accounts in confusion, with no depository for its funds, and the whole business of the Government deranged? or shall it be delayed until six months, or a year, or two years before the expiration of the charter? It is obvious that any new system which may be substitued in the place of the Bank of the United States could not be suddenly carried into effect on the termination of its existence without serious inconvenience to the Government and the people. Its vast amount of notes are then to be redeemed and withdrawn from circulation and its immense debt collected. These operations must be gradual, otherwise much suffering and distress will be brought upon the community. It ought to be not a work of months only, but of years, and the President thinks it cannot, with due attention to the interests of the people, be longer postponed. It is safer to begin it too soon than to delay it too long.

It is for the wisdom of Congress to decide upon the best substitute to be adopted in the place of the Bank of the United States; and the President would have felt himself relieved from a heavy and painful responsibility if in the charter to the bank Congress had reserved to itself the power of directing at its pleasure the public money to be elsewhere deposited, and had not devolved that power exclusively on one of the Executive Departments. It is useless now to inquire why this high and important power was surrendered by those who are peculiarly and appropriately the guardians of the public money. Perhaps it was an oversight. But as the President presumes that the charter to the bank is to be considered as a contract on the part of the Government, it is not now in the power of Congress to disregard its stipulations; and by the terms of that contract the public money is to be deposited in the bank during the continuance of its charter unless the Secretary of the Treasury shall otherwise direct. Unless, therefore, the Secretary of the Treasury first acts, Congress have no power over the subject, for they cannot add a new clause to the charter or strike one out of it without the consent of the bank; and consequently the public money must remain in that institution to the last hour of its existence unless the Secretary of the Treasury shall remove it at an earlier day. The responsibility is thus thrown upon the Executive branch of the Government of deciding how long before the expiration of the charter the public interest will require the deposits to be placed elsewhere. And although according to the frame and principle of our Government this decision would seem more properly to belong to the legislative power, yet as the law has imposed it upon the Executive department the duty ought to be faithfully and firmly met, and the decision made and executed upon the best lights that can be obtained and the best judgment that can be formed. It would ill become the Executive branch of the Government to shrink from any duty which the law imposes on it, to fix upon others the responsibility which justly belongs to itself. And while the President anxiously wishes to abstain from the exercise of doubtful powers and to avoid all interference with the rights and duties of others, he must yet with unshaken constancy discharge his own obligations, and cannot allow himself to turn aside in order to avoid any responsibility which the high trust with which he has been honored requires him to encounter; and it being the duty of one of the Executive departments to decide in the first instance, subject to the future action of the legislative power, whether the public deposits shall remain in the Bank of the United States until the end of its existence or be withdrawn some time before, the President has felt himself bound to examine the question carefully and deliberately in order to make up his judgment on the subject, and in his opinion the near approach of the termination of the charter and the public considerations heretofore mentioned are of themselves amply sufficient to justify the removal of the deposits, without reference to the conduct of the bank or their safety in its keeping.

But in the conduct of the bank may be found other reasons, very imperative in their character, and which require prompt action. Developments have been made from time to time of its faithlessness as a public agent, its misapplication of public funds, its interference in elections, its efforts by the machinery of committees to deprive the Government directors of a full knowledge of its concerns, and, above all, its flagrant misconduct as recently and unexpectedly disclosed in placing all the funds of the bank, including the money of the Government, at the disposition of the president of the bank, as means of operating upon public opinion and procuring a new charter, without requiring him to render a voucher for their disbursement. A brief recapitulation of the facts which justify these charges, and which have come to the knowledge of the public and the President, will, he thinks, remove every reasonable doubt as to the course which it is now the duty of the President to pursue.

We have seen that in sixteen months ending in May, 1832, the bank had extended its loans more than $28,000,000, although it knew the Government intended to appropriate most of its large deposit during that year in payment of the public debt. It was in May, 1832, that its loans arrived at the maximum, and in the preceding March so sensible was the bank that it would not be able to pay over the public deposit when it would be required by the Government that it commenced a secret negotiation, without the approbation or knowledge of the Government, with the agents for about $2,700,000 of the three per cent. stocks held in Holland, with a view of inducing them not to come forward for payment for one or more years after notice should be given by the Treasury Department. This arrangement would have enabled the bank to keep and use during that time the public money set apart for the payment of these stocks.

After this negotiation had commenced, the Secretary of the Treasury informed the bank that it was his intention to pay off one-half of the three per cents. on the first of the succeeding July, which amounted to about $6,500,000. The president of the bank, although the committee of investigation was then looking into its affairs at Philadelphia, came immediately to Washington, and upon representing that the bank was desirous of accommodating the importing merchants at New York (which it failed to do) and undertaking to pay the interest itself, procured the consent of the Secretary, after consultation with the President, to postpone the payment until the succeeding first of October.

Conscious that at the end of that quarter the bank would not be able to pay over the deposits and that further indulgence was not to be expected of the Government, an agent was dispatched to England secretly to negotiate with the holders of the public debt in Europe and induce them by the offer of an equal or higher interest than that paid by the Government to hold back their claims for one year, during which the bank expected thus to retain the use of $5,000,000 of the public money, which the Government should set apart for the payment of that debt. The agent made an arrangement on terms, in part, which were in direct violation of the charter of the bank; and when some incidents connected with this secret negotiation accidentally came to the knowledge of the public and the Government, then, and not before, so much of it as was palpably in violation of the charter was disavowed! A modification of the rest was attempted with the view of getting the certificates without payment of the money, and thus absolving the Government from its liability to the holders. In this scheme the bank was partially successful, but to this day the certificates of a portion of these stocks have not been paid and the bank retains the use of the money.

This effort to thwart the Government in the payment of the public debt that it might retain the public money to be used for their private interests, palliated by pretenses notoriously unfounded and insincere, would have justified the instant withdrawal of the public deposits. The negotiation itself rendered doubtful the ability of the bank to meet the demands of the Treasury, and the misrepresentations by which it was attempted to be justified proved that no reliance could be placed upon its allegations.

If the question of a removal of the deposits presented itself to the Executive in the same attitude that it appeared before the House of Representatives at their last session, their resolution in relation to the safety of the deposits would be entitled to more weight, although the decision of the question of removal has been confided by law to another department of the Government. But the question now occurs attended by other circumstances and new disclosures of the most serious import. It is true that in the message of the President which produced this inquiry and resolution on the part of the House of Representatives it was his object to obtain the aid of that body in making a thorough examination into the conduct and condition of the bank and its branches in order to enable the Executive department to decide whether the public money was longer safe in its hands. The limited power of the Secretary of the Treasury over the subject disabled him from making the investigation as fully and satisfactorily as it could be done by a committee of the House of Representatives, and hence the President desired the assistance of Congress to obtain for the Treasury Department a full knowledge of all the facts which were necessary to guide his judgment. But it was not his purpose, as the language of his message will show, to ask the representatives of the people to assume a responsibility which did not belong to them and relieve the Executive branch of the Government from the duty which the law had imposed upon it. It is due to the President that his object in that proceeding should be distinctly understood, and that he should acquit himself of all suspicion of seeking to escape from the performance of his own duties or of desiring to interpose another body between himself and the people in order to avoid a measure which he is called upon to meet. But although as an act of justice to himself he disclaims any design of soliciting the opinion of the House of Representatives in relation to his own duties in order to shelter himself from responsibility under the sanction of their counsel, yet he is at all times ready to listen to the suggestions of the representatives of the people, whether given voluntarily or upon solicitation, and to consider them with the profound respect to which all will admit that they are justly entitled. Whatever may be the consequences, however, to himself, he must finally form his own judgment where the Constitution and the law make it his duty to decide, and must act accordingly; and he is bound to suppose that such a course on his part will never be regarded by that elevated body as a mark of disrespect to itself; but that they will, on the contrary, esteem it the strongest evidence he can give of his fixed resolution conscientiously to discharge his duty to them and the country.

A new state of things has, however, arisen since the close of the last session of Congress, and evidence has since been laid before the President which he is persuaded would have led the House of Representatives to a different conclusion if it had come to their knowledge. The fact that the bank controls, and in some cases substantially *owns,* and by its money *supports* some of the leading presses of the country is now more clearly established. Editors to whom it loaned extravagant sums in 1831 and 1832, on unusual time and nominal security, have since turned out to be insolvent, and to others apparently in no better condition accommodations still more extravagant, on terms more unusual, and some without any security, have also been heedlessly granted.

The allegation which has so often circulated through these channels that the Treasury was bankrupt and the bank was sustaining it, when for many years there has not been less, on an average, than six millions of public money in that institution, might be passed over as a harmless misrepresentation; but when it is attempted by substantial acts to impair the credit of the Government and tarnish the honor of the country, such charges require more serious attention. With six millions of public money in its vaults, after having had the use of from five to twelve millions for nine years without interest, it became the purchaser of a bill drawn by our Government on that of France for about 900,000 dollars, being the first installment of the French indemnity. The purchase money was left in the use of the bank, being simply added to the Treasury deposit. The bank sold the bill in England, and the holder sent it to France for collection, and arrangements not having been made by the French Government for its payment, it was taken up by the agents of the bank in Paris with the funds of the bank in their hands. Under these circumstances it has through its organs openly assailed the credit of the Government, and has actually made and persists in a demand of fifteen per cent. or $158,842.77, as damages, when no damage, or none beyond some trifling expense, has in fact been sustained, and when the bank had in its own possession on deposit several millions of the public money which it was then using for its own profit. Is a fiscal agent of the Government, which thus seeks to enrich itself at the expense of the public, worthy of further trust?

There are other important facts not in the contemplation of the House of Representatives or not known to the members at the time they voted for the resolution.

Although the charter and the rules of the bank both declare that "not less than seven directors" shall be necessary to the transaction of business, yet the most important business, even that of granting discounts to any extent, is intrusted to a committee of five members, who do not report to the board.

To cut off all means of communication with the Government in relation to its most important acts at the commencement of the present year, not one of the Government directors was placed on any one committee. And although since, by an unusual remodeling of those bodies, some of those directors have been placed on some of the committees, they are yet entirely excluded from the committee of exchange, through which the greatest and most objectionable loans have been made.

When the Government directors made an effort to bring back the business of the bank to the board in obedience to the charter and the existing regulations, the board not only overruled their attempt, but altered the rule so as to make it conform to the practice, in direct violation of one of the most important provisions of the charter which gave them existence.

It has long been known that the president of the bank, by his single will, originates and executes many of the most important measures connected with the management and credit of the bank, and that the committee as well as the board of directors are left in entire ignorance of many acts done and correspondence carried on in their names, and apparently under their authority. The fact has been recently disclosed that an unlimited discretion has been and is now vested in the president of the bank to expend its funds in payment for preparing and circulating articles and purchasing pamphlets and newspapers, calculated by their contents to operate on elections and secure a renewal of its charter. It appears from the official report of the public directors that on the 30th November, 1830, the president submitted to the board an article published in the American Quarterly Review containing favorable notices of the bank, and suggested the expediency of giving it a wider circulation at the expense of the bank; whereupon the board passed the following resolution, viz:

Resolved, That the president be authorized to take such measures in regard to the circulation of the contents of the said article, either in whole or in part, as he may deem most for the interest of the bank.

By an entry in the minutes of the bank dated March 11, 1831, it appears that the president had not only caused a large edition of that article to be issued, but had also, before the resoultion of 30th November was adopted, procured to be printed and widely circulated numerous copies of the reports of General Smith and Mr. McDuffie in favor of the bank, and on that day he suggested the expediency of extending his power to the printing of other articles which might subserve the purposes of the institution, whereupon the following resolution was adopted, viz:

Resolved, That the president is hereby authorized to cause to be prepared and circulated such documents and papers as may communicate to the people information in regard to the nature and operations of the bank.

The expenditures purporting to have been made under authority of these resolutions during the years 1831 and 1832 were about $80,000. For a portion of these expenditures vouchers were rendered, from which it appears that they were incurred in the purchase of some hundred thousand copies of newspapers, reports and speeches made in Congress, reviews of the veto message and reviews of speeches against the bank, etc. For another large portion no vouchers whatever were rendered, but the various sums were paid on orders of the president of the bank, making reference to the resolution of the 11th of March, 1831.

On ascertaining these facts and perceiving that expenditures of a similar character were still continued, the Government directors a few weeks ago offered a resolution in the board calling for a specific account of these expenditures, showing the objects to which they had been applied and the persons to whom the money had been paid. This reasonable proposition was voted down.

They also offered a resolution rescinding the resolutions of November, 1830, and March, 1831. This also was rejected.

Not content with thus refusing to recall the obnoxious power or even to require such an account of the expenditure as would show whether the money of the bank had in fact been applied to the objects contemplated by these resolutions, as obnoxious as they were, the board renewed the power already conferred, and even enjoined renewed attention to its exercise by adopting the following in lieu of the propositions submitted by the Government directors, viz:

Resolved, That the board have confidence in the wisdom and integrity of the president and in the propriety of the resolutions of 30th November, 1830, and 11th March, 1831, and entertain a full conviction of the necessity of a renewed attention to the object of those resolutions, and that the president be authorized and requested to continue his exertions for the promotion of said object.

Taken in connection with the nature of the expenditures heretofore made, as recently disclosed, which the board not only tolerate, but approve, this resolution puts the funds of the bank at the disposition of the president for the purpose of employing the whole press of the country in the service of the bank, to hire writers and newspapers, and to pay out such sums as he pleases to what person and for what services he pleases without the responsibility of rendering any specific account. The bank is thus converted into a vast electioneering engine, with means to embroil the country in deadly feuds, and, under cover of expenditures, in themselves improper, extend its corruption through all the ramifications of society.

Some of the items for which accounts have been rendered show the construction which has been given to the resolutions and the way in which the power it confers has been exerted. The money has not been expended merely in the publication and distribution of speeches, reports of committees, or articles written for the purpose of showing the constitutionality or usefulness of the bank, but publications have been prepared and extensively circulated containing the grossest invectives against the officers of the Government; and the money which belongs to the stockholders and to the public has been freely applied in efforts to degrade in public estimation those who were supposed to be instrumental in resisting the wishes of this grasping and dangerous institution. As the president of the bank has not been required to settle his accounts, no one but himself knows how much more than the sum already mentioned may have been squandered, and for which a credit may hereafter be claimed in his account under this most extraordinary resolution. With these facts before us can we be surprised at the torrent of abuse incessantly poured out against all who are supposed to stand in the way of the cupidity or ambition of the Bank of the United States? Can we be surprised at sudden and unexpected changes of opinion in favor of an institution which has millions to lavish and avows its determination not to spare its means when they are necessary to accomplish its purposes? The refusal to render an account of the manner in which a part of the money expended has been applied gives just cause for the suspicion that it has been used for purposes which it is not deemed prudent to expose to the eyes of an intelligent and virtuous people. Those who act justly do not shun the light, nor do they refuse explanations when the propriety of their conduct is brought into question.

With these facts before him in an official report from the Government directors, the President would feel that he was not only responsible for all the abuses and corruptions the bank has committed or may commit, but almost an accomplice in a conspiracy against that Government which he has sworn honestly to administer, if he did not take every step within his constitutional and legal power likely to be efficient in putting an end to these enormities. If it be possible within the scope of human affairs to find a reason for removing the Government deposits and leaving the bank to its own resource for the mean of effecting its criminal designs, we have it here. Was it expected, when the moneys of the United States were directed to be placed in that bank, that they would be put under the control of one man empowered to spend millions without rendering a voucher or specifying the object? Can they be considered safe with the evidence before us that tens of thousands have been spent for highly improper if not corrupt purposes, and that the same motive may lead to the expenditure of hundreds of thousands, and even millions, more? And can we justify ourselves to the people by longer lending to it the money and power of the Government to be employed for such purposes?

It has been alleged by some as an objection to the removal of the deposits that the bank has the power, and in that event will have the disposition, to destroy the State banks employed by the Government, and bring distress upon the country. It has been the fortune of the President to encounter dangers which were represented as equally alarming, and he has seen them vanish before resolution and energy. Pictures equally appalling were paraded before him when this bank came to demand a new charter. But what was the result? Has the country been ruined, or even distressed? Was it ever more prosperous than since that act? The President verily believes the bank has not the power to produce the calamities its friends threaten. The funds of the Government will not be annihilated by being transferred. They will immediately be issued for the benefit of trade; and if the Bank of the United States curtails its loans the State banks, strengthened by the public deposits, will extend theirs. What comes in through one bank will go out through others, and the equilibrium will be preserved. Should the bank, for the mere purpose of producing distress, press its debtors more heavily than some of them can bear, the consequences will recoil upon itself, and in the attempts to embarrass the country it will only bring loss and ruin upon the holders of its own stock. But if the President believed the bank possessed all the power which has been attributed to it, his determination would only be rendered the more inflexible. If, indeed, this corporation now holds in its hands the happiness and prosperity of the American people, it is high time to take the alarm. If the despotism be already upon us and our only safety is in the mercy of the despot, recent developments in relation to his designs and the means he employs show how necessary it is to shake it off. The struggle can never come with less distress to the people or under more favorable auspices than at the present moment.

All doubt as to the willingness of the State banks to undertake the service of the Government to the same extent and on the same terms as it is now performed by the Bank of the United States is put to rest by the report of the agent recently employed to collect information, and from that willingness their own safety in the operation may be confidently inferred. Knowing their own resources better than they can be known by others, it is not to be supposed that they would be willing to place themselves in a situation which they cannot occupy without danger of annihilation or embarrassment. The only consideration applies to the safety of the public funds if desposited in those institutions, and when it is seen that the directors of many of them are not only willing to pledge the character and capital of the corporations in giving success to this measure, but also their own property and reputation, we cannot doubt that they at least believe the public deposits would be safe in their management. The President thinks that these facts and circumstances afford as strong a guarantee as can be had in human affairs for the safety of the public funds and the practicability of a new system of collection and disbursement through the agency of the State banks.

From all these considerations the President thinks that the State banks ought immediately to be employed in the collection and disbursement of the public revenue, and the funds now in the Bank of the United States drawn out with all convenient dispatch. The safety of the public moneys if deposited in the State banks must be secured beyond all reasonable doubts; but the extent and nature of the security, in addition to their capital, if any be deemed necessary, is a subject of detail to which the Treasury Department will undoubtedly give its anxious attention. The banks to be employed must remit the moneys of the Government without charge, as the Bank of the United States now does; must render all the services which that bank now performs; must keep the Government advised of their situation by periodical returns; in fine, in any arrangement with the State banks the Government must not in any respect be placed on a worse footing than it now is. The President is happy to perceive by the report of the agent that the banks which he has consulted have, in general, consented to perform the service on these terms, and that those in New York have further agreed to make payments in London without other charge than the mere cost of the bills of exchange.

It should also be enjoined upon any banks which may be employed that it will be expected of them to facilitate domestic exchanges for the benefit of internal commerce; to grant all reasonable facilities to the payers of the revenue; to exercise the utmost liberality toward the other State banks, and do nothing uselessly to embarrass the Bank of the United States.

As one of the most serious objections to the Bank of the United States is the power which it concentrates, care must be taken in finding other agents for the service of the Treasury not to raise up another power equally formidable. Although it would probably be impossible to produce such a result by any organization of the State banks which could be devised—yet it is desirable to avoid even the appearance. To this end it would be expedient to assume no more power over them and interfere no more in their affairs than might be absolutely necessary to the security of the public deposit and the faithful performance of their duties as agents of the Treasury. Any interference by them in the political contests of the country with a view to influence elections ought, in the opinion of the President, to be followed by an immediate discharge from the public service.

It is the desire of the President that the control of the banks and the currency shall as far as possible be entirely separated from the political power of the country as well as wrested from an institution which has already attempted to subject the Government to its will. In his opinion the action of the General Government on this subject ought not to extend beyond the grant in the Constitution, which only authorizes Congress "to coin money and regulate the value thereof"; all else belongs to the States and the people, and must be regulated by public opinion and the interests of trade.

In conclusion, the President must be permitted to remark that he looks upon the pending question as of higher consideration than the mere transfer of a sum of money from one bank to another. Its decision may affect the character of our Government for ages to come. Should the bank be suffered longer to use the public moneys in the accomplishment of its purposes, with the proofs of its faithlessness and corruption before our eyes, the patriotic among our citizens will despair of success in struggling against its power, and we shall be responsible for entailing it upon our country forever. Viewing it as a question of transcendent importance, both in the principles and consequences it involves, the President could not, in justice to the responsibility which he owes to the country, refrain from pressing upon the Secretary of the Treasury his view of the considerations which impel to immediate action. Upon him has been devolved by the Constitution and the suffrages of the American people the duty of superintending the operation of the Executive Departments of the Government and seeing that the laws are faithfully executed. In the performance of this high trust it is his undoubted right to express to those whom the laws and his own choice have made his associates in the administration of the Government his opinion of their duties under circumstances as they arise. It is this right which he now exercises. Far be it from him to expect or require that any member of the Cabinet should at his request, order, or dictation do any act which he believes unlawful or in his conscience condemns. From them and from his fellow-citizens in general he desires only that aid and support which their reason approves and their conscience sanctions.

In the remarks he has made on this all-important question he trusts the Secretary of the Treasury will see only the frank and respectful declarations of the opinions which the President has formed on a measure of great national interest deeply affecting the character and usefulness of his Administration, and not a spirit of dictation, which the President would be as careful to avoid as ready to resist. Happy will he be if the facts now disclosed produce uniformity of opinion and unity of action among the members of the Administration.

The President again repeats that he begs his Cabinet to consider the proposed measure as his own, in the support of which he shall require no one of them to make a sacrifice of opinion or principle. Its responsibility has been assumed after the most mature deliberation and reflection as necessary to preserve the morals of the people, the freedom of the press, and the purity of the elective franchise, without which all will unite in saying that the blood and treasure expended by our forefathers in the establishment of our happy system of government will have been vain and fruitless. Under these convictions he feels that a measure so important to the American people cannot be commenced too soon; and he therefore names the first day of October next as a period proper for the change of the deposits, or sooner, provided the necessary arrangements with the State banks can be made.

8

Texas

Stephen F. Austin: Address on Texas*

Texas became a magnet for the adventurous when the Louisiana Purchase, with its vague southwestern boundary, put the country west of the Sabine within American reach. The later renunciation of Texas by the United States in return for Florida and for Spanish recognition of an American interest on the Pacific coast only made the forbidden land seem more desirable. The Florida treaty was still awaiting ratification when Moses Austin secured a grant from the Spanish authorities to settle 300 American families in Texas.

Stephen Fuller Austin (1793-1836) took over the project on his father's death in 1821. The Texas story from that point up to the declaration of Texan independence is told by Austin himself in the *Address* reproduced here. Austin, in the states to raise money and recruit volunteers for the Texas revolution, did not yet know of the massacre at the Alamo, which came to its bloody end only the day before the address was delivered in Louisville, Kentucky. Later in the year Austin was defeated for the office of President of Texas by Sam Houston. He was serving as secretary of state in Houston's cabinet when he died suddenly in December 1836.

The most complete, and indeed the one indispensable volume on the subject, is Justin H. Smith, *The Annexation of Texas* (Corrected Edition; New York: Barnes and Noble, 1941). Older but readable and generally accurate are Eugene C. Barker, *The Life of Stephen F. Austin, Founder of Texas, 1739-1836* (Nashville: Cokesbury Press, 1925); and Marquis James, *The Raven: A Biography of Sam Houston* (Indianapolis: Bobbs-Merrill, 1929). In reading the *Address*, note (1) what theories of revolution and government Austin used to justify the Texas revolution; (2) what Austin assumed about the future relations of the United States and Texas; (3) the extent to which he referred to the institution of Negro slavery; (4) what re-

*Stephen F. Austin, *An Address delivered by S. F. Austin of Texas, to a very large audience of Ladies and Gentlemen in the Second Presbyterian Church, Louisville, Kentucky, on the 7th of March, 1836* (Lexington, 1836).

sources Texas possessed to support an independent existence; (5) what attitudes Austin displayed toward Mexicans and others of nonAnglo-Saxon heritage; and (6) what advantages both to Mexico and to the United States he thought would result from Texan independence.

IT IS WITH THE MOST UNFEIGNED AND HEARTFELT gratitude that I appear before this enlightened audience, to thank the citizens of Louisville, as I do in the name of the people of Texas, for the kind and generous sympathy they have manifested in favor of the cause of that struggling country; and to make a plain statement of facts explanatory of the contest in which Texas is engaged with the Mexican Government.

The public has been informed, through the medium of the newspapers, that war exists between the people of Texas and the present Government of Mexico. There are, however, many circumstances connected with this contest, its origin, its principles and objects which, perhaps, are not so generally known, and are indispensable to a full and proper elucidation of this subject.

When a people consider themselves compelled by circumstances or by oppression, to appeal to arms and resort to their natural rights, they necessarily submit their cause to the great tribunal of public opinion. The people of Texas, confident in the justice of their cause, fearlessly and cheerfully appeal to this tribunal. In doing this the first step is to show, as I trust I shall be able to do by a succinct statement of facts, that our cause is just, and is the cause of light and liberty:—the same holy cause for which our forefathers fought and bled:—the same that has an advocate in the bosom of every freeman, no matter in what country, or by what people it may be contended for.

But a few years back Texas was a wilderness, the home of the uncivilized and wandering Comanche and other tribes of Indians, who waged a constant and ruinous warfare against the Spanish settlements. These settlements at that time were limited to the small towns of Bexar (commonly called San Antonio) and Goliad, situated on the western limits. The incursions of the

Indians also extended beyond the Rio Bravo del Norte, and desolated that part of the country.

In order to restrain these savages and bring them into subjection, the Government opened Texas for settlement. Foreign emigrants were invited and called to that country. American enterprise accepted the invitation and promptly responded to the call. The first colony of Americans or foreigners ever settled in Texas was by myself. It was commenced in 1821 under a permission to my father, Moses Austin, from the Spanish Government previous to the Independence . of Mexico, and has succeeded by surmounting those difficulties and dangers incident to all new and wilderness countries infested with hostile Indians. These difficulties were many and at times appalling, and can only be appreciated by the hardy pioneers of this western country, who have passed through similar scenes.

The question here naturally occurs, what inducements, what prospects, what hopes could have stimulated us, the pioneers and settlers of Texas, to remove from the midst of civilized society, to expatriate ourselves from this land of liberty, from this our native country, endeared to us as it was, and still is, and ever will be, by the ties of nativity, the reminiscences of childhood and youth and local attachments, of friendship and relationship? Can it for a moment be supposed that we severed all these ties—the ties of nature and of education, and went to Texas to grapple with the wilderness and with savage foes, merely from a spirit of wild and visionary adventure, without guaranties of protection for our persons and property and political rights? No, it cannot be believed. No American, no Englishman, no one of any nation who has a knowledge of the people of the United States, or of the prominent characteristics of the Anglo-Saxon race to which we belong—a race that in all ages and in all countries wherever it has appeared has been marked for a jealous and tenacious watchfulness of its liberties, and for a cautious and calculating view of the probable events of the future—no one who has a knowledge of this race can or will believe that we removed to Texas without such guaranties, as free born and enterprising men naturally expect and require.

The fact is, we *had* such guaranties; for, in the first place the Government bound itself to protect us by the mere act of admitting us as citizens, on the general and long established principle, even in the dark ages, that *protection* and *allegiance* are reciprocal—a principle which in this enlightened age has been extended much further; for its received interpretation now is, that the object of government is the well being, security, and happiness of the governed, and that allegiance ceases whenever it is clear, evident, and palpable, that this object is in no respect effected.

But besides this general guarantee, we had others of a special, definite, and positive character—the colonization laws of 1823, '24, and '25, inviting emigrants generally to that country, specially guarantied protection for person and property, and the right of citizenship.

When the federal system and constitution were adopted in 1824, and the former provinces became States, Texas, by her representative in the Constitutional Congress, exercised the right which was claimed and exercised by all the provinces, of retaining within her own control, the rights and powers which appertained to her as one of the *unities* or district societies, which were confederated together to form the federal republic of Mexico. But not possessing at that time sufficient population to become a State by herself, she was with her own consent united provisionally with Coahuila, a neighboring province or society, to form the State of COAHUILA AND TEXAS, "*until Texas possessed the necessary elements to prove a separate State of herself.*" I quote the words of the constitutional or organic act passed by the Constituent Congress of Mexico, on the 7th of May, 1824, which establishes the State of Coahuila and Texas. This law, and the principles on which the Mexican federal compact was formed, gave to Texas a specific political existence, and vested in her inhabitants the special and well defined rights of self-government as a State of the Mexican confederation so soon as she "*possessed the necessary elements.*" Texas consented to the provisional union with Coahuila on the faith of this guaranty. It was therefore a solemn compact, which neither the State of Coahuila and Texas nor the general government of Mexico can change without the consent of the people of Texas.

In 1833 the people of Texas, after a full examination of their population and resources, and of the law and constitution, decided, in a general convention elected for that purpose, that the period had arrived contemplated by said law and compact of 7th May, 1824, and that the country possessed the necessary elements to form a State separate from Coahuila. A respectful and humble petition was accordingly drawn up by this convention, addressed to the general Congress of Mexico praying for the admission of Texas into the Mexican confederation as a State. I had the honor of being appointed by the convention the commissioner or agent of Texas to take this petition to the city of Mexico, and present it to the government. I discharged this duty to the best of my feeble abilities, and, as I believed, in a respectful manner. Many months passed and nothing was done with the petition, except to refer it to a committee of Congress, where it slept and was likely to sleep. I finally urged the just and constitutional claims of Texas to become a State in the most pressing manner, as I believed it to be my duty to do; representing also the necessity and good policy of this measure, owing to the almost total want of local good of any kind, the absolute want of a judiciary, the evident impossibility of being governed any longer by Coahuila (for three fourths of the Legislature were from there) and the consequent anarchy and discontent that existed in Texas. It was my misfortune to offend the high authorities of the nation—my frank and honest exposition of the truth was construed into threats.

At this time (September and October, 1833) a revolution was raging in many parts of the nation, and especially in the vicinity of the city of Mexico. I despaired of obtaining any thing, and wrote to Texas, recommending to the people there to organize as a State *de facto* without waiting any longer. This letter may have been imprudent, as respects the injury it might do me personally, but how far it was criminal or treasonable, considering the revolutionary state of the whole nation, and the peculiar claims and necessities of Texas, impartial men must decide. It merely expressed an opinion. This letter found its way from San Antonio de Bexar (where it was directed) to the government. I was arrested at Saltillo, two hundred leagues from Mexico, on my way home, taken back to that city and imprisoned one year, three months of the time in solitary confinement, without books or writing materials, in a dark dungeon of the former Inquisition prison. At the close of the year I was released from confinement, but detained six months in the city on heavy bail. It was nine months after my arrest before I was officially informed of the charges against me, or furnished with a copy of them. The constitutional requisites were not observed, my constitutional rights as a citizen were violated, the people of Texas were outraged by this treatment of their commissioner, and their respectful, humble and just petition was disregarded.

These acts of the Mexican government, taken in consideration with many others and with the general revolutionary situation of the interior of the republic, and the absolute want of local government in Texas, would have justified the people of Texas in organizing themselves as a State of the Mexican confederation, and if attacked for so doing in separating from Mexico. They would have been justifiable in doing this, because such acts were unjust, ruinous and oppressive, and because self-preservation required a local government in Texas suited to the situation and necessities of the country and the character of its inhabitants. Our forefathers in '76 flew to arms for much less. They resisted a *principle*, *"the theory of oppression,"* but in our case it was the *reality*—it was a denial of justice and our guarantied rights—it was oppression itself.

Texas, however, even under these aggravated circumstances forbore and remained quiet. The constitution, although outraged by the sport of faction and revolution, still existed in name, and the people of Texas still looked to it with the hope that it would be sustained and executed, and the vested rights of Texas respected, I will now proceed to show how this hope was defeated by the total prostration of the constitution, the destruction of the federal system, and the dissolution of the federal compact.

It is well known that Mexico has been in constant revolutions and confusion, with only a few short intervals, ever since its separation from Spain in 1821. This unfortunate state of things has been produced by the efforts of the ecclesiastical and aristocratical party to oppose republicanism, overturn the federal system and constitution, and establish a monarchy or a consolidated government of some kind.

In 1834, the President of the Republic, Gen. Santa Anna, who heretofore was the leader and champion of the republican party and system became the head and leader of his former antagonists—the aristocratic and church party. With this accession and strength, this party triumphed. The constitutional general Congress of 1834, which was decidedly republican and federal, was dissolved in May of that year by a military order of the President before its constitutional term had expired. The council of government composed of half the Senate which, agreeably to the constitution, ought to have been installed the day after closing the session of Congress, was also dissolved; and a new revolutionary and unconstitutional Congress was convened by another military order of the President. This Congress met on the 1st of January, 1835. It was decidedly aristocratic, ecclesiastical and central in its politics. A number of petitions were presented to it from several towns and villages, praying that it would change the federal form of government and establish a central form. These petitions were all of a revolutionary character, and were called *"pronunciamientos,"* or pronouncements for centralism. They were formed by partial and revolutionary meetings gotten up by the military and priests. Petitions in favor of the federal system and constitution, and protests against such revolutionary measures, were also sent in by the people and by some of the State Legislatures, who still retained firmness to express their opinions. The latter were disregarded and their authors persecuted and imprisoned. The former were considered sufficient to invest Congress with plenary powers. It accordingly, by a decree, deposed the constitutional Vice President, Gomez Farias, who was a leading federalist, without any impeachment or trial, or even the form of a trial, and elected another of their own party, Gen. Barragan, in his place. By another decree it united the Senate with the House of Representatives in one chamber, and, thus constituted, it declared itself invested with full powers as a national convention. In accordance with these usurped powers, it proceeded to annul the federal constitution and system, and to establish a central or consolidated government. How far it has progressed in the details of this new system is unknown to us. The decree of the 3rd October last, which fixes the outlines of the new government, is however sufficient to show that the federal system and compact is dissolved and

ccntralism established. The States are converted into departments. . . .

These revolutionary measures of the party who had usurped
the government in Mexico, were resisted by the people in the
States of Pueblo, Oaxaco, Mexico, Jalisco, and other parts of the
nation. The State of Zacatecas took up arms, but its efforts were
crushed by an army headed by the President General Santa Anna
in person, and the people of that State were disarmed and subjected to a military government. In October last a military force
was sent to Texas under Gen. Cos for the purpose of enforcing
these unconstitutional and revolutionary measures, as had been
done in Zacatecas and other parts of the nation. This act roused
the people of Texas and the war commenced.

Without exhausting the patience by a detail of numerous other
vexatious circumstances and violations of our rights, I trust
that what I have said on this point is sufficient to show that the
federal social compact of Mexico is dissolved; that we have just
and sufficient cause to take up arms against the revolutionary
government which has been established; that we have forborne
until the cup was full to overflowing; and that further forbearance or submission on our part would have been both ruinous
and degrading; and that it was due to the great cause of liberty,
to ourselves, to our posterity, and to the free blood which, I am
proud to say, fills our veins, to insist and proclaim *war* against
such acts of usurpation and oppression.

The justice of our cause being clearly shown, the most important question that naturally presents itself to the intelligent and
inquiring mind is, *what are the objects and intentions of the
people of Texas?*

To this we reply that our object is *freedom*—civil and religious freedom—emancipation from that government and that people who, after fifteen years experiment since they have been
separated from Spain, have shown that they were incapable of
self government, and that all hopes of any thing like stability or
rational liberty in their political institutions—at least for many
years—are vain and fallacious.

This object we expect to obtain by a total separation from
Mexico as an independent community—a new republic—or by
becoming a State of the United States. Texas would have been

satisfied to have been a State of the Mexican Confederation, and she made every constitutional effort in her power to become one. But that is no longer practicable, for that confederation no longer exists. One of the two alterations above-mentioned, therefore, is the only recourse which the revolutionary government of Mexico has left her. Either will secure the liberties and prosperity of Texas, for either will secure to us the right of self-government over a country which we have redeemed from the wilderness, and conquered without any aid or protection whatever from the Mexican government (for we never received any) and which is clearly ours. Ours by every principle by which original titles to countries are, and ever have been founded. We have explored and pioneered it, developed its resources, made it known to the world, and given to it a high and rapidly increasing value. The federal republic of Mexico had a *constitutional* right to participate *generally* in this value, but it had not, and cannot have any other; and this one has evidently been forfeited and destroyed by unconstitutional acts and usurpation, and by the total dissolution of the social compact. Consequently, the true and legal owners of Texas, the only legitimate sovereigns of that country, are the people of Texas.

It is also asked, *what is the present situation of Texas, and what are our resources to effect our objects and defend our rights?*

The present position of Texas is an *absolute Declaration of Independence*—a *total separation* from Mexico. This declaration was made on the 7th of November last. It is as follows:

Whereas, Gen. Antonio Lopez de Santa Anna, and other military chieftains, have by force of arms, overthrown the federal institutions of Mexico, and dissolved the social compact which existed between Texas and the other members of the Mexican Confederacy, now the good people of Txeas, availing themselves of their natural rights, SOLEMNLY DECLARE,

1st. That they have taken up arms in defence of their rights and liberties, which were threatened by encroachments of military despots, and in defence of the republican principles of the federal constitution of Mexico of 1824.

2d. That Texas is no longer morally or civilly bound by the compact of Union; yet stimulated by the generosity and sympathy common to a free people, they offer their support and assistance to such of the members of the Mexican Confederacy, as will take up arms against military despotism.

3d. That they do not acknowledge that the present authorities of the nominal Mexican Republic have the right to govern within the limits of Texas.

4th. That they will not cease to carry on war against the said authorities, whilst their troops are within the limits of Texas.

5th. That they hold it to be their right, during the disorganization of the federal system and the reign of despotism, to withdraw from the Union, to establish an independent government, or to adopt such measures as they may deem best calculated to protect their rights and liberties; but that they will continue faithful to the Mexican government, so long as that nation is governed by the constitution and laws that were framed for the government of the political association.

6th. That Texas is responsible for the expenses of her armies, now in the field.

7th. That the public faith of Texas is pledged for the payment of any debts contracted by her agents.

8th. That she will reward by donations in land all who volunteer their services in her present struggle, and receive them as citizens.

These declarations we solemnly avow to the world, and call God to witness their truth and sincerity, and invoke defeat and disgrace upon our heads, should we prove guilty of duplicity.

It is worthy of particular attention that this declaration affords another and an unanswerable proof of the forbearance of the Texans and of their firm adherence, even to the last moment, to the constitution which they had sworn to support, and to their political obligations as Mexican citizens. For, although at this very time the federal system and constitution of 1824 had been overturned and trampled under foot by military usurpation in all other parts of the republic, and although our country was actually invaded by the usurpers for the purpose of subjecting us to the military rule, the people of Texas still said to the Mexican nation—"restore the federal constitution and govern in conformity to the social compact which we are all bound by our oaths to sustain, and we will continue to be a member of the Mexican Confederation." This noble and generous act, for such it certainly was under the circumstances, is of itself sufficient to repel and silence the false charges which the priests and despots of Mexico have made of the ingratitude of the Texans. In what does this ingratitude consist? I cannot see, unless it be in our enterprise and perseverance in giving value to a country that the Mexicans considered valueless, and thus exciting their jealousy and cupidity.

To show more strongly the absurdity of this charge of ingratitude, etc. made by the general government of Mexico, and of the pretended claims to liberality, which they set up, for having given fortunes in land to the settlers of Texas. It must be remembered that, with the exception of the first three hundred families settled by myself, the general government have never granted or given one foot of land in Texas. The vacant land belonged to the State of Coahuila and Texas so long as they remained united, and to Texas so soon as she was a State separate from Coahuila. Since the adoption of the federal system in 1824, the general government have never had any power or authority whatever to grant, sell, or give any land in Texas, nor in any other State. This power was vested in the respective States. The lands of Texas have therefore been distributed by the State of Coahuila and Texas (with the exception of the three hundred families above mentioned) and not by the general government, and, consequently, it is truly absurd for that government to assume any credit for an act in which it had no participation, and more especially when it has for years past thrown every obstacle in the way to impede the progress of Texas, as is evident from the 11th article of the law of the 6th April, 1830, which absolutely prohibited the emigration to Texas of citizens of the United States; and many other acts of a similar nature—such as vexatious custom-house regulations, passports, and garrisoning the settled parts of the country where troops were not needed to protect it from the Indians, nor from any other enemy. It is therefore clear that if any credit for liberality is due, it is to the State government, and how far *it* is entitled to this credit, men of judgment must decide, with the knowledge of the fact that it *sold* the lands of Texas at from thirty to fifty dollars per square league, Mexican measure, which is four thousand four hundred and twenty-eight acres English, and considering they were getting a high price and full value for it.

The true interpretation of this charge of ingratitude is as follows: The Mexican government have at last discovered that the enterprising people who were induced to remove to Texas by certain promises and guaranties, have by their labors given value to Texas and its lands. An attempt is therefore now made to take them from us and to annul all those guaranties, and we are ungrateful because we are not sufficiently *"docile"* to submit to this usurpation and injustice as the *"docile"* Mexicans have in other parts of the nation.

To close this matter about *ingratitude,* I will ask—if it was not ingratitude in the people of the United States to resist the "throng of oppression" and separate from England?—can it be ingratitude in the people of Texas to resist *oppression* and *usurpation* by separating from Mexico?

To return to the declaration of the 7th of November last, it will be observed that it is a total separation from Mexico—an absolute declaration of independence—in the event of the destruction of the federal compact or system, and the establishment of centralism. This event has taken place. The federal compact is dissolved, and a central or consolidated government is established. I therefore repeat that the present position of Texas is absolute independence:—a position in which we have been placed by the unconstitutional and revolutionary acts of the Mexican government. The people of Texas firmly adhered to the last moment, to the constitution which they and the whole nation had sworn to support.

The government of Mexico have not—the party now in power have overturned the constitutional government and violated their oaths—they have separated from their obligations, from their duty and from *the people of Texas;* and, consequently, they are the true rebels. So far from being grateful, as they ought to be, to the people of Texas for having given value to that country, and for having adhered to their duty and constitutional obligations, the Mexicans charge us with these very acts as evidence of ingratitude. Men of judgment and impartiality must decide this point, and determine who has been, and now is ungrateful.

In order to make the position of Texas more clear to the world, a convention has been called to meet the first of March, and is no doubt now in session, for the express purpose of publishing a positive and unqualified declaration of independence and organizing a permanent government.

Under the declaration of 7th November, a provincial government has been organized, compounded of an executive head or governor, a legislative council, and a judiciary. A regular army has been formed, which is now on the western frontiers prepared to repel an invasion should one be attempted. A naval force has been fitted out which is sufficient to protect our coast. We have met the invading force that entered Texas in October under Gen. Cos, and beaten him in every contest and skirmish, and driven every hostile soldier out of Texas. In San Antonio de Bexar he was entrenched in strong fortifications, defended by heavy cannon and a strong force of regular troops greatly superior to ours in number, which was of undisciplined militia without any experienced officer. This place was besieged by the militia of Texas. The enemy was driven into his works; his provisions cut off, and the spirits and energies of his soldiers worn down, with the loss of only one man to the Texans, and the place was then taken by storm. A son of Kentucky, a noble and brave spirit from this land of liberty and of chivalry, led the storm. He conquered, and died, as such a spirit wished to die, in the cause of liberty, and in the arms of victory. Texas weeps for her Milam; Kentucky has cause to be proud of her son. His free spirit appeals to his countrymen to embark in the holy cause of liberty for which he died, and to avenge his death.

I pass to an examination of the resources of Texas. We consider them sufficient to effect and sustain our independence. We have one of the finest countries in the world, a soil surpassed by none for agriculture and pasturage, not even by the fairest portions of Kentucky—a climate that may be compared to Italy; within the cotton or sugar region, intersected by navigable rivers, and bounded by the coast of the Gulf of Mexico, on which there are several fine bays and harbors suitable for all the purposes of commerce—a population of about seventy thousand, which is rapidly increasing, and is generally compounded of men of very reputable education and property, enterprising, bold and energetic, devotedly attached to liberty and their country, inured to the use of arms, and at all times ready to use them, and defend their homes inch by inch if necessary. The exportations of cotton are large. Sheep, cattle and hogs are very abundant and cheap. The revenue from importations and direct taxes will be considerable and rapidly increasing, the vacant lands are very extensive and valuable, and may be safely relied upon as a great source of revenues and as bounties to emigrants. The credit of Texas is good, as is proven by the extensive loans already negotiated. The country and army are generally well supplied with arms and ammunition, and the organized force in February last in the field exceeded two thousand, and is rapidly increasing. But besides these resources, we have one which ought not, and certainly will not fail us—*it is our cause*—the cause of light and liberty, of religious toleration and pure religion. To suppose that such a cause will fail, when defended by Anglo-Saxon blood, by Americans, and on the limits, and at the very door of this free and philanthropic and magnanimous nation, would be calumny against republicanism and freedom, against a noble race, and against the philanthropic principles of the people of the United States. I therefore repeat that we consider our resources sufficient to effect our independence against the Mexicans, who are disorganized and enfeebled by revolutions, and almost destitute of funds or credit. Another interesting question which naturally occurs to every one is, what great benefits and advantages are to result to philanthropy and religion, or to the people of these United States from the emancipation of Texas? To this we reply, that ours is most truly and emphatically the cause of liberty, which is the cause of philanthropy, of religion, of mankind; for in its train follow freedom of conscience, pure morality, enterprise, the arts and sciences, all that is dear to the noble minded and the free, all that renders life precious. On this principle the Greeks and the Poles, and all others who have struggled for liberty, have received the sympathies or aid of the people of the United States; on this principle the liberal party in priest-ridden Spain, is now receiving the aid of high-minded and free born Englishmen; on this same principle Texas expects to receive the sympathies and aid of their brethren, the people of the United States, and of the freemen of all nations. But the Greeks and the Poles are not parallel cases with ours—they are not the sons and daughters of Anglo-Americans. We are. We look to this happy land as to a fond mother from whose bosom we have imbibed those great principles of liberty which are now nerving us, although comparatively few in numbers and weak in resources, to contend against the whole Mexican nation in defence of our rights.

The emancipation of Texas will extend the principles of self-government over a rich and neighboring country, and open a vast field there for enterprise, wealth, and happiness, and for those who wish to escape from the frozen blasts of a northern climate by removing to a more congenial one. It will promote and accelerate the march of the present age, for it will open a door through which a bright and constant stream of light and intelligence will flow from this great northern fountain over the benighted region of Mexico.

That nation of our continent will be regenerated; freedom of conscience and rational liberty will take root in that distant and, by nature, much favored land, which for ages past the upas [poisonous or harmful] banner of the inquisition, of intolerance, and of despotism has paralized, and sickened, and deadened every effort in favor of civil and religious liberty.

But apart from these great principles of philanthropy, and narrowing down this question to the contracted limits of cold and prudent political calculation, a view may be taken of it, which doubtless has not escaped the penetration of the sagacious and cautious politicians of the United States. It is the great importance of Americanizing Texas, by filling it with a population from this country who will harmonize in language, in political education, in common origin, in every thing, with their neighbors to the east and north. By this means Texas will become a great outwork on the west to protect the outlet of this western world, the mouths of the Mississippi, as Alabama and Florida are on the east; and to keep far away from the southwestern frontier—the weakest and most vulnerable in the nation, all enemies who might make Texas a door for invasion, or use it as a theatre from which mistaken philanthropists, and wild fanatics might attempt a system of intervention in the domestic concerns of the South, which might lead to a servile war, or at least jeopardize the tranquillity of Louisiana and the neighboring States.

This view of the subject is a very important one, so much so that a bare allusion to it is sufficient to direct the mind to the various interests and results, immediate and remote, that are involved.

To conclude, I have shown that our cause is just and righteous, that it is the great cause of mankind, and as such merits the approbation and moral support of this magnanimous and free people. That our object is independence as a new republic, or to become a State of these United States; that our resources are sufficient to sustain the principles we are defending; that the results will be the promotion of the great cause of liberty, of philanthropy and religion, and the protection of a great and important interest to the people of the United States.

With these claims to the approbation and moral support of the free of all nations—the people of Texas have taken up arms in self-defence, and they submit their cause to the judgment of an impartial world, and to the protection of a just and omnipotent God.

9

The Democratic Principle

The Democratic Review: A Confession of Faith*

For half a century after the adoption of the Constitution, political theorizing in America sprang directly out of political controversy, and was couched too often in terms of federal power versus states' rights. So vocal were the proponents on both sides that this legalistic and largely negative dispute tended to obscure another and more fundamental development in American thought—the rise of a truly democratic philosophy. The founding fathers, most of them, did not really believe that the common man could or should govern himself; by Jackson's time almost everyone believed it, with the exception of a small if vocal group of southern slaveholders.

The document reprinted here is one of the best contemporary expressions of the democratic idea, with a small "d" even though the language is often that of party. The essay, probably written by editor John L. O'Sullivan (1813-95), is more than a confession of faith by the new periodical, the *United States Magazine and Democratic Review*. It is a challenge to Americans to rededicate themselves to a concept of government of, by, and for the people. It is a forthright appeal to a new and confident generation, already both physically and morally on the move.

For more wide-ranging discussion of the development of American democratic ideas, the reader should consult Charles M. Wiltse, *The Jeffersonian Tradition in American Democracy* (New ed.; New York: Hill and Wang, 1960); Ralph H. Gabriel, *The Course of American Democratic Thought* (2nd ed.; New York: Ronald Press, 1956); and Arthur A. Ekirch, *The American Democratic Tradition* (New York: Macmillan, 1963). In the selection reprinted here note (1) evidence of the author's familiarity with the history of political thought; (2) what he regarded as the great argument against democracy; (3) what ideas he advanced in support of democracy; (4) his

*"Introduction," *United States Magazine and Democratic Review*, Vol. I, No. 1 (October, 1837).

attitudes toward the role of the State in society; (5) what the author said concerning religion in relation to government and to democracy; (6) what mission the author thought had been given to the American nation; and (7) what limitations hampered American literature in its tasks and what prescription the author proposed.

The Democratic Principle—the Importance of Its Assertion, and Application to Our Political System and Literature

THE CHARACTER AND DESIGN OF THE WORK OF WHICH the first number is here offered to the public, are intended to be shadowed forth in its name, the "United States Magazine and *Democratic Review*." It has had its origin in a deep conviction of the necessity of such a work, at the present critical stage of our national progress, for the advocacy of that high and holy DEMOCRATIC PRINCIPLE which was designed to be the fundamental element of the new social and political system created by the 'American experiment;' for the vindication of that principle from the charges daily brought against it, of responsibility for every evil result growing out, in truth, of adventitious circumstances, and the adverse elements unhappily combined with it in our institutions; for its purification from those corruptions and those hostile influences, by which we see its beneficent and glorious tendencies, to no slight extent, perverted and paralysed; for the illustration of truth, which we see perpetually darkened and confused by the arts of wily error; for the protection of those great interests, not alone of our country, but of humanity, looking forward through count-less ages of the future, which we believe to be vitally committed with the cause of American Democracy. This is, in broad terms, the main motive in which this undertaking has had its origin: this is the object towards which, in all its departments, more or less directly, its efforts will tend.

There is a great deal of mutual misunderstanding between our parties; but in truth, there does not exist in the people, with reference to its great masses, that irreconcileable hostility of opinions and leading principles which would be the natural inference from the violence of the party warfare in which we are perpetually engaged. There does exist, it is true, an essential opposition of principles, proceeding from opposite points of departure, between the respective political creeds or systems of our two great parties, the Democratic and the Whig; but we feel well assured that the great body of the latter party, those who supply their leaders and leading interests with their votes, do not rightly understand the questions at issue, in their true popular bearings; and that, if these could but be exhibited in their proper lights, to their sound minds and honest hearts, they would soon be found ranged, by the hundreds of thousands, under the broad and bright folds of our democratic banner.

So many false ideas have insensibly attached themselves to the term "democracy," as connected with our party politics, that we deem it necessary here, at the outset, to make a full and free profession of the cardinal principles of political faith on which we take our stand; principles to which we are devoted with an unwavering force of conviction and earnestness of enthusiasm which, ever since they were first presented to our minds, have constantly grown and strengthened by contemplation of them, and of the incalculable capabilities of social improvement of which they contain the germs.

We believe, then, in the principle of *democratic republicanism*, in its strongest and purest sense. We have an abiding confidence in the virtue, intelligence, and full capacity for self-government, of the great mass of our people—our industrious, honest, manly, intelligent millions of freemen.

We are opposed to all self-styled "wholesome restraints" on the free action of the popular opinion and will, other than those which have for their sole object the prevention of precipitate legislation. This latter object is to be attained by the expedient of the division of power, and by causing all legislation to pass through the ordeal of successive forms; to be sifted through the discussions of co-ordinate legislative branches, with mutual suspensive veto powers. Yet all should be dependant with equal directness and promptness on the influence of public opinion; the popular will should be equally the animating and moving spirit of them all, and ought never to find in any of its own creatures a self-imposed power, capable (when misused either by corrupt ambition or honest error) of resisting itself, and defeating its own determined object. We cannot, therefore, look with an eye of favor on any such forms of representation as, by length of tenure of delegated power, tend to weaken that universal and unrelaxing responsibility to the vigilance of public opinion, which is the true conservative principle of our institutions.

The great question here occurs, which is of vast importance to this country (was it not once near dissolving the Union, and plunging it into the abyss of civil war?)—of the relative rights of majorities and minorities. Though we go for the republican principle of the supremacy of the will of the majority, we acknowledge, in general, a strong sympathy with minorities, and consider that their rights have a high moral claim on the respect and justice of majorities; a claim not always fairly recognised in practice by the latter, in the full sway of power, when flushed with triumph, and impelled by strong interests. This has ever been the point of the democratic cause most open to assault, and most difficult to defend. This difficulty does not arise from any intrinsic weakness. The democratic theory is perfect and harmonious in all its parts; and if this point is not so self-evidently clear as the rest is generally, in all candid discussion, conceded to be, it is because of certain false principles of government, which have, in all practical experiments of the theory, been interwoven with the democratic portions of the system, being borrowed from the example of anti-democratic systems of government. We shall always be willing to meet this question frankly and fairly. The great argument against pure democracy, drawn from this source, is this:

Though the main object with reference to which all social institutions ought to be modelled is undeniably, as stated by the democrat, "the greatest good of the greatest number," yet it by no means follows that the greatest number always rightly understands its own greatest good. Highly pernicious error has often possessed the minds of nearly a whole nation; while the philosopher in his closet, and an enlightened few about him, powerless against the overwhelming current of popular prejudice and excitement, have alone possessed the truth, which the next generation may perhaps recognise and practice, though its author, now sainted, has probably, in his own time, been its martyr. The original adoption of the truth would have saved perhaps oceans of blood, and mountains of misery and crime. How much stronger, then, the case against the absolute supremacy of the opinion and will of the majority, when its numerical preponderance is, as often happens, comparatively small. And if the larger proportion of the more wealthy and cultivated classes of the society are found on the side of the minority, the disinterested observer may well be excused if he hesitate long before he awards the judgment, in a difficult and complicated question, in favor of the mere numerical argument. Majorities are often as liable to error of opinion, and not always free from a similar proneness to selfish abuse of power, as minorities; and a vast amount of injustice may often be perpetrated, and consequent general social injury be done, before the evil reaches that extreme at which it rights itself by revolution, moral or physical.

We have here, we believe, correctly stated the anti-democratic side of the argument on this point. It is not to be denied that it possesses something more than plausibility. It has certainly been the instrument of more injury to the cause of the democratic principle than all the bayonets and cannon that have ever been arrayed in support of it against that principle. The inference from it is, that the popular opinion and will must not be trusted with the supreme and absolute direction of the general interests; that it must be subjected to the "conservative checks" of minority interests, and to the regulation of the "more enlightened wisdom" of the "better classes," and those to whom the possession of a property "test of merit" gives what they term "a stake in the community." And here we find ourselves in the face of the great stronghold of the anti-democratic, or *aristocratic,* principle.

It is not our purpose, in this place, to carry out the discussion of this question. The general scope and tendency of the present work are designed to be directed towards the refutation of this sophistical reasoning and inference. It will be sufficient here to allude to the leading ideas by which they are met by the advocate of the pure democratic cause.

In the first place, the greatest number are *more likely*, at least, as a general rule, to understand and follow their own greatest good, than is the minority.

In the second, a minority is much more likely to abuse power for the promotion of its own selfish interests, at the expense of the majority of numbers—the substantial and producing mass of the nation—than the latter is to oppress unjustly the former. The social evil is also, in that case, proportionately greater. This is abundantly proved by the history of all aristocratic interests that have existed, in various degrees and modifications, in the world. A majority cannot subsist upon a minority; while the natural, and in fact uniform, tendency of a minority entrusted with governmental authority is, to surround itself with wealth, splendor, and power, at the expense of the producing mass, creating and perpetuating those artificial social distinctions which violate the natural equality of rights of the human race, and at the same time offend and degrade the true dignity of human nature.

In the third place, there does not naturally exist any such original superiority of a minority class above the great mass of a community, in intelligence and competence for the duties of government—even putting out of view its constant tendency to abuse from selfish motives, and the safer honesty of the mass. The general diffusion of education; the facility of access to every species of knowledge important to the great interests of the community; the freedom of the press, whose very licentiousness cannot materially impair its permanent value, in this country at least, make the pretensions of those self-styled "better classes" to the sole possession of the requisite intelligence for the management of public affairs, too absurd to be entitled to any other treatment than an honest, manly contempt. As far as superior knowledge and talent confer on their possessor a natural charter of privilege to control his associates, and exert an influence on the direction of the general affairs of the community, the free and natural action of that privilege is best secured by a perfectly free democratic system, which will abolish all artificial distinctions, and, preventing the accumulation of any social obstacles to advancement, will permit the free developement of every germ of talent, wherever it may chance to exist, whether on the proud mountain summit, in the humble valley, or by the wayside of common life.

But the question is not yet satisfactorily answered, how the relation between majorities and minorities, in the frequent case of a collision of sentiments and particular interests, is to be so adjusted as to secure a mutual respect of rights, to preserve harmony and good will, and save society from the *malum extremum discordia,* from being as a house divided against itself—and thus to afford free scope to that competition, discussion, and mutual moral influence, which cannot but result, in the end, in the ascendency of the truth, and in "the greatest good of the greatest number." On the one side, it has only been shown that the absolute government of the majority does not always afford a perfect guarantee against the misuse of its numerical power over the weakness of the minority. On the other, it has been shown that this chance of misuse is, as a general rule, far less than in the opposite relation of the ascendency of a minority; and that the evils attendant upon it are infinitely less, in every point of view, in the one case than the other. But this is not yet a complete or satisfactory solution of the problem. Have we but a choice of evils? Is there, then, such a radical deficiency in the moral elements implanted by its Creator in human society, that no other alternative can be devised by which both evils shall be avoided, and a result attained more analogous to the beautiful and glorious harmony of the rest of his creation?

It were scarcely consistent with a true and living faith in the existence and attributes of that Creator, so to believe; and such is not the democratic belief. The reason of the plausibility with which appeal may be made to the experience of so many republics, to sustain this argument against democratic institutions, is, that the true theory of national self-government has been hitherto but imperfectly understood; bad principles have been mixed up with the good; and the republican government has been administered on ideas and in a spirit borrowed from the strong governments of the other forms; and to the corruptions and manifold evils which have never failed, in the course of time, to evolve themselves out of these seeds of destruction, is ascribable the eventual failure of those experiments, and the consequent doubt and discredit which have attached themselves to the democratic principles on which they were, in the outset, mainly based.

It is under the word *government,* that the subtle danger lurks. Understood as a central consolidated power, managing and directing the various general interests of the society, all government is evil, and the parent of evil. A strong and active democratic *government,* in the common sense of the term, is an evil, differing only in degree and mode of operation, and not in nature, from a strong despotism. This difference is certainly vast, yet, inasmuch as these strong governmental powers must be wielded by human agents, even as the powers of despotism, it is, after all, only a difference in degree; and the tendency to demoralization and tyranny is the same, though the development of the evil results is much more gradual and slow in the one case than in the other. Hence the demagogue—hence the faction —hence the mob—hence the violence, licentiousness, and instability—hence the ambitious struggles of parties and their leaders for power—hence the abuses of that power by majorities and their leaders—hence the indirect oppressions of the general by partial interests—hence (fearful symptom) the demoralization of the great men of the nation, and of the nation itself, proceeding (unless checked in time by the more healthy and patriotic portion of the mind of the nation rallying itself to reform the principles and sources of the evil) gradually to that point of maturity at which relief from the tumult of moral and physical confusion is to be found only under the shelter of an energetic armed despotism.

The best government is that which governs least. No human depositories can, with safety, be trusted with the power of legislation upon the general interests of society so as to operate directly or indirectly on the industry and property of the community. Such power must be perpetually liable to the most pernicious abuse, from the natural imperfection, both in wisdom of judgment and purity of purpose, of all human legislation, exposed constantly to the pressure of partial interests; interests which, at the same time that they are essentially selfish and tyrannical, are ever vigilant, persevering, and subtle in all the arts of deception and corruption. In fact, the whole history of human society and government may be safely appealed to, in evidence that the abuse of such power a thousand fold more than overbalances its beneficial use. Legislation has been the fruitful parent of nine-tenths of all the evil, moral and physical, by which mankind has been afflicted since the creation of the world, and by which human nature has been self-degraded, fettered, and oppressed. Government should have as little as possible to do with the general business and interests of the people. If it once undertake these functions as its rightful province of action, it is impossible to say to it "thus far shalt thou go, and no farther." It will be impossible to confine it to the public interests of the *commonwealth*. It will be perpetually tampering with private interests, and sending forth seeds of corruption which will result in the demoralization of the society. Its domestic action should be confined to the administration of justice, for the protection of the natural equal rights of the citizen, and the preservation of social order. In all other respects, the VOLUNTARY PRINCIPLE, the principle of FREEDOM, suggested to us by the analogy of the divine government of the Creator, and already recognised by us with perfect success in the great social interest of Religion, affords the true "golden rule" which is alone abundantly competent to work out the best possible general result of order and happiness from that chaos of characters, ideas, motives, and interests—human society. Afford but the single nucleus of a system of administration of justice between man and man, and, under the sure operation of this principle, the floating atoms will distribute and combine themselves, as we see in the beautiful natural process of crystallization, into a far more perfect and harmonious result than if government, with its "fostering hand," undertake to disturb, under the plea of directing, the process. The natural laws which will establish themselves and find their own level are the best laws. The same hand was the Author of the moral, as of the physical world; and we feel clear and strong in the assurance that we cannot err in trusting, in the former, to the same fundamental principles of spontaneous action and self-regulation which produce the beautiful order of the latter.

This is then, we consider, the true theory of government, the one simple result towards which the political science of the world is gradually tending, after all the long and varied experience by which it will have dearly earned the great secret—the elixir of political life. This is the fundamental principle of the philosophy of democracy, to furnish a system of administration of justice, and then leave all the business and interests of society to themselves, to free competition and association—in a word, to the VOLUNTARY PRINCIPLE—

> Let man be fettered by no duty, save
> His brother's right—like his, inviolable.

It is borrowed from the example of the perfect self-government of the physical universe, being written in letters of light on every page of the great bible of Nature. It contains the idea of full and fearless faith in the providence of the Creator. It is essentially involved in Christianity, of which it has been well said that its pervading spirit of democratic equality among men is its highest fact, and one of its most radiant internal evidences of the divinity of its origin. It is the essence and the one general result of the science of political economy. And this principle alone, we will add, affords a satisfactory and perfect solution of the great problem, otherwise unsolved, of the relative rights of majorities and minorities.

This principle, therefore, constitutes our "point of departure." It has never yet received any other than a very partial and imperfect application to practice among men, all human society having been hitherto perpetually chained down to the ground by myriads of lilliputian fetters of artificial government and prescription. Nor are we yet prepared for its full adoption in this country. Far, very far indeed, from it; yet is our gradual tendency toward it clear and sure. How many generations may yet be required before our theory and practice of government shall be sifted and analysed down to the lowest point of simplicity consistent with the preservation of some degree of national organization, no one can presume to prophecy. But that we are on the path toward that great result, to which mankind is to be guided down the long vista of future years by the democratic principle,—walking hand in hand with the sister spirit of Christianity,—we feel a faith as implicit as that with which we believe in any other great moral truth.

This is all generalization, and therefore, though necessary, probably dull. We have endeavored to state the theory of the

Jeffersonian democracy, to which we profess allegiance, in its abstract essence, however unpopular it appears to be, in these latter days, to "theorize." These are the original ideas of American democracy; and we would not give much for that "practical knowledge" which is ignorant of, and affects to disregard, the essential and abstract principles which really constitute the animating soul of what were else lifeless and naught. The application of these ideas to practice, in our political affairs, is obvious and simple. Penetrated with a perfect faith in their eternal truth, we can never hesitate as to the direction to which, in every practical case arising, they must point with the certainty of the magnetized needle; and we have no desire to shrink from the responsibility, at the outset, of a frank avowal of them in the broadest general language.

But having done so, we will not be further misunderstood, and we hope not misrepresented, as to immediate practical views. We deem it scarcely necessary to say that we are opposed to all precipitate radical changes in social institutions. Adopting "Nature as the best guide," we cannot disregard the lesson which she teaches, when she accomplishes her most mighty results of the good and beautiful by the silent and slow operation of great principles, without the convulsions of too rapid action. *Festina lente* is an invaluable precept, if it be not abused. On the other hand, that specious sophistry ought to be no less watchfully guarded against, by which old evils always struggle to perpetuate themselves by appealing to our veneration for "the wisdom of our fathers," to our inert love of present tranquillity, and our natural apprehension of possible danger from the untried and unknown—

> Better to bear the present ills we know,
> Than fly to others that we know not of.

We are not afraid of that much dreaded phrase, "untried experiment," which looms so fearfully before the eyes of some of our most worthy and valued friends. The whole history of the progress hitherto made by humanity, in every respect of social amelioration, records but a series of "*experiments.*" The American revolution was the greatest of "experiments," and one of which it is not easy at this day to appreciate the gigantic boldness. Every step in the onward march of improvement by the human race is an "experiment"; and the present is most emphatically an age of "experiments." The eye of man looks naturally *forward;* and as he is carried onward by the progress of time and truth, he is far more likely to stumble and stray if he turn his face backward, and keep his looks fixed on the thoughts and things of the past. We feel safe under the banner of the democratic principle, which is borne onward by an unseen hand of Providence, to lead our race toward the high destinies of which every human soul contains the God-implanted germ; and of the advent of which—certain, however distant—a dim prophetic presentiment has existed, in one form or another, among all nations in all ages. We are willing to make every reform in our institutions that may be commanded by the test of the democratic principle—to *democratize* them—but only so rapidly as shall appear, to the most cautious wisdom, consistent with a due regard to the existing developement of public opinion and to the permanence of the progress made. Every instance in which the action of *government* can be simplified, and one of the hundred giant arms curtailed, with which it now stretches around its fatal protecting grasp over almost all the various interests of society, to substitute the truly healthful action of the free voluntary principle—every instance in which the operation of the public opinion and will, fairly signified, can be brought to bear more directly upon the action of delegated powers—we would regard as so much gained for the true interest of the society and of mankind at large. In this path we cannot go wrong; it is only necessary to be cautious not to go too fast.

Such is, then, our democracy. It of course places us in the school of the strictest construction of the constitution; and in that appears to be involved a full committal of opinion on all the great political questions which now agitate the public mind, and to which we deem it unnecessary here to advert in detail. One necessary inference from the views expressed above is, that we consider the preservation of the present ascendency of the democratic party as of great, if not vital, importance to the future destinies of this holy cause. Most of its leading members we know to possess all the qualifications that should entitle men to the confidence and attachment of their country; and the arduous functions of the executive department of the government are administered with an efficiency, and a strictness and purity of principle, which, considering their nature, extent, and complexity, are indeed remarkable. And even without a particular knowledge of the men, the principle alone would still of necessity attach us to that party. The acquisition of the vast influence of the executive department by the present Opposition principles, we could not look upon but as a staggering blow to the cause of democracy, and all the high interests committed with it; from which it would take a long and indefinite period of years to recover—even if the loss of time in national progress would not, in that event, have to be reckoned by generations! We shall therefore, while devoting ourselves to preserve and improve the purity of our democratic institutions, labor to sustain the present democratic administration, by fair appeal to argument, with all the earnestness due to the gravity of the principles and interests involved.

We are admonished by the prescribed limits of this introductory article, to curtail various topics of interest to which we had intended to allude in it. The important subject of national literature cannot, however, be passed without a slight notice.

What is the cause, is sometimes asked among the disciples of the democratic school of political philosophy, of that extensive anti-democratic corruption of sentiment in some portions of our people, especially in the young mind of the nation, which is certainly so just a subject of surprise and alarm? It has lately been a topic of newspaper remark, that nineteen-twentieths of the youth of one of the colleges of Virginia were opposed to the democratic principles. The very exaggeration is good evidence of the lamentable truth; and it is well known that a very large proportion of the young men who annually leave our colleges, carry with them a decided anti-popular bias, to swell the ranks of that large majority of the *"better classes"* already ranged on that side, and to exercise the influence of their cultivated talents in a cause at variance with the genius of our country, the spirit of the age, the best interests and true dignity of humanity, and the highest truths of the science of political morals.

And yet the democratic cause is one which not only ought to engage the whole mind of the American nation, without any serious division of its energies,—to carry forward the noble mission entrusted to her, of going before the nations of the world as the representative of the democratic principle and as the constant living exemplar of its results; but which ought peculiarly to commend itself to the generosity of youth, its ardent aspirations after the good and beautiful, its liberal and unselfish freedom from narrow prejudices of interest.

For Democracy is the cause of Humanity. It has faith in human nature. It believes in its essential equality and fundamental goodness. It respects, with a solemn reverence to which the proudest artificial institutions and distinctions of society have no claim, the human soul. It is the cause of philanthropy. Its object is to emancipate the mind of the mass of men from the degrading and disheartening fetters of social distinctions and advantages; to bid it walk abroad through the free creation "in its own majesty;" to war against all fraud, oppression, and violence; by striking at their root, to reform all the infinitely varied human misery which has grown out of the old and false ideas by which the world has been so long misgoverned; to dismiss the hireling soldier; to spike the cannon, and bury the bayonet; to burn the gibbet, and open the debtor's dungeon; to substitute harmony and mutual respect for the jealousies and discord now subsisting between different classes of society, as the consequence of their artificial classification. It is the cause of Christianity, to which a slight allusion has been already made, to be more fully developed hereafter. And that portion of the peculiar friends and ministers of religion who now, we regret to say, cast the weight of their social influence against the cause of democracy, under the false prejudice of an affinity between it and infidelity (no longer, in this century, the case, and which, in the last, was but a consequence of the overgrown abuses of religion found, by the reforming spirit that then awakened in Europe, in league with despotism) understand but little either its true spirit, or that of their own faith. It is, moreover, a cheerful creed, a creed of high hope and universal love, noble and ennobling; while all others, which imply a distrust of mankind, and of the natural moral principles infused into it by its Creator, for its own self-development and self-regulation, are as gloomy and selfish, in the tone of moral sentiment which pervades them, as they are degrading in their practical tendency, and absurd in theory, when examined by the light of original principles.

Then whence this remarkable phenomenon, of the young mind of our country so deeply tainted with anti-democratic sentiment— a state of things lamentable in itself, and portentous of incalculable future evil?

Various partial causes may be enumerated in explanation of it; among which we may refer to the following: In the first place, the possession of the executive power (as it exists in our system) is, in one point of view, a great disadvantage to the principles of that ascendant party. The Administration occupies a position of defence; the Opposition, of attack. The former is by far the more arduous task. The lines of fortification to be maintained against the never relaxing onsets from every direction, are so extensive and exposed, that a perpetual vigilance and devotion to duty barely suffice to keep the enemy at bay. The attacking cause, ardent, restless, ingenious, is far more attractive to the imagination of youth than that of the defence. It is, moreover, difficult, if not impossible, to preserve a perfect purity from abuse and corruption throughout all the countless ramifications of the action of such an executive system as ours, however stern may be the integrity, and high the patriotism, of the presiding spirit which, from its head, animates the whole. Local abuses in the management of party affairs are the necessary consequence of the long possession of the ascendancy. The vast official patronage of the executive department is a weight and clog under which it is not easy to bear up. This must lay any administration open to perpetual assault at great disadvantage; and especially if the great party campaign present at any time such a phase as may render it necessary to put forth, to the full limits of constitutional right, the energies of the executive department, to resist the accumulated pressure of attack, bearing along in its train evils, to avert which almost any means would seem justifiable. This we have seen, in a remarkable manner, the case during the two terms of the late administration. Our natural jealousy of power affords a string to which, when played upon by the bold and skilful hands that are never found wanting, the very spirit of democratic freedom never fails to respond; and many are confused by sophistry and clamor, and carried away by the power of eloquence—divine, even though misused—to array themselves against their own best and most honest friends, under leaders, in truth, the worst enemies of the American principles for which they believe themselves contending.

In the second place, we may refer to a cause which we look upon with deep pain, as one of the worst fruits of the evil principles to which allusion has already been made above as existing in our system—the demoralization of many of the great men of the nation. How many of these master-spirits of their day, to whom their country had long been accustomed to look with generous affection as her hope and pride, have we not seen seduced from the path of their early promise by the intrigues of party and the allurements of ambition, in the pursuit of that too dazzling prize, and too corrupting both in the prospect and the possession—the presidential office! To how many a one could we point, within the history of the last quarter of a century, to whom we might well apply Milton's famous description of Lucifer, the Son of the Morning:

> He above the rest,
> In shape and gesture proudly eminent,
> Stood like a tower; his form had not yet lost
> All her original brightness, nor appeared
> Less than archangel ruined, and the excess
> Of glory obscured; as when the sun new risen
> Looks through the horizontal misty air,
> Shorn of his beams, or from behind the moon,
> In dim eclipse, disastrous twilight sheds
> On half the nations, and with fear of change
> Perplexes monarchs.   Darkened so, yet shone
> Above them all the archangel; but his face
> Deep scars of thunder had entrench'd, and care
> Sat on his faded cheek, but under brows
> Of dauntless courage and considerate pride,
> Waiting revenge, etc.

The influence of such men (especially on the minds of the young) commanding by their intellectual power, misleading by their eloquence, and fascinating by the natural sympathy which attaches itself to greatness still proud in its "fallen estate," produces certainly a powerful effect in our party contests.

We might also refer to the fact, that the anti-democratic cause possesses at least two-thirds of the press of the country, and that portion of it which is best supported by talent and the resources of capital, under the commercial patronage of our cities. To the strong influence that cities,—where wealth accumulates, where luxury gradually unfolds its corrupting tendencies, where aristocratic habits and social classifications form and strengthen themselves, where the congregation of men stimulates and exaggerates all ideas,—to the influence that cities exert upon the country, no inconsiderable effect is to be ascribed. From the influence of the mercantile classes, too (extensively anti-democratic) on the young men of the professions, especially that of the law, creating an insensible bias, from the dependence of the latter mainly on the patronage of the former, these young men becoming again each the centre of a small sphere of social influence; from that of the religious ministry, silently and insensibly exerted, from the false prejudice slightly touched upon above; from these and some other minor influences, on which we cannot here pause, a vast and active power on public opinion is perpetually in operation. And it is only astonishing that the democratic party should be able to bear up against them all so successfully as we in fact witness. This is to be ascribed (under that Providence whose unseen hand we recognise in all human affairs) only to the sterling honesty and good sense of the great industrious mass of our people, its instinctive perception of, and yearning after, the democratic truth, and the unwavering generosity of its support of those public servants whom it has once tried well and long, and with whom it has once acknowledged the genuine sympathy of common sentiments and a common cause. Yet still the democratic principle can do little more than hold its own. The moral energies of the national mind are, to a great extent, paralyzed by division; and instead of bearing forward the ark of democratic truth, entrusted to us as a chosen people, towards the glorious destiny of its future, we must fain be content, if we can but stem with it the perpetual tide of attack which would bear it backward towards the ideas and habits of past dark ages.

But a more potent influence than any yet noticed, is that of our national literature. Or rather we have no national literature. We depend almost wholly on Europe, and particularly England, to think and write for us, or at least to furnish materials and models

after which we shall mould our own humble attempts. We have
a considerable number of writers; but not in that consists a
national literature. The vital principle of an American national
literature must be democracy. Our mind is enslaved to the past
and present literature of England. Rich and glorious as is that
vast collection of intellectual treasure, it would have been far
better for us had we been separated from it by the ocean of a
difference of language, as we are from the country itself by our
sublime Atlantic. Our mind would then have been compelled to
think for itself and to express itself, and its animating spirit
would have been our democracy. As it now is, we are cowed by
the mind of England. We follow feebly and afar in the splendid
track of a literature moulded on the whole (notwithstanding a
number of noble exceptions) by the ideas and feelings of an utterly anti-democratic social system. We give back but a dim
reflection—a faint echo of the expression of the English mind. No
one will misunderstand us as disparaging the literature of our
mother language—far from it. We appreciate it with a profound
veneration and gratitude, and would use it, without abusing it
by utterly submitting our own minds to it; but we look upon it,
as we do upon the political system of the country, as a something
magnificent, venerable, splendid, and powerful, and containing a
considerable infusion of the true principle; yet the one no more
suitable to be adopted as our own, or as a model for slavish
imitation, than the other. In the spirit of her literature we can
never hope to rival England. She is immeasurably in advance of
us, and is rich with ever active energies, and resources of literary
habits and capital (so to speak) which mock our humble attempts at imitation. But we should not follow in her wake; a
radiant path invites us forward in another direction. We have a
principle—an informing soul—of our own, our democracy, though
we allow it to languish uncultivated; this must be the animating
spirit of our literature, if, indeed, we would have a national
American literature. There is an immense field open to us, if we
would but enter it boldly and cultivate it as our own. All history
has to be re-written; political science and the whole scope of all
moral truth have to be considered and illustrated in the light of
the democratic principle. All old subjects of thought and all new
questions arising, connected more or less directly with human

existence, have to be taken up again and re-examined in this point of view. We *ought* to exert a powerful moral influence on Europe, and yet we are entirely unfelt; and as it is only by its literature that one nation can utter itself and make itself known to the rest of the world, we are really entirely unknown. In the present general fermentation of popular ideas in Europe, turning the public thoughts naturally to the great democracy across the Atlantic, the voice of America might be made to produce a powerful and beneficial effect on the developement of truth; but as it is, American writings are never translated, because they almost always prove to be a diluted and tardy second edition of English thought.

The anti-democratic character of our literature, then, is a main cause of the evil of which we complain; and this is both a mutual cause and effect, constantly acting and re-acting. Our "better educated classes" drink in an anti-democratic habit of feeling and thinking from the copious, and it must be confessed delicious, fountain of the literature of England; they give the same spirit to our own, in which we have little or nothing that is truly democratic and American. Hence this tone of sentiment of our literary institutions and of our learned professions, poisoning at the spring the young mind of our people.

If the "United States Magazine and Democratic Review" shall be able, by the influence of example and *the most liberal* encouragement, to contribute in any degree towards the remedy of this evil (as of the other evils in our institutions which may need reform) by vindicating the true glory and greatness of the democratic principle, by infusing it into our literature, and by rallying the mind of the nation from the state of torpor and even of demoralization in which so large a proportion of it is sunk, one of the main objects of its establishment will have been achieved.

10

Education

Horace Mann: First Annual Report of the Secretary of the Massachusetts Board of Education*

The idea of universal public education came naturally to people committed to the principle of self-government, but as is the case with so many other corollaries of democracy, theory was far ahead of practice. The concept of public welfare as envisaged by the Constitution was not yet broad enough to bring education within the jurisdiction of the federal government, and the states were too often indifferent. The impulse to do something about it paralleled the extension of the franchise in the 1820's and 1830's, with Massachusetts, in keeping with the flowering of her own culture, leading the way. Leading Massachusetts was the singleminded, driving personality of Horace Mann (1796-1859).

A lawyer by training and a politician by instinct, Mann was a member of the state senate when education became his dominant interest. He sponsored and drove to passage in 1837 an act setting up a state board of education, after which he resigned his senate seat to become its secretary and administrative head. In the dozen years he occupied that position his influence spread from his own state to the nation, and beyond. He returned to politics in 1848 when he was elected to J. Q. Adams' honored seat in Congress, but declined a nomination for governor four years later to become president of Antioch College in Ohio. Horace Mann's first annual report as secretary of the Massachusetts Board of Education deals largely with the problems of reorganizing the common school system. One of those problems, discussed in the excerpt reprinted here, concerned the competence of teachers.

For additional reading, R. Freeman Butts and Lawrence A. Cremin, *A History of Education in American Culture* (New York: Holt, 1953) is excellent. Both Merle E. Curti, *The Social Ideas of American Edu-*

---

*Horace Mann, *Lectures and Annual Reports on Education* (Cambridge, 1867), pp. 420-32.

cators (New York: Scribner, 1935), and Neil G. McClusky, *Public Schools and Moral Education; the Influence of Horace Mann, William Torrey Harris and John Dewey* (New York: Columbia, 1959), are particularly good. In reading the excerpt note (1) what Mann had to say concerning the competence of teachers in Massachusetts; (2) what he found regarding teachers' pay; (3) his observations concerning moral instruction in the schools; (4) what proposals he advanced for improving instruction; and (5) who in his judgment was ultimately responsible for the success of any educational system.

ANOTHER COMPONENT ELEMENT IN THE PROSPERITY of schools is the competency of teachers. Teaching is the most difficult of all arts, and the profoundest of all sciences. In its absolute perfection, it would involve a complete knowledge of the whole being to be taught, and of the precise manner in which every possible application would affect it; that is, a complete knowledge of all the powers and capacities of the individual, with their exact proportions and relations to each other, and a knowledge, how, at any hour or moment, to select and apply, from a universe of means, the one then exactly apposite to its ever-changing condition. But in a far more limited and practical sense, it involves a knowledge of the principal laws of physical, mental, and moral growth, and of the tendency of means, not more to immediate than to remote results. Hence to value schools, by length instead of quality, is a matchless absurdity. Arithmetic, grammar, and the other rudiments, as they are called, comprise but a small part of the teachings in a school. The rudiments of feeling are taught not less than the rudiments of thinking. The sentiments and passions get more lessons than the intellect. Though their open recitations may be less, their secret rehearsals are more. And even in training the intellect, much of its chance of arriving, in after-life, at what we call sound judgment, or common sense, much of its power of perceiving ideas as distinctly as though they were colored diagrams, depends upon the tact and philosophic sagacity of the teacher. He has a far deeper duty to perform than to correct the erroneous results of intellectual processes. The error in the individual case is of little consequence. It is the false projecting

power in the mind—the power which sends out the error—that
is to be discovered and rectified; otherwise the error will be repeated as often as opportunities recur. It is no part of a teacher's
vocation to spend day after day in moving the hands on the
dial-plate backwards and forwards, in order to adjust them to
the true time: but he is to adjust the machinery and the regu-
lator, so that they may indicate the true time; so that they may
be a standard and measure for other things, instead of needing
other things as a standard and measure for them. Yet how can
a teacher do this, if he be alike ignorant of the mechanism and
the propelling power of the machinery he superintends?

The law lays its weighty injunctions upon teachers, in the following solemn and impressive language: *"It shall be the duty
of all instructors of youth to exert their best endeavors to impress on the minds of children and youth, committed to their
care and instruction, the principles of piety, justice, and a sacred
regard to truth, love to their country, humanity, and universal
benevolence, sobriety, industry, and frugality, chastity, moderation, and temperance, and those other virtues, which are the
ornament of human society, and the basis upon which a republican constitution is founded; and it shall be the duty of such
instructors to endeavor to lead their pupils, as their ages and
capacities will admit, into a clear understanding of the tendency
of the above-mentioned virtues to preserve and perfect a republican constitution, and secure the blessings of liberty, as well as
to promote their future happiness, and also to point out to them
the evil tendency of the opposite vices."* Is it not worthy of the
most solemn deliberation, whether, under our present system, or
rather our present want of system, in regard to the qualifications
and appointment of teachers, we are in any way of realizing,
to a reasonable and practicable extent, a fulfilment of the elevated purposes contemplated by the law? And will not an impartial posterity inquire what measures had been adopted by
the lawgiver to insure the execution of the duties which he had
himself so earnestly and solemnly enjoined?

Wherever the discharge of my duties has led me through the
State, with whatever intelligent men I have conversed, the conviction has been expressed with entire unanimity, that there is

an extensive want of competent teachers for the Common Schools. This opinion casts no reproach upon that most worthy class of persons, engaged in the sacred cause of education; and I should be unjust to those, whose views I am here reporting, should I state the fact more distinctly than the qualification. The teachers are as good as public opinion has demanded. Their attainments have corresponded with their opportunities; and the supply has answered the demand as well in quality as in number. Yet, in numerous instances, school committees have alleged, in justification of their approval of incompetent persons, the utter impossibility of obtaining better for the compensation offered. It was stated publicly by a member of the school committee of a town, containing thirty or more school districts, that one-half at least of the teachers approved by them would be rejected, only that it would be in vain to expect better teachers for present remuneration. And, without a change in prices, is it reasonable to expect a change in competency, while talent is invited, through so many other avenues, to emolument and distinction? From the Abstract of the School Returns of this Commonwealth (which I have this day submitted to the Board), including Boston, Salem, Lowell, Charlestown, and other towns, with their liberal salaries, it appears that the average wages per month paid to male teachers throughout the State, inclusive of board, is twenty-five dollars and forty-four cents; and to female teachers, eleven dollars and thirty-eight cents. Considering that many more than half of the whole number of teachers are employed in the counties bordering on the sea, it is supposed that two dollars and fifty cents a week for males, and one dollar and fifty cents a week for females, would be a very low estimate for the average price of their board, respectively, throughout the State. In the country, there would not be this difference between males and females, but in the populous towns and cities it would probably be greater. That of females is purposely put rather low, because there were several towns where it was not included, by the returns, in the wages. On this basis of computation, the average wages of male teachers throughout the State is fifteen dollars and forty-four cents a month, exclusive of board, or at the rate of one hundred and eighty-five dollars and twenty-eight cents by the year; and the average wages of female teachers, exclusive of board, is five dollars and thirty-eight cents a month, or at the rate of sixty-four dollars and fifty-six cents by the year.

In regard to moral instruction, the condition of our public schools presents a singular, and, to some extent at least, an alarming phenomenon. To prevent the school from being converted into an engine of religious proselytism; to debar successive teachers in the same school from successively inculcating hostile religious creeds, until the children in their simple-mindedness should be alienated, not only from creeds, but from religion itself; the statute of 1826 specially provided that no school-books should be used in any of the public schools, "calculated to favor any particular religious sect or tenet." The language of the Revised Statutes is slightly altered, but the sense remains the same. Probably, no one would desire a repeal of this law while the danger impends which it was designed to repel. The consequence of the enactment, however, has been, that among the vast libraries of books, expository of the doctrines of revealed religion, none have been found, free from that advocacy of particular "tenets" or "sects," which includes them within the scope of the legal prohibition; or, at least, no such books have been approved by committees, and introduced into the schools. Independently, therefore, of the immeasurable importance of moral teaching, in itself considered, this entire exclusion of religious teaching, though justifiable under the circumstances, enhances and magnifies, a thousand-fold, the indispensableness of moral instruction and training. Entirely to discard the inculcation of the great doctrines of morality and of natural theology has a vehement tendency to drive mankind into opposite extremes; to make them devotees on one side, or profligates on the other; each about equally regardless of the true constituents of human welfare. Against a tendency to these fatal extremes, the beautiful and sublime truths of ethics and of natural religion have a poising power. Hence it will be learnt with sorrow, that of the multiplicity of books used in our schools, only three have this object in view; and these three are used in only *six* of the two thousand nine hundred and eighteen schools from which returns have been received.

I have adverted to this topic in this connection, not only on account of its intrinsic importance, but on account of its relationship to the one last considered. Under our present system, indeed, this is only a branch of the preceding topic. If children are not systematically instructed in the duties they now owe, as sons and daughters, as brothers and sisters, as school-fellows and associates; in the duties also which they will so soon owe, when, emerging from parental restraint and becoming a part of the sovereignty of the State, they will be enrolled among the arbiters of a nation's destiny; is not the importance immeasurably augmented, of employing teachers, who will, themselves, be a living lesson to their pupils, of decorous behavior, of order, of magnanimity, of justice, of affection; and who, if they do not directly teach the principles, will still, by their example, transfuse and instil something of the sentiment of virtue? Engaged in the Common Schools of this State, there are now, out of the city of Boston, but few more than a hundred male teachers, who devote themselves to teaching as a regular employment or profession. The number of females is a little, though not materially, larger. Very few even of these have ever had any special training for their vocation. The rest are generally young persons, taken from agricultural or mechanical employments, which have no tendency to qualify them for the difficult station; or they are undergraduates of our colleges, some of whom, there is reason to suspect, think more of what they are to receive at the end of the stipulated term, than what they are to impart during its continuance. To the great majority of them all, however, I concede, because I sincerely believe it is their due, higher motives of action than those which govern men in the ordinary callings of life; yet still, are they not, inevitably, too inexperienced to understand and to act upon the idea, that the great secret of insuring a voluntary obedience to duty consists in a skilful preparation of motives beforehand? Can they be expected, as a body, to be able to present to their older pupils a visible scale, as it were, upon which the objects of life, so far forth as this world is concerned, are marked down, according to their relative values? Among the pagan Greeks, the men most venerated for their wisdom, their Platos and Socrates, were the educators of their youth. And after such teachers as we employ are introduced into the schools, they address themselves to the culture of the intellect mainly. The fact that children have moral natures and social affections, then in the most rapid state of development, is scarcely recognized. One page of the daily manual teaches the power of commas; another, the spelling of words; another, the rules of cadence and emphasis; but the pages are missing which teach the laws of forbearance under injury, of sympathy with misfortune, of impartiality in our judgments of men, of love and fidelity to truth; of the ever-during relations of men, in the domestic circle, in the organized government, and of stranger to stranger. How can it be expected that such cultivation will scatter seeds, so that, in the language of Scripture, *"instead of the thorn shall come up the fir-tree, and instead of the briar shall come up the myrtle-tree"*? If such be the general condition of the schools, is it a matter of surprise, that we see lads and young men thickly springing up in the midst of us, who startle at the mispronunciation of a word, as though they were personally injured, but can hear volleys of profanity, unmoved; who put on arrogant airs of superior breeding, or sneer with contempt, at a case of false spelling or grammar, but can witness spectacles of drunkenness in the streets with entire composure? Such elevation of the subordinate, such casting-down of the supreme, in the education of children, is incompatible with all that is worthy to be called the prosperity of their manhood. The moral universe is constructed upon principles, not admissive of welfare under such an administration of its laws. In such early habits, there is a gravitation and proclivity to ultimate downfall and ruin. If persevered in, the consummation of a people's destiny may still be a question of time, but it ceases to be one of certainty. To avert the catastrophe, we must look to a change in our own measures, not to any repeal or suspension of the ordinances of Nature. These, as they were originally framed in wisdom, need no amendment. Whoever wishes for a change in effects without a corresponding change in causes, wishes for a violation of Nature's laws. He proposes, as a remedy for the folly of men, an abrogation of the wisdom of Providence.

One of the greatest and most exigent wants of our schools at the present time, is a book, portraying, with attractive illustration and with a simplicity adapted to the simplicity of childhood, the obligations arising from social relationships; making them stand out, with the altitude of mountains, above the level of the engrossments of life;—not a book written for the copyright's sake, but one emanating from some comprehension of the benefits of supplying children, at an early age, with simple and elementary notions of right and wrong in feeling and in conduct, so that the appetites and passions, as they spring up in the mind, may, by a natural process, be conformed to the principles, instead of the principles made to conform to the passions and appetites.

It is said, by a late writer on the present condition of France, to have been ascertained, after an examination of great extent and minuteness, that most crimes are perpetrated in those provinces where most of the inhabitants can read and write. Nor is this a mere general fact, but the ratio is preserved with mathematical exactness; the proportion of those who can read and write, directly representing the proportion of criminals, and conversely. Their morals have been neglected, and the cultivated intellect presents to the uncultivated feelings, not only a larger circle of temptations, but better instruments for their gratification.

It is thought by some, that the State cannot afford any advance upon the present salaries of teachers, which we have seen to be on an average, exclusive of board, fifteen dollars and forty-four cents per month for males, and five dollars and thirty-eight cents for females. The valuation of the State, according to the census of 1830, was $208,360,407.54. During the past season, it has been repeatedly stated, in several of the public papers, and, so far as I have seen, without contradiction or question, that it is now equal to three hundred millions. The amount raised by taxes the current year, for the support of Common Schools, in the towns heard from, is four hundred and sixty-five thousand two hundred and twenty-eight dollars and four cents, which, if we assume the correctness of the above estimate respecting the whole property in the State, is less than one mill and six-tenths of a mill on the dollar.

Would it not seem, as though the question were put, not in sobriety, but in derision, if it were asked, whether something more than one six-hundredth part of the welfare of the State might not come from the enlightenment of its intellect and the soundness of its morals ? and yet this would, to some extent certainly, involve the question whether the State could afford any increase of its annual appropriations for schools.

There are other topics, connected with this subject, worthy of exposition, did time permit. I can enumerate but one or two of them in closing this report.

The law of 1836, respecting children employed in factories, is believed to have been already most salutary in its operation. I have undoubted authority for saying, that, in one place, four hundred children went to school, last winter, who never had been before, and whose attendance then was solely attributable to that law. Sufficient time has not yet elapsed (as the law took effect April 1, 1837) to determine whether there is a general disposition to comply with its requirements. So far as I have learned, the accounts hold out an encouraging prospect of compliance on the part of the owners and agents of manufacturing establishments, notwithstanding attempts to evade it by some parents, who hold their children to be articles of property, and value them by no higher standard than the money they can earn.

From the best information I have been able to obtain, I am led to believe that there are not more than fifty towns in the State, where any thing worthy the name of apparatus is used in schools. With few exceptions, Holbrook's Common-School apparatus, and occasionally a globe, conclude the list. Thus the natural superiority of the eye over all the other senses, in quickness, in precision, in the vastness of its field of operations, in its power of penetrating into any interstices where light can go and come, and of perceiving, in their just collocations, the different parts of complex objects, is foregone. Children get dim and imperfect notions about many things, where, with visible illustrations, they might acquire living and perfect ones at a glance. This great defect will undoubtedly be, to a considerable extent, supplied by the law of April 12, 1837, which authorizes school districts to raise money by taxation, to be expended for the purchase of apparatus and Common-School Libraries, in sums not exceeding thirty dollars the first year, and ten for any succeeding year.

In every county where I have been, excepting two, county associations for the improvement of Common Schools have been formed. In the two excepted counties, there were teachers' associations previously existing. Measures were taken to make these associations auxiliary to the Board of Education in the general plan of State operations. These county associations will open a channel of communication in both directions, between the Board as a central body, and the several towns and school districts in the State; and through the Board, between all the different parts of the State; so that improvements, devised or discovered in any place, instead of being wholly lost, may be universally diffused, and sound views, upon this great subject, may be multiplied by the number of minds capable of understanding them. Several excellent addresses have already emanated from committees, appointed by these associations, or by the conventions which originated them.

If, in addition to these county associations, town associations could be formed, consisting of teachers, school-committee-men, and the friends of education generally, who should meet to discuss the relative merits of different modes of teaching—thus discarding the worst, and improving even the best—but little, perhaps nothing more, could be desired in the way of systematic organization. It should be a special duty of all the members of the town associations, to secure, as far as possible, a regular and punctual attendance of the children upon the schools.

Some means of obtaining more precise information respecting the number of scholars attending the public schools, and the regularity of that attendance, is most desirable. The practice of keeping registers in the schools, indispensable as it is to statistical accuracy, seems to be very often neglected. In preparing the abstract, evidence has been constantly occurring of the want of information, which such registers would have supplied. Sometimes, the committee resort to conjecture; sometimes they frankly avow their ignorance of the desired fact; and sometimes all the sums, set down in several columns of considerable length, have a common multiple, which is incompatible with the diversity of actual occurrences. On the whole, there is, undoubtedly, a very close approximation of truth; and where particulars are so numerous, errors on one side will often balance and cancel errors on the other; excepting where there is some standing bias, when the errors will all be on the gravitating side. Still exactness should be aimed at, as statistics are every day becoming more and more the basis of legislation and economical science. While the State, in the administration of its military functions, establishes a separate department, fills the statute-books with pages of minute regulations and formidable penalties, commissions various grades of officers, so that the fact of every missing gun-flint and priming-wire may be detected, transmitted, and recorded among its archives, it prescribes no means of ascertaining how many of its children are deserters from what should be the nurseries of intelligence and morality. This is mentioned here with no view of disparaging what is done, but only to contrast it with what is omitted.

Not a little inconvenience results from the fact, that school committees are elected at the annual town-meetings in the spring, and are obliged to make their returns in October following. Their returns, therefore, cover but half the time of their own continuance in office, while they cover half the time of the official existence of their predecessors. It is for the Legislature to say whether there be any good reason, why the time covered by these returns should not be coincident with their duration in office.

In closing this report, I wish to observe, that, should it ever fall under the notice, either of individuals or of classes, who may suspect that some imputation is cast upon them by any of its statements, I wish to assure them, that no word of it has been dictated by a feeling of unkindness to any one. The object of whatever has been said was to expose defects in a system so substantially excellent, as to requite any labor for its reformation; and all the remarks which may seem accusatory of persons connected with it have caused me more pain to write, than they can any one to read. To have spoken in universal commendation of the system and of its administrators would have been most grateful, could it have been, also, true; but, in the discharge of a duty, respecting one of the most valuable and enduring of human interests, I have felt that it would be unworthy the sacred character of the cause, if, to purchase any temporary gratification for others or for myself, I could have sacrificed one particle of the permanent utility of truth.

11

The Eastern States, 1841-42

Sir Charles Lyell: Travels in North America*

European visitors were coming to study the United States before the ink was dry on the articles of British capitulation at Yorktown. Some came to criticize, some came in hopes of making money, some on legitimate business, and a few with a genuine desire to see and to understand. The list for the first half of the nineteenth century is long and distinguished, including such names as Charles Dickens, Frederick Marryat, Harriet Martineau, Alexis de Tocqueville, and Fanny Kemble. One of the most perceptive—and most charitable—was Charles Lyell (1797-1875), already a world-famous geologist when he first visited the United States in 1841 to lecture at the Lowell Institute in Boston.

Both insatiably curious and unusually articulate, Lyell could resist neither the opportunity to see for himself the wonders of this new land, nor the temptation to write a book about it. Using Boston as a base of operation, he visited Niagara Falls by way of the Erie Canal; studied with scientific eye the coal fields of Pennsylvania; sat in on Congress on his way to visit the South. On another trip he traveled down the Ohio River from Pittsburgh to Cincinnati by steamboat, returning by way of Cleveland and the lakes.

Lyell's observations may be usefully supplemented by reference to a standard historical geography, such as Ralph H. Brown, *Historical Geography of the United States* (New York: Harcourt, Brace, 1948). For comparative purposes such travel anthologies as Allan Nevins, ed., *America Through British Eyes* (Rev. ed.; New York: Oxford, 1948), and Oscar Handlin, ed., *This Was America* (Cambridge: Harvard, 1949) are excellent. Jane Louise Mesick's *The English Traveller in America, 1785-1835* (New York: Columbia U. P., 1922), provides a useful background for the early nineteenth-century British observers of the states. In the excerpts printed here, the reader should

---

*Sir Charles Lyell, *Travels in North America*. Two vols. (London: John Murray, 1845), pp. I, 4-5, 10-11, 14, 15-16, 21-22, 101-03, 127-28, 130-31, 135, 153-54, 156-58, 183, 193-95; II, 73-74, 76-77.

note (1) the extent to which Sir Charles felt at home in Boston and why; (2) what he observed concerning the state of the economy in general and of transportation facilities in particular; (3) what he thought of the social and cultural life of Washington, D. C.; (4) what he learned about the South as a destination for European immigrants; (5) his reception among southerners; (6) what suggestions he made for improving the lot of the Negroes; (7) what he thought of Ohio's progress; and (8) his sentiments while contemplating the advance of Europeans across the North American continent.

AUGUST 2.—A RUN OF ABOUT THIRTY HOURS CARRIED us to Boston, which we reached in twelve and a half days after leaving Liverpool. The heat here is intense, the harbour and city beautiful, the air clear and entirely free from smoke, so that the shipping may be seen far off, at the end of many of the streets. The Tremont Hotel merits its reputation as one of the best in the world. Recollecting the contrast of everything French when I first crossed the straits of Dover, I am astonished, after having traversed the wide ocean, at the resemblance of every thing I see and hear to things familiar at home. It has so often happened to me in our own island, without travelling into those parts of Wales, Scotland, or Ireland, where they talk a perfectly distinct language, to encounter provincial dialects which it is difficult to comprehend, that I wonder at finding the people here so very English. . . .

Aug. 9.—After a week spent very agreeably at Boston, we started for New Haven in Connecticut, going the first hundred miles on an excellent railway in about five hours, for three dollars each. The speed of the railways in this state, the most populous in the Union, is greater than elsewhere, and I am told that they are made with American capital, and for the most part pay good interest. There are no tunnels, and so few embankments that they afford the traveller a good view of the country. The number of small lakes and ponds, such as are seen in the country between Lund and Stockholm in Sweden, affords a pleasing variety to the scenery, and they are as useful as they are ornamental. The water is beautifully clear, and when frozen to the depth of many feet in winter, supplies those large cubical masses of ice, which are sawed and transported to the principal cities throughout the Union, and even shipped to Calcutta, crossing the equator twice in their outward voyage. It has been truly said, that this part of New England owes its wealth to its industry, the soil being sterile, the timber small, and there being no staple commodities of native growth, except ice and granite. . . .

The city of New Haven, with a population of 14,000 souls possesses, like Springfield, fine avenues of trees in its streets, which mingle agreeably with the buildings of the university, and the numerous churches, of which we counted near twenty steeples. When attending service, according to the Presbyterian form, in the College chapel on Sunday, I could scarcely believe I was not in Scotland. . . .

Aug. 13.—A large steamer carried us from New Haven to New York, a distance of about ninety miles, in less than six hours. We had Long Island on the one side, and the main land on the other, the scenery at first tame from the width of the channel, but very lively and striking when this became more contracted, and at length we seemed to sail into the very suburbs of the great city itself, passing between green islands, some of them covered with buildings and villas. We had the same bright sunshine which we have enjoyed ever since we landed, and an atmosphere unsullied by the chimnies of countless steam-boats, factories, and houses of a population of more than 300,000 souls, thanks to the remoteness of all fuel save anthracite and wood.

Aug. 16.—Sailed in the splendid new steam-ship the Troy, in company with about 500 passengers, from New York to Albany, 145 miles, at the rate of about 16 miles an hour. When I was informed that "seventeen of these vessels went to a mile," it seemed incredible, but I found that in fact the deck measured 300 feet in length. To give a sufficient supply of oxygen to the anthracite, the machinery is made to work two bellows which blow a strong current of air into the furnace. The Hudson is an arm of the sea or estuary about twelve fathoms deep, above New York, and its waters are inhabited by a curious mixture of marine and fresh-water plants and mollusca. At first on our left, or on the western bank, we had a lofty precipice of columnar basalt from 400 to 600 feet in height, called the Palisades, extremely picturesque. This basalt rests on sandstone, which is of the same age as that mentioned before near New Haven, but has an opposite or westward dip. On arriving at the Highlands, the winding channel is closed in by steep hills of gneiss on both sides, and the vessel often holds her course as if bearing directly on the land. The stranger cannot guess in which direction he is to penetrate the rocky gorge, but he soon emerges again into a broad valley, the blue Catskill mountains appearing in the distance. The scenery deserves all the praise which has been lavished upon it, and when the passage is made in nine hours it is full of variety and contrast. . . .

A few years ago it was a fatiguing tour of many weeks to reach the Falls of Niagara from Albany. We are now carried along at the rate of sixteen miles an hour, on a railway often supported on piles, through large swamps covered with aquatic trees and shrubs, or through dense forests, with occasional clearings where orchards are planted by anticipation among the stumps, before they have even had time to run up a log house. The traveller views with surprise, in the midst of so much unoccupied land, one flourishing town after another, such as Utica, Syracuse, and Auburn. At Rochester he admires the streets of large houses, inhabited by 20,000 souls, where the first settler built his log-cabin in the wilderness only twenty-five years ago. At one point our train stopped at a handsome new built station-house, and looking out at one window, we saw a group of Indians of the Oneida tribe, lately owners of the broad lands around, but now humbly offering for sale a few trinkets, such as baskets ornamented with porcupine quills, moccasins of moose-deer skin, and boxes of birch bark. At the other window stood a well-dressed waiter handing ices and confectionery. When we reflect that some single towns of which the foundations were laid by persons still living, can already number a population, equal to all the aboriginal hunter tribes who possessed the forests for hundreds of miles around, we soon cease to repine at the extraordinary revolution, however much as may commiserate the unhappy fate of the disinherited race. . . .

Lyell returned to New York by way of Albany and the Hudson River. He then combined a visit to Philadelphia with a trip into the Pennsylvania coal region which, as a geologist, was of special interest to him.

OCTOBER 7, 1841.—The steep slopes, as well as the summits of the ridges in the anthracite region of Pennsylvania, are so densely covered with wood, that the surveyors were obliged to climb to the tops of trees, in order to obtain general views of the country, and construct a geographical map on the scale of two inches to a mile, on which they laid down the result of their geological observations. Under the trees, the ground is covered with Rhododendron, Kalmia, and another evergreen called Sweet Fern, the leaves of which have a very agreeable odour, resembling that of our bog-myrtle, but fainter. The leaves are so like those of a fern or Pteris in form, that the miners call the impressions of the fossil Pecopteris, in the coal-shales "sweet fern."

We found the German language chiefly spoken in this mountainous region, and preached in most of the churches, as at Reading. It is fast degenerating into a patois, and it is amusing to see many Germanized English words introduced even into the newspapers, such as *turnpeik* for turnpike, *fense* for fence, *flauer* for flour, or others, such as jail, which have been adopted without alteration.

From the Lehigh Summit Mine, we descended for nine miles on a railway impelled by our own weight, in a small car at the rate of twenty miles an hour. A man sat in front checking our speed by a drag on the steeper declivities, and oiling the wheels without stopping. The coal is let down by the same railroad, sixty mules being employed to draw up the empty cars every day. In the evening the mules themselves are sent down standing four abreast and feeding out of mangers the whole way. We saw them start in a long train of waggons, and were told, that so completely do they acquire the notion that it is their business through life to pull weights up hill, and ride down at their ease, that if any of them are afterwards taken away from the mine and set to other occupations, they willingly drag heavy loads up steep ascents, but obstinately refuse to pull any vehicle down hill, coming to a dead halt at the commencement of the slightest slope.

The general effect of the long unbroken summits of the ridges of the Alleghany Mountains is very monotonous and unpicturesque; but the scenery is beautiful, where we meet occasionally with a transverse gorge through which a large river escapes.

After visiting the Beaver Meadow coal field, we left the mountains by one of these openings, called the Lehigh Gap, wooded on both sides, and almost filled up by the Lehigh River, a branch of the Delaware, the banks of which we now followed to Trenton in New Jersey. . . .

Lyell was back in Boston in November when a heavy snowfall on the twenty-ninth of that month convinced him the time had come for a trip to the southern states.

. . . Pursuing my course southwards, I found that the snowstorm had been less heavy at New York, still less at Philadelphia, and after crossing the Susquehanna (Dec. 13) the weather began to resemble that of an English spring. In the suburbs of Baltimore, the locomotive engines being detached, our cars were drawn by horses on a railway into the middle of the town. Maryland was the first slave state we had visited; and at Baltimore we were reminded for the first time of the poorer inhabitants of a large European city by the mean dwellings and dress of some of the labouring class, both coloured and white.

At Washington I was shown the newly-founded national museum, in which the objects of natural history and other treasures collected during the late voyage of discovery to the Antarctic regions, the South Seas, and California, are deposited. Such a national repository would be invaluable at Philadelphia, New York, or Boston, but here there is no university, no classes of students in science or literature, no philosophical societies, no people who seem to have any leisure. The members of Congress rarely have town residences in this place, but, leaving their families in large cities, where they may enjoy more refined society, they live here in boarding-houses until their political duties and the session are over. If the most eminent legislators and statesmen, the lawyers of the supreme courts, and the foreign ambassadors, had all been assembled here for a great part of the year with their families, in a wealthy and flourishing metropolis, the social and political results of a great centre of influence and authority could not have failed to be most beneficial. . . . After being presented to the President, and visiting several persons to whom we had letters, we were warned by a light sprinkling of snow that it was time to depart and migrate further southwards.

Crossing the Potomac, therefore, I proceeded to Richmond, in Virginia, where I resolved to sail down the James River, in order to examine the geology of the tertiary strata on its shores. . . .

On entering the station-house of the railway which was to carry us to our place of embarkation, we found a room with only two chairs in it. One of these was occupied by a respectable-looking woman, who immediately rose, intending to give it up to me, an act betraying that she was English, and newly-arrived, as an American gentleman, even if already seated, would have felt it necessary to rise and offer the chair to any woman, whether mistress or maid, and she, as a matter of course, would have accepted the proffered seat. After I had gone out, she told my wife that she and her husband had come a few months before from Hertfordshire, hoping to get work in Virginia, but she had discovered that there was no room here for poor white people, who were despised by the very negroes if they laboured with their own hands. She had found herself looked down upon, even for carrying her own child, for they said she ought to hire a black nurse. These poor emigrants were now anxious to settle in some free state.

As another exemplification of the impediments to improvement existing here, I was told that a New England agriculturist had bought a farm on the south side of the James river, sold off all the slaves, and introduced Irish labourers, being persuaded that their services would prove more economical than slave-labour. The scheme was answering well, till, by the end of the third year, the Irish became very dissatisfied with their position, feeling degraded by losing the respect of the whites, and being exposed to the contempt of the surrounding negroes. They had, in fact, lowered themselves by the habitual performance of offices which, south of the Potomac, are assigned to hereditary bondsmen.

All the planters in this part of Virginia, to whose houses I went without letters of introduction, received me politely and hospitably. To be an Englishman engaged in scientific pursuits was a sufficient passport, and their servants, horses, and carriages, were most liberally placed at my disposal.

DEC. 28.—Charleston, South Carolina. We arrived here after a journey of 160 miles through the pine forests of North Carolina, between Weldon and Wilmington, and a voyage of about 17 hours, in a steam ship, chiefly in the night between Wilmington and this place. Here we find ourselves in a genial climate, where the snow is rarely seen, and never lies above an hour or two upon the ground. The rose, the narcissus, and other flowers, are still lingering in the gardens, the woods still verdant with the magnolia, live oak, and long-leaved pine, while the dwarf fan palm or palmetto, frequent among the underwood, marks a more southern region. In less than four weeks since we left Boston, we have passed from the 43d to the 33d degree of latitude, carried often by the power of steam for several hundred miles together through thinly peopled wildernesses, yet sleeping every night in good inns, and contrasting the facilities of locomotion in this new country with the difficulties we had contended with the year before when travelling in Europe, through populous parts of Touraine, Brittany, and other provinces of France. . . . About forty miles below Augusta at Demery's Ferry, the place where we disembarked the waters were so high that we were carried on shore by two stout negroes. In the absence of the proprietor to whom I had letters, we were hospitably received by his overseer, who came down to the river bank, with two led horses, on one of which was a lady's saddle. He conducted us through a beautiful wood, where the verdure of the evergreen oaks, the pines, and hollies, and the mildness of the air, made it difficult for us to believe that it was mid-winter, and that we had been the month before in a region of snow storms and sledges. We crossed two creeks, and after riding several miles reached the house, and were shown into a spacious room, where a great wood fire was kept up constantly on the hearth, and the doors on both sides left open day and night.

Returning home to this hospitable mansion in the dusk of the evening of the day following, I was surprised to see, in a grove of trees near the court-yard of the farm, a large wood-fire blazing on the ground. Over the fire hung three cauldrons, filled, as I afterwards learned, with hog's lard, and three old negro women, in their usual drab-coloured costume, were leaning over the cauldrons, and stirring the lard to clarify it. The red glare of the fire was reflected from their faces, and I need hardly say how much they reminded me of the scene of the witches in Macbeth. Beside them, moving slowly backwards and forwards in a rock-ing-chair, sat the wife of the overseer, muffled up in a cloak, and suffering from a severe cold, but obliged to watch the old slaves, who are as thoughtless as children, and might spoil the lard if she turned away her head for a few minutes. When I inquired the meaning of this ceremony I was told it was "killing time," this being the coldest season of the year, and that since I left the farm in the morning thirty hogs had been sacrificed by the side of a running stream not far off. These were destined to serve as winter provisions for the negroes, of whom there were about a hundred on this plantation. To supply all of them with food, clothes, and medical attendants, young, old, and impotent, as well as the able-bodied, is but a portion of the expense of slave-labour. They must be continually superintended by trustworthy whites, who might often perform no small part of the task, and far more effectively, with their own hands. . . .

South Carolina is one of the few states where there is a numerical preponderance of slaves. One night, at Charleston, I went to see the guard-house, where there is a strong guard kept constantly in arms, and on the alert. Every citizen is obliged to serve in person, or find a substitute; and the maintenance of such a force, the strict laws against importing books relating to emancipation, and the prohibition to bring back slaves who have been taken by their masters into free states, show that the fears of the owner, whether well-founded or not, are real.

A philanthropist may well be perplexed when he desires to devise some plan of interference which may really promote the true interests of the negro. But the way in which the planters would best consult their own interests appears to me very clear. They should exhibit more patience and courage towards the abolitionists, whose influence and numbers they greatly overrate, and lose no time in educating the slaves, and encouraging private manumission to prepare the way for general emancipation. All seem agreed that the states most ripe for this great reform are Maryland, Virginia, North Carolina, Tennessee, Kentucky, and Missouri. Experience has proved in the northern States that emancipation immediately checks the increase of the coloured population, and causes the relative number of the whites to augment very rapidly. Every year, in proportion as the north-western States fill up, and as the boundary of the new settlers

in the west is removed farther and farther, beyond the Mississippi and Missouri, the cheaper and more accessible lands south
of the Potomac will offer a more tempting field for colonization
to the swarms of New Englanders, who are averse to migrating
into slave states. Before this influx of white labourers, the coloured race will give way, and it will require the watchful care
of the philanthropist, whether in the north or south, to prevent
them from being thrown out of employment and reduced to
destitution.

If due exertions be made to cultivate the minds, and protect
the rights and privileges of the negroes, and it nevertheless be
found that they cannot contend, when free, with white competitors, but are superseded by them, still the cause of humanity will
have gained. The coloured people, though their numbers remain
stationary, or even diminish, may in the meantime be happier
than now, and attain to a higher moral rank. They would, moreover, escape the cruelty and injustice which are the invariable
consequences of the exercise of irresponsible power, especially
where authority must be sometimes delegated by the planter to
agents of inferior education and coarser feelings. And last not
least, emancipation would effectually put a stop to the breeding,
selling, and exporting of slaves to the sugar-growing States of
the South, where, unless the accounts we usually read of slavery
be exaggerated and distorted, the life of the Negro is shortened
by severe toil and suffering.

Lyell returned to Charleston from Savannah by steamboat. He
continued his journey north by the same mode of transportation
as far as Wilmington, North Carolina, thence by rail to South
Washington on the Pamlico River, where he boarded another
steamboat for Washington, D.C. From Washington he returned
to Boston by rail. He resumed his travels in the spring of 1842,
and in May of that month we find him in Cincinnati, having
reached that city by river boat from Pittsburgh.

MAY 29.—We left Cincinnati for Cleveland on Lake Erie, a
distance of 250 miles, and our line of route took us through the
centre of the State of Ohio, by Springfield, Mount Vernon, and
Wooster, at all which places we slept, reaching Cleveland on the
fifth day. . . .

In passing from the southern to the northern frontier of Ohio, we left a handsome and populous city and fine roads, and found the towns grow smaller and the high roads rougher, as we advanced. When more than half way across the State, and after leaving Mount Vernon, we saw continually new clearings, where the felling, girdling, and burning of trees was going on, and where oats were growing amidst the blackened stumps on land which had never been ploughed, but only broken up with the harrow. The carriage was then jolted for a short space over a corduroy road, constructed of trunks of trees laid side by side, while the hot air of burning timber made us impatient of the slow pace of our carriage. We then lost sight for many leagues of all human habitations, except here and there some empty wooden building, on which "Mover's House" was inscribed in large letters. Here we were told a family of emigrants might pass the night on payment of a small sum. At last the road again improved, and we came to the termination of the table land of Ohio, at a distance of about sixteen miles from Lake Erie. From this point on the summit of Stony Hill we saw at our feet a broad and level plain covered with wood; and beyond, in the horizon, Lake Erie, extending far and wide like the ocean. We then began our descent, and in about three hours reached Cleveland. . . .

Ohio was a wilderness exclusively occupied by the Indians, until near the close of the last century. In 1800 its population amounted to 45,365, in the next ten years it had increased fivefold, and in the ten which followed it again more than doubled. In 1840 it had reached 1,600,000 souls, all free, and almost without any admixture of the coloured race. In this short interval the forest had been transformed into a land of steamboats, canals, and flourishing towns; and would have been still more populous had not thousands of its new settlers migrated still farther west to Indiana and Illinois. A portion of the public works which accelerated this marvellous prosperity, were executed with foreign capital, but the interest of the whole has been punctually paid by direct taxes. There is no other example in history, either in the old or new world, of so sudden a rise of a large country to opulence and power. The State contains nearly as wide an extent of arable land as England, all of moderate elevation, so rich in its alluvial plains as to be cropped thirty or forty years without

manure, having abundance of fine timber, a temperate climate,
many large navigable rivers, a ready communication through Lake
Erie with the north and east, and by the Ohio with the south and
west, and, lastly, abundance of coal in its eastern counties.

I am informed that, in the beginning of the present year (1842),
the foremost bands of emigrants have reached the Platte River, a
tributary of the Missouri. This point is said to be only half way
between the Atlantic and the Rocky Mountains, and the country
beyond the present frontier is as fertile as that already occupied.
De Tocqueville calculated that along the borders of the United
States, from Lake Superior to the Gulf of Mexico, extending a
distance of more than 1200 miles as the bird flies, the whites advance every year at a mean rate of seventeen miles; and he truly
observes that there is a grandeur and solemnity in this gradual
and continuous march of the European race towards the Rocky
Mountains. He compares it to "a deluge of men rising unabatedly,
and daily driven onwards by the hand of God.". . .

12

Oregon, 1843

John Charles Fremont:
Report of the Expedition to Oregon*

By 1843 the Oregon country, jointly occupied for a quarter of a century by the United States and Great Britain, was becoming an object of controversy between the two nations. American farmers were moving in significant numbers into the Willamette valley, where rich, well-watered land could be had for the taking, when Lieutenant John Charles Fremont (1813-90) of the Army Corps of Topographical Engineers was sent to explore Oregon and California. His orders were rescinded while he was still outfitting at Westport, Missouri, but his young wife of two years, Jessie Benton Fremont, daughter of the politically powerful Missouri Senator, intercepted the cancellation at St. Louis and forwarded in its stead an urgent message to be off and ask no questions.

Fremont's report of his explorations was widely used as an official guide to the West, with which the explorer himself was soon completely identified. In California when the Mexican War broke out, his assumption of command over all United States forces in the area led to a clash with General Kearney, and to a court martial. He was acquitted but resigned from the Army, returning to California in time to be elected one of the state's first senators. In 1856 he was the new Republican party's first presidential nominee. He was appointed a major general in 1861, but was soon at odds with Lincoln and was shelved. He was not again active, either in military life or in politics.

The standard life of Fremont is Allan Nevins, *Fremont, Pathmaker of the West* (New ed.; New York: Longmans, 1955). Francis Parkman's *The Oregon Trail*, reprinted in numerous editions since it first appeared in 1849, is a vivid firsthand description of the earlier section of the trail. The most recent work is David Lavender, *Westward Vision: The Story of the Oregon Trail* (New York: McGraw-Hill,

*John Charles Fremont, *Report of the Exploring Expedition to the Rocky Mountains in the Year 1842, and to Oregon and Northern California in the Years 1843-44.* 28th Congress, 2nd Session, House Executive Document 166.

185]

1963). In the excerpts reproduced here, note (1) the mood and style in which the report was written; (2) the extent to which Fremont noted natural surroundings, climate, temperature, and resources; (3) how Fremont described the condition of the Indians encountered; (4) the extent to which he concerned himself with the emigrants and potential settlers who would follow after he had blazed the trail; and (5) the nature of the receptions accorded him along the way and at his destination.

OCTOBER 13 [1843].—The morning was bright, with the temperature at sunset 28°. The horses had strayed off during the night, probably in search of grass; and, after a considerable delay, we had succeeded in finding all but two, when, about 9 o'clock, we heard the sound of an Indian song and drum approaching; and, shortly after, three Cayuse Indians appeared in sight, bringing with them the two animals. They belonged to a party which had been on a buffalo hunt in the neighborhood of the Rocky mountains, and were hurrying home in advance. We presented them with some tobacco, and other things, with which they appeared well satisfied, and, moderating their pace, travelled in company with us.

We were now about to leave the valley of the great southern branch of the Columbia river, to which the absence of timber, and the scarcity of water, give the appearance of a desert, to enter a mountainous region where the soil is good, and in which the face of the country is covered with nutritious grasses, and dense forest—land embracing many varieties of trees peculiar to the country, and on which the timber exhibits a luxuriance of growth unknown to the eastern part of the continent and to Europe. This mountainous region connects itself in the southward and westward with the elevated country belonging to the Cascade or California range; and, as will be remarked in the course of the narrative, forms the eastern limit of the fertile and timbered lands along the desert and mountainous region included within the Great Basin—a term which I apply to the intermediate region between the Rocky mountains and the next range, containing many lakes, with their own system of rivers and creeks, (of which the Great Salt is the principal,) and which have no connexion with the ocean, or the great rivers which flow into it. This Great Basin is yet to be adequately explored. And here, on quitting the banks of a sterile river, to enter on arable mountains, the remark may be made, that, on this western slope of our continent, the usual order or distribution of good and bad soil is often reversed; the river and creek bottoms being often sterile, and darkened with the gloomy and barren artemisia; while the mountain is often fertile, and covered with rich grass, pleasant to the eye, and good for flocks and herds. . . .

OCT. 15.—The thermometer at daylight was 42°, and at sunrise 40°; clouds, which were scatterred over all the sky, disappeared with the rising sun. The trail did not much improve until we had crossed the dividing grounds between the *Brulé* (Burnt) and Powder rivers. The rock displayed on the mountains, as we approached the summit, was a compact trap, decomposing on the exposed surfaces, and apparently an altered argillaceous sandstone, containing small crystalline nodules of anolcime, apparently filling cavities originally existing. From the summit here, the whole horizon shows high mountains; no high plain or level is to be seen; and on the left, from south around by the west to north, the mountains are black with pines; while, through the remaining space to the eastward, they are bald with the exception of some scattered pines. You will remark that we are now entering a region where all the elevated parts are covered with dense and heavy forests. From the dividing grounds we descended by a mountain road to Powder river, on an old bed of which we encamped. Descending from the summit, we enjoyed a picturesque view of high rocky mountains on the right, illuminated by the setting sun.

From the heights we had looked in vain for a well-known landmark on Powder river, which had been described to me by Mr. Payette as *l'arbre seul* (the lone tree;) and, on arriving at the river, we found a fine tall pine stretched on the ground, which had been felled by some inconsiderate emigrant axe. It had been a beacon on the road for many years past. Our Cayuses had become impatient to reach their homes, and travelled on ahead to-day; and this afternoon we were visited by several Indians, who belonged to the tribes on the Columbia. They were on horseback, and were out on a hunting excursion, but had

obtained no better game than a large gray hare, of which each
had some six or seven hanging to his saddle. We were also visited
by an Indian who had his lodge and family in the mountain to
the left. He was in want of ammunition, and brought with him
a beaver skin to exchange, and which he valued at six charges of
powder and ball. I learned from him that there are very few of
these animals remaining in this part of the country. . . .

OCT. 18.—It began to rain an hour before sunrise, and
continued until 10 o'clock; the sky entirely overcast, and the
temperature at sunrise 48°.

We resumed our journey somewhat later than usual, travelling
in a nearly north direction across this beautiful valley; and about
noon reached a place on one of the principal streams, where I
had determined to leave the emigrant trail, in the expectation of
finding a more direct and better road across the Blue mountains.
At this place the emigrants appeared to have held some consul-
tation as to their further route, and finally turned directly off to
the left; reaching the foot of the mountain in about three miles,
which they ascended by a hill as steep and difficult as that by
which we had yesterday descended to the Rond. Quitting,
therefore, this road, which, after a very rough crossing, issues
from the mountains by the heads of the *Umatilah* river, we continued our northern course across the valley, following an Indian
trail which had been indicated to me by Mr. Payette, and encamped at the northern extremity of the Grand Rond, on a
slough-like stream of very deep water, without any apparent
current. There are some pines here on the low hills at the creek;
and in the northwest corner of the Rond is a very heavy body
of timber, which descends into the plain. The clouds, which had
rested very low along the mountain sides during the day, rose
gradually up in the afternoon; and in the evening the sky was
almost entirely clear, with a temperature at sunset of 47°. Some
indifferent observations placed the camp in longitude 117°28'26",
latitude 45°26'47"; and the elevation was 2,600 feet above the
sea.

OCT. 19.—This morning the mountains were hidden by fog;
there was a heavy dew during the night, in which the exposed
thermometer at daylight stood at 32°, and at sunrise the temperature was 35°.

We passed out of the Grand Rond by a fine road along the creek, which, for a short distance, runs in a kind of rocky chasm. Crossing a low point, which was a little rocky, the trail conducted into the open valley of the stream—a handsome place for farms; the soil, even of the hills, being rich and black. Passing through a point of pines, which bore evidences of being much frequented by the Indians, and in which the trees were sometimes apparently 200 feet high and 3 to 7 feet in diameter, we halted for a few minutes in the afternoon at the foot of the Blue mountains, on a branch of the Grand Rond river, at an elevation of 2,700 feet. Resuming our journey, we commenced the ascent of the mountain through an open pine forest of large and stately trees, among which the balsam pine made its appearance; the road being good, with the exception of one steep ascent, with a corresponding descent, which might both have been easily avoided by opening a way for a short distance through the timber. It would have been well had we encamped on the stream where we had halted below, as the night overtook us on the mountain, and we were obliged to encamp without water, and tie up the animals to the trees for the night. We had halted on a smooth open place of a narrow ridge, which descended very rapidly to a ravine or piney hollow, at a considerable distance below; and it was quite a pretty spot, had there been water near. But the fires at night look very cheerless after a day's march, when there is no preparation for supper going on; and, after sitting some time around the blazing logs, Mr. Preuss and Carson, with several others, volunteered to take the India rubber buckets and go down into the ravine in search of water. It was a very difficult way in the darkness down the slippery side of the steep mountain, and harder still to climb about half a mile up again; but they found the water, and the cup of coffee (which it enabled us to make) and bread were only enjoyed with greater pleasure. . . .

OCT. 22.—The white frost this morning was like snow on the ground; the ice was a quarter of an inch thick on the creek, and the thermometer at sunrise was at 20°. But, in a few hours, the day became warm and pleasant, and our road over the mountains was delightful and full of enjoyment.

The trail passed sometimes through very thick young timber,

in which there was much cutting to be done; but, after travelling
a few miles, the mountains became more bald, and we reached a
point from which there was a very extensive view in the northwest. We were here on the western verge of the Blue mountains,
long spurs of which, very precipitous on either side, extended
down into the valley, the waters of the mountain roaring between them. On our right was a mountain plateau, covered with
a dense forest; and to the westward, immediately below us, was
the great *Nez Percé* (pierced nose) prairie, in which dark lines
of timber indictaed the course of many affluents to a considerable
stream that was seen pursuing its way across the plain towards
what appeared to be the Columbia river. This I knew to be the
Walahwalah river, and occasional spots along its banks, which
resembled clearings, were supposed to be the mission or Indian
settlements; but the weather was smoky and unfavorable to far
views with the glass. The rock displayed here in the escarpments
is a compact amorphous trap, which appears to constitute the
mass of the Blue mountains in this latitude; and all the region
of country through which we have travelled since leaving the
Snake river has been the seat of violent and extensive igneous
action. Along the Burnt river valley, the strata are evidently
sedimentary rocks, altered by the intrusion of volcanic products,
which in some instances have penetrated and essentially changed
their original condition. Along our line of route from this point
to the California mountains, there seems but little essential
change. All our specimens of sedimentary rocks show them to be
much altered, and volcanic productions appear to prevail
throughout the whole intervening distance.

The road now led along the mountain side, around heads of
the precipitous ravines; and, keeping men ahead to clear a road,
we passed alternately through bodies of timber and small open
prairies, and encamped in a large meadow, in view of the great
prairie below.

At sunset the thermometer was at 40°, and the night was very
clear and bright. Water was only to be had here by descending
a bad ravine, into which we drove our animals, and had much
trouble with them, in a very close growth of small pines. Mr.
Preuss had walked ahead, and did not get into camp this evening. The trees here maintained their size, and one of the black

spruces measured 15 feet in circumference. In the neighborhood of the camp, pines have reappeared here among the timber.

OCT. 23.—The morning was very clear; there had been a heavy white frost during the night, and at sunrise the thermometer was at 31°.

After cutting through two thick bodies of timber, in which I noticed some small trees of *hemlock* spruce (*perusse*) the forest became more open, and we had no longer any trouble to clear a way. The pines here were 11 or 12 feet in circumference, and about 110 feet high, and appeared to love the open grounds. The trail now led along one of the long spurs of the mountain, descending gradually towards the plain; and after a few miles travelling, we emerged finally from the forest, in full view of the plain below, and saw the snowy mass of Mount Hood, standing high out above the surrounding country, at the distance of 180 miles. The road along the ridge was excellent, and the grass very green and good; the old grass having been burnt off early in the autumn. About 4 o'clock in the afternoon we reached a little bottom on the Walahwalah river, where we found Mr. Preuss, who yesterday had reached this place, and found himself too far in advance of the camp to return. The stream here has just issued from the narrow ravines, which are walled with precipices, in which the rock has a brown and more burnt appearance than above.

At sunset the thermometer was at 48°; and our position was in longitude 118°00′39″, and in latitude 45°53′35″.

The morning was clear, with a temperature at sunrise of 24°. Crossing the river, we travelled over a hilly country with good bunch grass; the river bottom, which generally contains the best soil in other countries, being here a sterile level of rock and pebbles. We had found the soil in the Blue mountains to be of excellent quality, and it appeared also to be good here among the lower hills. Reaching a little eminence, over which the trail passed, we had an extensive view along the course of the river, which was divided and spread over its bottom in a net work of water, receiving several other tributaries from the mountains. There was a band of several hundred horses grazing on the hills about two miles ahead; and as we advanced on the road we met other bands, which Indians were driving out to pasture also on

the hills. True to its general character, the reverse of other countries, the hills and mountains here were rich in grass, the bottoms
barren and sterile.

In six miles we crossed a principal fork, below which the
scattered water of the river was gathered into one channel; and,
passing on the way several unfinished houses, and some cleared
patches, where corn and potatoes were cultivated, we reached,
in about eight miles farther, the missionary establishment of Dr.
Whitman, which consisted, at this time, of one *adobe* house—i. e.
built of unburnt bricks, as in Mexico.

I found Dr. Whitman absent on a visit to the *Dalles* of the
Columbia; but had the pleasure to see a fine-looking large family
of emigrants, men, women, and children, in robust health, all
indemnifying themselves for previous scanty fare, in a hearty
consumption of potatoes, which are produced here of a remarkably good quality. We were disappointed in our expectation of
obtaining corn meal or flour at this station, the mill belonging to
the mission having been lately burnt down; but an abundant
supply of excellent potatoes banished regrets, and furnished a
grateful substitute for bread. A small town of Nez Percé Indians
gave an inhabited and even a populous appearance to the station; and, after remaining about an hour, we continued our
route, and encamped on the river about four miles below, passing on the way an emigrant encampment.

Temperature at sunset, 49°.

oct. 25.—The weather was pleasant, with a sunrise temperature of 36°. Our road to-day had in it nothing of interest;
and the country offered to the eye only a sandy, undulating
plain, through which a scantily timbered river takes its course.
We halted about three miles above the mouth, on account of
grass; and the next morning arrived at the Nez Percé fort, one of
the trading establishments of the Hudson Bay Company, a few
hundred yards above the junction of the Walahwalah with the
Columbia river. Here we had the first view of this river, and
found it about 1,200 yards wide, and presenting the appearance
of a fine navigable stream. We made our camp in a little grove
of willows on the Walahwalah, which are the only trees to be
seen in the neighborhood; but were obliged to send the animals
back to the encampment we had left, as there was scarcely a

blade of grass to be found. The post is on the bank of the Columbia, on a plain of bare sands, from which the air was literally filled with clouds of dust and sand, during one of the few days we remained here; this place being one of the several points on the river which are distinguished for prevailing high winds, which come from the sea. The appearance of the post and country was without interest, except that we here saw, for the first time, the great river on which the course of events for the last half century has been directing attention and conferring historical fame. The river is, indeed, a noble object, and has here attained its full magnitude. About nine miles above, and in sight from the heights about the post, is the junction of the two great forks which constitute the main stream—that on which we had been travelling from Fort Hall, and known by the names of Lewis's fork, Shoshonee, and Snake river; and the North fork, which has retained the name of Columbia, as being the main stream.

We did not go up to the junction, being pressed for time; but the union of two large streams, coming one from the southeast, and the other from the northeast, and meeting in what may be treated as the geographical centre of the Oregon valley, thence doubling the volume of water to the ocean, while opening two great lines of communication with the interior continent, constitutes a feature in the map of the country which cannot be overlooked; and it was probably in reference to this junction of waters, and these lines of communication, that this post was established. They are important lines, and, from the structure of the country, must forever remain so—one of them leading to the South Pass, and to the valley of the Mississippi; the other to the pass at the head of the Athabasca river, and to the countries drained by the waters of the Hudson Bay. The British fur companies now use both lines; the Americans, in their emigration to Oregon, have begun to follow the one which leads towards the United States. Batteaus from tide water ascend to the junction, and thence high up the North fork, or Columbia. Land conveyance only is used upon the line of Lewis's fork. To the emigrants to Oregon, the Nez Percé is a point of interest, as being, to those who choose it, the termination of their overland journey. The broad expanse of the river here invites them to embark on its bosom; and the lofty trees of the forest furnish the means of doing so.

From the South Pass to this place is about 1,000 miles; and as it is about the same distance from that pass to the Missouri river at the mouth of the Kansas, it may be assumed that 2,000 miles is the *necessary* land travel in crossing from the United States to the Pacific ocean on this line. From the mouth of the Great Platte it would be about 100 miles less.

Mr. McKinley, the commander of the post, received us with great civility; and both to myself, and the heads of the emigrants who were there at the time, extended the rites of hospitality in a comfortable dinner to which he invited us.

By a meridional altitude of the sun, the only observation that the weather permitted us to obtain, the mouth of the Walah-walah river is in latitude 46°03′46″; and, by the road we had travelled, 612 miles from Fort Hall. At the time of our arrival, a considerable body of the emigrants under the direction of Mr. Applegate, a man of considerable resolution and energy, had nearly completed the building of a number of Mackinaw boats, in which they proposed to continue their further voyage down the Columbia. I had seen, in descending the Walahwalah river, a fine drove of several hundred cattle, which they had exchanged for Californian cattle, to be received at Vancouver, and which are considered a very inferior breed. The other portion of the emigration had preferred to complete their journey by land along the banks of the Columbia, taking their stock and wagons with them.

Having reinforced our animals with eight fresh horses, hired from the post, and increased our stock of provisions with dried salmon, potatoes, and a little beef, we resumed our journey down the left bank of the Columbia, being guided on our road by an intelligent Indian boy, whom I had engaged to accompany us as far as the Dalles.

The sketch of a rock which we passed in the course of the morning is annexed, to show the manner in which the basaltic rock, which constitutes the geological formation of the Columbia valley, now presents itself. From an elevated point over which the road led, we obtained another far view of Mount Hood, 150 miles distant. We obtained on the river bank an observation of the sun at noon, which gave for the latitude 45°58′08″. The country to-day was very unprepossessing, and our road bad; and as we toiled slowly along through deep loose sands, and over fragments of black volcanic rock, our laborious travelling was strongly contrasted with the rapid progress of Mr. Applegate's fleet of boats, which suddenly came gliding swiftly down the broad river, which here chanced to be tranquil and smooth. At evening we encamped on the river bank, where there was very little grass, and less timber. We frequently met Indians on the road, and they were collected at every favorable spot along the river. . . .

NOV. 2.—The river here entered among bluffs, leaving no longer room for a road; and we accordingly left it, and took a more inland way among the river hills; on which we had no sooner entered, than we found a great improvement in the country. The sand had disappeared, and the soil was good, and covered with excellent grass, although the surface was broken into high hills, with uncommonly deep valleys. At noon we crossed John Day's river, a clear and beautiful stream, with a swift current and a bed of rolled stones. It is sunk in a deep valley, which is characteristic of all the streams in this region; and the hill we descended to reach it well deserves the name of mountain. Some of the emigrants had encamped on the river, and others at the summit of the farther hill, the ascent of which had probably cost their wagons a day's labor; and others again had halted for the night a few miles beyond, where they had slept without water. We also encamped in a grassy hollow without water; but as we had been forewarned of this privation by the guide, the animals had all been watered at the river, and we had brought with us a sufficient quantity for the night.

NOV. 3.—After two hours' ride through a fertile, hilly country, covered as all the upland here appears to be with good green grass, we descended again into the river bottom, along which we resumed our sterile road, and in about four miles reached the ford of the Fall river (*Rivière aux Chutes*) a considerable tributary to the Columbia. We had heard, on reaching the Nez Percé fort, a repetition of the account in regard to the unsettled character of the Columbia Indians at the present time; and to our little party they had at various points manifested a not very friendly disposition, in several attempts to steal our horses. At this place I expected to find a badly disposed band, who had plundered a party of 14 emigrant men a few days before, and taken away their horses; and accordingly we made the necessary preparations for our security, but happily met with no difficulty.

The river was high, divided into several arms, with a rocky island at its outlet into the Columbia, which at this place it rivalled in size, and apparently deserved its highly characteristic name, which is received from one of its many falls some forty miles up the river. It entered the Columbia with a roar of falls and rapids, and is probably a favorite fishing station among the Indians, with whom both banks of the river were populous; but they scarcely paid any attention to us. The ford was very difficult at this time, and, had they entertained any bad intentions, they were offered a good opportunity to carry them out, as I drove directly into the river, and during the crossing the howitzer was occasionally several feet under water, and a number of the men appeared to be more often below than above. Our guide was well acquainted with the ford, and we succeeded in getting every thing safe over to the left bank. We delayed here only a short time to put the gun in order, and, ascending a long mountain hill, left both rivers, and resumed our route again among the interior hills.

The roar of the *Falls of the Columbia* is heard from the heights, where we halted a few moments to enjoy a fine view of the river below. In the season of high water it would be a very interesting object to visit, in order to witness what is related of the annual submerging of the fall under the waters which back up from the basin below, constituting a great natural lock at this place. But time had become an object of serious consideration; and the Falls, in their present state, had been seen and described by many.

After a day's journey of 17 miles, we encamped among the hills on a little clear stream, where, as usual, the Indians immediately gathered round us. Among them was a very old man, almost blind from age, with long and very white hair. I happened of my own accord to give this old man a present of tobacco, and was struck with the impression which my unpropitiated notice made on the Indians, who appeared in a remarkable manner acquainted with the real value of goods, and to understand the equivalents of trade. At evening, one of them spoke a few words to his people, and, telling me that we need entertain no uneasiness in regard to our animals, as none of them would be disturbed, they went all quietly away. In the morning, when they again came to the camp, I expressed to them the gratification we felt at their reasonable conduct, making them a present of some large knives and a few smaller articles.

NOV. 4.—The road continued among the hills, and, reaching an eminence, we saw before us in a little green valley, watered by a clear stream, a tolerably large valley, through which the trail passed.

In comparison with the Indians of the Rocky mountains and the great eastern plain, these are disagreeably dirty in their habits. Their huts were crowded with half-naked women and children, and the atmosphere within any thing but pleasant to persons who had just been riding in the fresh morning air. We were somewhat amused with the scanty dress of one woman, who, in common with the others, rushed out of the huts on our arrival, and who, in default of other covering, used a child for a fig leaf.

The road in about half an hour passed near an elevated point, from which we overlooked the valley of the Columbia for many miles, and saw in the distance several houses surrounded by fields, which a chief, who had accompanied us from the village, pointed out to us as the Methodist missionary station.

In a few miles we descended to the river, which we reached at one of its remarkably interesting features, known as the *Dalles of the Columbia.* The whole volume of the river at this place passed between the walls of a chasm, which has the appearance of having been rent through the basaltic strata which form the valley rock of the region. At the narrowest place we found the breadth, by measurement, 58 yards, and the average height of the walls above the water 25 feet; forming a trough between the rocks—whence the name, probably applied by a Canadian voyageur. The mass of water, in the present low state of the river, passed swiftly between, deep and black, and curled into many small whirlpools and counter currents, but unbroken by foam, and so still that scarcely the sound of a ripple was heard. The rock, for a considerable distance from the river, was worn over a large portion of its surface into circular holes and well-like cavities, by the abrasion of the river, which, at the season of high waters, is spread out over the adjoining bottoms. . . .

We passed rapidly three or four miles down the level valley, and encamped near the mission. The character of the forest growth here changed, and we found ourselves, with pleasure, again among oaks and other forest trees of the east, to which we had long been strangers; and the hospitable and kind reception with which we were welcomed among our country people at the mission aided the momentary illusion of home.

Two good-looking wooden dwelling houses, and a large school house, with stables, barn, and garden, and large cleared fields between the houses and the river bank, on which were scattered the wooden huts of an Indian village, gave to the valley the cheerful and busy air of civilization, and had in our eyes an appearance of abundant and enviable comfort.

Our land journey found here its western termination. . . .

Being now upon the ground explored by the South Sea expedition under Captain Wilkes, and having accomplished the object of uniting my survey with his, and thus presenting a connected exploration from the Mississippi to the Pacific, and the winter being at hand, I deemed it necessary to economize time by voyaging in the night, as is customary here, to avoid the high winds, which rise with the morning, and decline with the day.

Accordingly, after an hour's halt, we again embarked, and resumed our pleasant voyage down the river. The wind rose to a gale after several hours; but the moon was very bright, and the wind was fair, and the canoe glanced rapidly down the stream, the waves breaking into foam alongside; and our night voyage, as the wind bore us rapidly along between the dark mountains, was wild and interesting. About midnight we put to the shore on a rocky beach, behind which was a dark-looking pine forest. We built up large fires among the rocks, which were in large masses round about; and, arranging our blankets on the most sheltered places we could find, passed a delightful night.

After an early breakfast, at daylight we resumed our journey, the weather being clear and beautiful, and the river smooth and still. On either side the mountains are all pine-timbered, rocky, and high. We were now approaching one of the marked features of the lower Columbia, where the river forms a great *cascade,* with a series of rapids, in breaking through the range of mountains to which the lofty peaks of Mount Hood and St. Helens belong, and which rise as great pillars of snow on either side of the passage. The main branch of the *Sacramento* river, and the *Tlamath,* issue in cascades from this range; and the Columbia, breaking through it in a succession of cascades, gives the idea of cascades to the whole range; and hence the name of the CASCADE RANGE, which it bears, and distinguishes it from the Coast Range lower down. In making a short turn to the south, the river forms the cascades in breaking over a point of agglomerated masses of rock, leaving a handsome bay to the right, with several rocky pine-covered islands, and the mountains sweep at a distance around a cove where several small streams enter the bay. In less than an hour we halted on the left bank, about five minutes' walk above the cascades, where there were several Indian huts, and where our guides signified it was customary to hire Indians to assist in making the *portage.* . . .

In the morning, the first object that attracted my attention was the barque Columbia, lying at anchor near the landing. She was about to start on her voyage to England, and was now ready for sea; being detained only in waiting the arrival of the express batteaus, which descend the Columbia and its north fork with the overland mail from Canada and Hudson's bay, which had been delayed beyond their usual time. I immediately waited upon Dr. McLaughlin, the executive officer of the Hudson Bay Company in the territory west of the Rocky mountains, who received me with the courtesy and hospitality for which he has been eminently distinguished, and which makes a forcible and delightful impression on a traveller from the long wilderness from which we had issued. I was immediately supplied by him with the necessary stores and provisions to refit and support my party in our contemplated winter journey to the States; and also with a Mackinaw boat and canoes, manned with Canadian

and Iroquois voyageurs and Indians, for their transportation to
the Dalles of the Columbia. In addition to this efficient kindness
in furnishing me with these necessary supplies, I received from
him a warm and gratifying sympathy in the suffering which his
great experience led him to anticipate for us in our homeward
journey, and a letter of recommendation and credit for any officers of the Hudson Bay Company into whose posts we might be
driven by unexpected misfortune. . . .

13

Literature and Criticism

Ralph Waldo Emerson: New England Reformers*

The United States of the 1840's was in intellectual ferment. American inventiveness had been stimulated by the depression following the Panic of 1837, while American imagination had been aroused by events in Texas and the vast sweeps of Oregon. At the same time the American conscience, stung by the presence of slavery, set men to thinking of reform—political, social, religious. Steamships and the graceful clippers were cutting the passage to Europe to less than two weeks and a furious exchange of ideas was under way. Among the more influential of the imported doctrines were French socialism and German transcendentalism.

Out of these crosscurrents came a new, more creative literature, no longer parochial, no longer an imitation of European forms, but an amalgam of indigenous themes with the broad cultural heritage now moving freely across the Atlantic in both directions. Most representative of this new literature was Ralph Waldo Emerson (1803-82), who had abandoned the ministry in 1832 to preach thereafter from the lecture platform. Through his essays and lectures he brought the best of European thought to America and interpreted his countrymen for Europe.

For broad treatment of early literature and criticism in America, the reader should consult two old but highly useful works: Vernon L. Parrington, *Main Currents in American Thought* (3 vols.; New York: Harcourt, Brace, 1927-30), and Merle E. Curti, *The Growth of American Thought* (3rd ed.; New York: Harper, 1951). More strictly confined to literature is Van Wyck Brooks, *The Flowering of New England* (New York: Dutton, 1936). Ralph L. Rusk has written an adequate biography, *The Life of Ralph Waldo Emerson* (New York: Charles Scribner's Sons, 1949). The lecture reproduced here, delivered by Emerson in March 1844, displays him as critic of his society

---

*Ralph Waldo Emerson, *Works* (Riverside Edition; Boston, 1883), III, pp. 239-70.

and prophet of a better day, as man of letters, as historian, as philosopher, and as moralist. In reading the selection note (1) what were some of the "isms" that had attracted Emerson's attention; (2) his analysis of the shift in New England from spiritual to practical concerns; (3) his comments on education; (4) evidences of Emerson's radical individualism; (5) what Emerson thought of the past in comparison to the present and future; (6) his reflections on the communal societies, based on the teachings of Fourier and others, that flourished at this time (including Brook Farm in which Emerson himself participated); (7) evidences of his transcendentalism; and (8) what advice he had for those who wished for a reformation of the ills besetting society.

WHOEVER HAS HAD OPPORTUNITY OF ACQUAINTANCE with society in New England during the last twenty-five years, with those middle and with those leading sections that may constitute any just representation of the character and aim of the community, will have been struck with the great activity of thought and experimenting. His attention must be commanded by the signs that the Church, or religious party, is falling from the Church nominal, and is appearing in temperance and non-resistance societies; in movements of abolitionists and of socialists; and in very significant assemblies called Sabbath and Bible Conventions; composed of ultraists, of seekers, of all the soul of the soldiery of dissent, and meeting to call in question the authority of the Sabbath, of the priesthood, and of the Church. In these movements nothing was more remarkable than the discontent they begot in the movers. The spiirt of protest and of detachment drove the members of these Conventions to bear testimony against the Church, and immediately afterwards to declare their discontent with these Conventions, their independence of their colleagues, and their impatience of the methods whereby they were working. They defied each other, like a congress of kings, each of whom had a realm to rule, and a way of his own that made concert unprofitable. What a fertility of projects for the salvation of the world! One apostle thought all men should go to farming, and another that no man should buy or sell, that the use of money was the cardinal evil; another that the mischief was in our diet, that we eat and drink damnation. These made unleavened bread, and were foes to the death to fermentation. It was in vain urged by the housewife that God made yeast, as well as dough, and loves fermentation just as dearly as he loves vegetation; that fermentation develops the saccharine element in the grain, and makes it more palatable and more digestible. No; they wish the pure wheat, and will die but it shall not ferment. Stop, dear nature, these incessant advances of thine; let us scotch these ever-rolling wheels! Others attacked the system of agriculture, the use of animal manures in farming, and the tyranny of man over brute nature; these abuses polluted his food. The ox must be taken from the plough and the horse from the cart, the hundred acres of the farm must be spaded, and the man must walk, wherever boats and locomotives will not carry him. Even the insect world was to be defended,— that had been too long neglected, and a society for the protection of ground-worms, slugs, and mosquitos was to be incorporated without delay. With these appeared the adepts of homœopathy, of hydropathy, of mesmerism, of phrenology, and their wonderful theories of the Christian miracles! Others assailed particular vocations, as that of the lawyer, that of the merchant, of the manufacturer, of the clergyman, of the scholar. Others attacked the institution of marriage as the fountain of social evils. Others devoted themselves to the worrying of churches and meetings for public worship; and the fertile forms of antinomianism among the elder puritans seemed to have their match in the plenty of the new harvest of reform.

With this din of opinion and debate there was a keener scrutiny of institutions and domestic life than any we had known; there was sincere protesting against existing evils, and there were changes of employment dictated by conscience. No doubt there was plentiful vaporing, and cases of backsliding might occur. But in each of these movements emerged a good result, a tendency to the adoption of simpler methods, and an assertion of the sufficiency of the private man. Thus it was directly in the spirit and genius of the age, what happened in one instance when a church censured and threatened to excommunicate one of its members on account of the somewhat hostile part to the church which his conscience led him to take in the anti-slavery business; the threatened individual immediately excommunicated the church,

in a public and formal process. This has been several times repeated: it was excellent when it was done the first time, but of
course loses all value when it is copied. Every project in the
history of reform, no matter how violent and surprising, is good
when it is the dictate of a man's genius and constitution, but
very dull and suspicious when adopted from another. It is right
and beautiful in any man to say, "I will take this coat, or this
book, or this measure of corn of yours,"—in whom we see the act
to be original, and to flow from the whole spirit and faith of him;
for then that taking will have a giving as free and divine; but
we are very easily disposed to resist the same generosity of speech
when we miss originality and truth to character in it.

There was in all the practical activities of New England for
the last quarter of a century, a gradual withdrawal of tender
consciences from the social organizations. There is observable
throughout, the contest between mechanical and spiritual methods, but with a steady tendency of the thoughtful and virtuous
to a deeper belief and reliance on spiritual facts.

In politics for example it is easy to see the progress of dissent.
The country is full of rebellion; the country is full of kings.
Hands off! let there be no control and no interference in the
administration of the affairs of this kingdom of me. Hence the
growth of the doctrine and of the party of Free Trade, and the
willingness to try that experiment, in the face of what appear
incontestable facts. I confess, the motto of the Globe newspaper
is so attractive to me that I can seldom find much appetite to
read what is below it in its columns: "The world is governed
too much." So the country is frequently affording solitary examples of resistance to the government, solitary nullifiers, who
throw themselves on their reserved rights; nay, who have reserved all their rights; who reply to the assessor and to the clerk
of court that they do not know the State, and embarrass the
courts of law by non-juring and the commander-in-chief of the
militia by non-resistance.

The same disposition to scrutiny and dissent appeared in civil,
festive, neighborly, and domestic society. A restless, prying, conscientious criticism broke out in unexpected quarters. Who gave
me the money with which I bought my coat? Why should professional labor and that of the countinghouse be paid so dis-

proportionately to the labor of the porter and woodsawyer? This whole business of Trade gives me to pause and think, as it constitutes false relations between men; inasmuch as I am prone to count myself relieved of any responsibility to behave well and nobly to that person whom I pay with money; whereas if I had not that commodity, I should be put on my good behavior in all companies, and man would be a benefactor to man, as being himself his only certificate that he had a right to those aids and services which each asked of the other. Am I not too protected a person? is there not a wide disparity between the lot of me and the lot of thee, my poor brother, my poor sister? Am I not defrauded of my best culture in the loss of those gymnastics which manual labor and the emergencies of poverty constitute? I find nothing healthful or exalting in the smooth conventions of society; I do not like the close air of saloons. I begin to suspect myself to be a prisoner, though treated with all this courtesy and luxury. I pay a destructive tax in my conformity.

The same insatiable criticism may be traced in the efforts for the reform of Education. The popular education has been taxed with a want of truth and nature. It was complained that an education to things was not given. We are students of words: we are shut up in schools, and colleges, and recitation-rooms, for ten or fifteen years, and come out at last with a bag of wind, a memory of words, and do not know a thing. We cannot use our hands, or our legs, or our eyes, or our arms. We do not know an edible root in the woods, we cannot tell our course by the stars, nor the hour of the day by the sun. It is well if we can swim and skate. We are afraid of a horse, of a cow, of a dog, of a snake, of a spider. The Roman rule was to teach a boy nothing that he could not learn standing. The old English rule was, "All summer in the field, and all winter in the study." And it seems as if a man should learn to plant, or to fish, or to hunt, that he might secure his subsistence at all events, and not be painful to his friends and fellow-men. The lessons of science should be experimental also. The sight of a planet through a telescope is worth all the course on astronomy; the shock of the electric spark in the elbow, outvalues all the theories; the taste of the nitrous oxide, the firing of an artificial volcano, are better than volumes of chemistry.

One of the traits of the new spirit is the inquisition it fixed on our scholastic devotion to the dead languages. The ancient languages, with great beauty of structure, contain wonderful remains of genius, which draw, and always will draw, certain likeminded men,—Greek men, and Roman men,—in all countries, to their study; but by a wonderful drowsiness of usage they had exacted the study of *all* men. Once (say two centuries ago), Latin and Greek had a strict relation to all the science and culture there was in Europe, and the Mathematics had a momentary importance at some era of activity in physical science. These things became stereotyped as *education*, as the manner of men is. But the Good Spirit never cared for the colleges, and though all men and boys were now drilled in Latin, Greek, and Mathematics, it had quite left these shells high and dry on the beach, and was now creating and feeding other matters at other ends of the world. But in a hundred high schools and colleges this warfare against common sense still goes on. Four, or six, or ten years, the pupil is parsing Greek and Latin, and as soon as he leaves the University, as it is ludicrously styled, he shuts those books for the last time. Some thousands of young men are graduated at our colleges in this country every year, and the persons who, at forty years, still read Greek, can all be counted on your hand. I never met with ten. Four or five persons I have seen who read Plato.

But is not this absurd, that the whole liberal talent of this country should be directed in its best years on studies which lead to nothing? What was the consequence? Some intelligent persons said or thought, "Is that Greek and Latin some spell to conjure with, and not words of reason? If the physician, the lawyer, the divine, never use it to come at their ends, I need never learn it to come at mine. Conjuring is gone out of fashion, and I will omit this conjugating, and go straight to affairs." So they jumped the Greek and Latin, and read law, medicine, or sermons, without it. To the astonishment of all, the self-made men took even ground at once with the oldest of the regular graduates, and in a few months the most conservative circles of Boston and New York had quite forgotten who of their gownsmen was college-bred, and who was not.

One tendency appears alike in the philosophical speculation

and in the rudest democratical movements, through all the petulance and all the puerility, the wish, namely, to cast aside the superfluous and arrive at short methods; urged, as I suppose, by an intuition that the human spirit is equal to all emergencies, alone, and that man is more often injured than helped by the means he uses.

I conceive this gradual casting off of material aids, and the indication of growing trust in the private self-supplied powers of the individual, to be the affirmative principle of the recent philosophy, and that it is feeling its own profound truth and is reaching forward at this very hour to the happiest conclusions. I readily concede that in this, as in every period of intellectual activity, there has been a noise of denial and protest; much was to be resisted, much was to be got rid of by those who were reared in the old, before they could begin to affirm and to construct. Many a reformer perishes in his removal of rubbish; and that makes the offensiveness of the class. They are partial; they are not equal to the work they pretend. They lose their way; in the assault on the kingdom of darkness they expend all their energy on some accidental evil, and lose their sanity and power of benefit. It is of little moment that one or two or twenty errors of our social system be corrected, but of much that the man be in his senses.

The criticism and attack on institutions, which we have witnessed, has made one thing plain, that society gains nothing whilst a man, not himself renovated, attempts to renovate things around him: he has become tediously good in some particular but negligent or narrow in the rest; and hypocrisy and vanity are often the disgusting result.

It is handsomer to remain in the establishment better than the establishment, and conduct that in the best manner, than to make a sally against evil by some single improvement, without supporting it by a total regeneration. Do not be so vain of your one objection. Do you think there is only one? Alas! my good friend, there is no part of society or of life better than any other part. All our things are right and wrong together. The wave of evil washes all our institutions alike. Do you complain of our Marriage? Our marriage is no worse than our education, our diet, our trade, our social customs. Do you complain of the laws of

Property? It is a pedantry to give such importance to them. Can we not play the game of life with these counters, as well as with those? in the institution of property, as well as out of it? Let into it the new and renewing principle of love, and property will be universality. No one gives the impression of superiority to the institution, which he must give who will reform it. It makes no difference what you say, you must make me feel that you are aloof from it; by your natural and supernatural advantages do easily see to the end of it,—do see how man can do without it. Now all men are on one side. No man deserves to be heard against property. Only Love, only an Idea, is against property as we hold it.

I cannot afford to be irritable and captious, nor to waste all my time in attacks. If I should go out of church whenever I hear a false sentiment I could never stay there five minutes. But why come out? the street is as false as the church, and when I get to my house, or to my manners, or to my speech, I have not got away from the lie. When we see an eager assailant of one of these wrongs, a special reformer, we feel like asking him, What right have you, sir, to your one virtue? Is virtue piecemeal? This is a jewel amidst the rags of a beggar.

In another way the right will be vindicated. In the midst of abuses, in the heart of cities, in the aisles of false churches, alike in one place and in another,—wherever, namely, a just and heroic soul finds itself, there it will do what is next at hand, and by the new quality of character it shall put forth it shall abrogate that old condition, law or school in which it stands, before the law of its own mind.

If partiality was one fault of the movement party, the other defect was their reliance on Association. Doubts such as those I have intimated drove many good persons to agitate the questions of social reform. But the revolt against the spirit of commerce, the spirit of aristocracy, and the inveterate abuses of cities, did not appear possible to individuals; and to do battle against numbers they armed themselves with numbers, and against concert they relied on new concert.

Following or advancing beyond the ideas of St. Simon, of Fourier, and of Owen, three communities have already been formed in Massachusetts on kindred plans, and many more in the country at large. They aim to give every member a share in the manual labor, to give an equal reward to labor and to talent, and to unite a liberal culture with an education to labor. The scheme offers, by the economies of associated labor and expense, to make every member rich, on the same amount of property that, in separate families, would leave every member poor. These new associations are composed of men and women of superior talents and sentiments; yet it may easily be questioned whether such a community will draw, except in its beginnings, the able and the good; whether those who have energy will not prefer their chance of superiority and power in the world, to the humble certainties of the association; whether such a retreat does not promise to become an asylum to those who have tried and failed, rather than a field to the strong; and whether the members will not necessarily be fractions of men, because each finds that he cannot enter it without some compromise. Friendship and association are very fine things, and a grand phalanx of the best of the human race, banded for some catholic object; yes, excellent; but remember that no society can ever be so large as one man. He, in his friendship, in his natural and momentary associations, doubles or multiplies himself; but in the hour in which he mortgages himself to two or ten or twenty, he dwarfs himself below the stature of one.

But the men of less faith could not thus believe, and to such, concert appears the sole specific of strength. I have failed, and you have failed, but perhaps together we shall not fail. Our housekeeping is not satisfactory to us, but perhaps a phalanx, a community, might be. Many of us have differed in opinion, and we could find no man who could make the truth plain, but possibly a college, or an ecclesiastical council, might. I have not been able either to persuade my brother or to prevail on myself to disuse the traffic or the potation of brandy, but perhaps a pledge of total abstinence might effectually restrain us. The candidate my party votes for is not to be trusted with a dollar, but he will be honest in the Senate, for we can bring public opinion to bear on him. Thus concert was the specific in all cases. But concert is neither better nor worse, neither more nor less potent, than individual force. All the men in the world cannot make a statue walk and speak, cannot make a drop of blood, or a blade of grass, any more than one man can. But let there be one man, let there be truth in two men, in ten men, then is concert for the first time possible; because the force which moves the world is a new quality, and can never be furnished by adding whatever quantities of a different kind. What is the use of the concert of the false and the disunited? There can be no concert in two, where there is no concert in one. When the individual is not *individual*, but is dual; when his thoughts look one way and his actions another; when his faith is traversed by his habits; when his will, enlightened by reason, is warped by his sense; when with one hand he rows and with the other backs water, what concert can be?

I do not wonder at the interest these projects inspire. The world is awaking to the idea of union, and these experiments show what it is thinking of. It is and will be magic. Men will live and communicate, and plough, and reap, and govern, as by added ethereal power, when once they are united; as in a celebrated experiment, by expiration and respiration exactly together, four persons lift a heavy man from the ground by the little finger only, and without sense of weight. But this union must be inward, and not one of covenants, and is to be reached by a reverse of the methods they use. The union is only perfect when all the uniters are isolated. It is the union of friends who live in different streets or towns. Each man, if he attempts to join himself to others, is on all sides cramped and diminished of his proportion; and the stricter the union the smaller and more pitiful he is. But leave him alone, to recognize in every hour and place the secret soul; he will go up and down doing the works of a true member, and, to the astonishment of all, the work will be done with concert, though no man spoke. Government will be adamantine without any governor. The union must be ideal in actual individualism.

I pass to the indication in some particulars of that faith in man, which the heart is preaching to us in these days, and which engages the more regard, from the consideration that the speculations of one generation are the history of the next following.

In alluding just now to our system of education, I spoke of the deadness of its details. But it is open to graver criticism than the palsy of its members: it is a system of despair. The disease with which the human mind now labors is want of faith. Men do not believe in a power of education. We do not think we can speak to divine sentiments in man, and we do not try. We renounce all high aims. We believe that the defects of so many perverse and so many frivolous people who make up society, are organic, and society is a hospital of incurables. A man of good sense but of little faith, whose compassion seemed to lead him to church as often as he went there, said to me that "he liked to have concerts, and fairs, and churches, and other public amusements go on." I am afraid the remark is too honest, and comes from the same origin as the maxim of the tyrant, "If you would rule the world quietly, you must keep it amused." I notice too that the ground on which eminent public servants urge the claims of popular education is fear; "This country is filling up with thousands and millions of voters, and you must educate them to keep them from our throats." We do not believe that any education, any system of philosophy, any influence of genius, will ever give depth of insight to a superficial mind. Having settled ourselves into this infidelity, our skill is expended to procure alleviations, diversion, opiates. We adorn the victim with manual skill, his tongue with languages, his body with inoffensive and comely manners. So have we cunningly hid the tragedy of limitation and inner death we cannot avert. Is it strange that society should be devoured by a secret melancholy which breaks through all its smiles and all its gayety and games?

But even one step farther our infidelity has gone. It appears that some doubt is felt by good and wise men whether really the happiness and probity of men is increased by the culture of the mind in those disciplines to which we give the name of education. Unhappily too the doubt comes from scholars, from persons who have tried these methods. In their experience the scholar was not raised by the sacred thoughts amongst which he dwelt, but used them to selfish ends. He was a profane person, and became a showman, turning his gifts to a marketable use, and not to his own sustenance and growth. It was found that the intellect could be independently developed, that is, in separation from the man, as any single organ can be invigorated, and the result was monstrous. A canine appetite for knowledge was gen-

erated, which must still be fed but was never satisfied, and this
knowledge, not being directed on action, never took the character of substantial, humane truth, blessing those whom it entered. It gave the scholar certain powers of expression, the power
of speech, the power of poetry, of literary art, but it did not
bring him to peace or to beneficence.

When the literary class betray a destitution of faith, it is not
strange that society should be disheartened and sensualized by
unbelief. What remedy? Life must be lived on a higher plane.
We must go up to a higher platform, to which we are always
invited to ascend; there, the whole aspect of things changes. I
resist the skepticism of our education and of our educated men.
I do not believe that the differences of opinion and character in
men are organic. I do not recognize, beside the class of the good
and the the wise, a permanent class of skeptics, or a class of
conservatives, or of malignants, or of materialists. I do not believe in two classes. You remember the story of the poor woman
who importuned King Philip of Macedon to grant her justice,
which Philip refused: the woman exclaimed, "I appeal:" the
king, astonished, asked to whom she appealed: the woman
replied, "From Philip drunk to Philip sober." The text will suit
me very well. I believe not in two classes of men, but in man in
two moods, in Philip drunk and Philip sober. I think, according
to the good-hearted word of Plato, "Unwillingly the soul is
deprived of truth." Iron conservative, miser, or thief, no man is
but by a supposed necessity which he tolerates by shortness or
torpidity of sight. The soul lets no man go without some visita-
tions and holydays of a diviner presence. It would be easy to
show, by a narrow scanning of any man's biography, that we are
not so wedded to our paltry performances of every kind but that
every man has at intervals the grace to scorn his performances,
in comparing them with his belief of what he should do;—that he
puts himself on the side of his enemies, listening gladly to what
they say of him, and accusing himself of the same things.

What is it men love in Genius, but its infinite hope, which
degrades all it has done? Genius counts all its miracles poor and
short. Its own idea it never executed. The Iliad, the Hamlet, the
Doric column, the Roman arch, the Gothic minster, the German
anthem, when they are ended, the master casts behind him. How

sinks the song in the waves of melody which the universe pours over his soul! Before that gracious Infinite out of which he drew these few strokes, how mean they look, though the praises of the world attend them. From the triumphs of his art he turns with desire to this greater defeat. Let those admire who will. With silent joy he sees himself to be capable of a beauty that eclipses all which his hands have done; all which human hands have ever done.

Well, we are all the children of genius, the children of virtue, —and feel their inspirations in our happier hours. Is not every man sometimes a radical in politics? Men are conservatives when they are least vigorous, or when they are most luxurious. They are conservatives after dinner, or before taking their rest; when they are sick, or aged: in the morning, or when their intellect or their conscience has been aroused; when they hear music, or when they read poetry, they are radicals. In the circle of the rankest tories that could be collected in England, Old or New, let a powerful and stimulating intellect, a man of great heart and mind act on them, and very quickly these frozen conservators will yield to the friendly influence, these hopeless will begin to hope, these haters will begin to love, these immovable statues will begin to spin and revolve. I cannot help recalling the fine anecdote which Warton relates of Bishop Berkeley, when he was preparing to leave England with his plan of planting the gospel among the American savages. "Lord Bathurst told me that the members of the Scriblerus club being met at his house.at dinner, they agreed to rally Berkeley, who was also his guest, on his scheme at Bermudas. Berkeley, having listened to the many lively things they had to say, begged to be heard in his turn, and displayed his plan with such an astonishing and animating force of eloquence and enthusiasm that they were struck dumb, and, after some pause, rose up all together with earnestness, exclaiming, 'Let us set out with him immediately.'" Men in all ways are better than they seem. They like flattery for the moment, but they know the truth for their own. It is a foolish cowardice which keeps us from trusting them and speaking to them rude truth. They resent your honesty for an instant, they will thank you for it always. What is it we heartily wish of each other? Is it to be pleased and flattered? No, but to be convicted and exposed, to be shamed out of our nonsense of all kinds, and made men of, instead of ghosts and phantoms. We are weary of gliding ghostlike through the world, which is itself so slight and unreal. We crave a sense of reality, though it come in strokes of pain. I explain so—by this manlike love of truth—those excesses and errors into which souls of great vigor, but not equal insight, often fall. They feel the poverty at the bottom of all the seeming affluence of the world. They know the speed with which they come straight through the thin masquerade, and conceive a disgust at the indigence of nature: Rousseau, Mirabeau, Charles Fox, Napoleon, Byron—and I could easily add names nearer home, of raging riders, who drive their steeds so hard, in the violence of living to forget its illusion: they would know the worst, and tread the floors of hell. The heroes of ancient and modern fame, Cimon, Themistocles, Alcibiades, Alexander, Caesar, have treated life and fortune as a game to be well and skilfully played, but the stake not to be so valued but that any time it could be held as a trifle light as air, and thrown up. Caesar, just before the battle of Pharsalia, discourses with the Egyptian priest concerning the fountains of the Nile, and offers to quit the army, the empire, and Cleopatra, if he will show him those mysterious sources.

The same magnanimity shows itself in our social relations, in the preference, namely, which each man gives to the society of superiors over that of his equals. All that a man has will he give for right relations with his mates. All that he has will he give for an erect demeanor in every company and on each occasion. He aims at such things as his neighbors prize, and gives his days and nights, his talents and his heart, to strike a good stroke, to acquit himself in all men's sight as a man. The consideration of an eminent citizen, of a noted merchant, of a man of mark in his profession; a naval and military honor, a general's commission, a marshal's baton, a ducal coronet, the laurel of poets, and, anyhow procured, the acknowledgment of eminent merit—have this lustre for each candidate that they enable him to walk erect and unashamed in the presence of some persons before whom he felt himself inferior. Having raised himself to this rank, having established his equality with class after class of those with whom he would live well, he still finds certain others before whom he cannot possess himself, because they have somewhat fairer, somewhat grander, somewhat purer, which extorts homage of him. Is his ambition pure? then will his laurels and his possessions seem worthless: instead of avoiding these men who make his fine gold dim, he will cast all behind him and seek their society only, woo and embrace this his humiliation and mortification, until he shall know why his eye sinks, his voice is husky, and his brilliant talents are paralyzed in this presence. He is sure that the soul which gives the lie to all things will tell none. His constitution will not mislead him. If it cannot carry itself as it ought, high and unmatchable in the presence of any man; if the secret oracles whose whisper makes the sweetness and dignity of his life do here withdraw and accompany him no longer—it is time to undervalue what he has valued, to dispossess himself of what he has acquired, and with Caesar to take in his hand the army, the empire, and Cleopatra, and say, "All these will I relinquish, if you will show me the fountains of the Nile." Dear to us are those who love us; the swift moments we spend with them are a compensation for a great deal of misery; they enlarge our life;—but dearer are those who reject us as unworthy, for they add another life: they build a heaven before us whereof we had not dreamed, and thereby supply to us new powers out of the recesses of the spirit, and urge us to new and unattempted performances.

As every man at heart wishes the best and not inferior society, wishes to be convicted of his error and to come to himself—so he wishes that the same healing should not stop in his thought, but should penetrate his will or active power. The selfish man suffers more from his selfishness than he from whom that selfishness withholds some important benefit. What he most wishes is to be lifted to some higher platform, that he may see beyond his present fear the transalpine good, so that his fear, his coldness, his custom may be broken up like fragments of ice, melted and carried away in the great stream of good will. Do you ask my aid? I also wish to be a benefactor. I wish more to be a benefactor and servant than you wish to be served by me; and surely the greatest good fortune that could befall me is precisely to be so moved by you that I should say, "Take me and all mine, and use me and mine freely to your ends!" for I could not say it otherwise than because a great enlargement had come to my heart and mind, which made me superior to my fortunes. Here we are paralyzed with fear; we hold on to our little properties, house and land, office and money, for the bread which they have in our experience yielded us, although we confess that our being does not flow through them. We desire to be made great; we desire to be touched with that fire which shall command this ice to stream, and make our existence a benefit. If therefore we start objections to your project, O friend of the slave, or friend of the poor or of the race, understand well that it is because we wish to drive you to drive us into your measures. We wish to hear ourselves confuted. We are haunted with a belief that you have a secret which it would highliest advantage us to learn, and we would force you to impart it to us, though it should bring us to prison or to worse extremity.

Nothing shall warp me from the belief that every man is a lover of truth. There is no pure lie, no pure malignity in nature. The entertainment of the proposition of depravity is the last profligacy and profanation. There is no skepticism, no atheism but that. Could it be received into common belief, suicide would unpeople the planet. It has had a name to live in some dogmatic theology, but each man's innocence and his real liking of his neighbor have kept it a dead letter. I remember standing at the polls one day when the anger of the political contest gave a certain grimness to the faces of the independent electors, and a good man at my side, looking on the people, remarked, "I am satisfied that the largest part of these men, on either side, mean to vote right." I suppose considerate observers, looking at the masses of men in their blameless and in their equivocal actions, will assent, that in spite of selfishness and frivolity, the general purpose in the great number of persons is fidelity. The reason why any one refuses his assent to your opinion, or his aid to your benevolent design, is in you: he refuses to accept you as a bringer of truth, because though you think you have it, he feels that you have it not. You have not given him the authentic sign.

If it were worth while to run into details this general doctrine of the latent but ever soliciting Spirit, it would be easy to adduce illustration in particulars of a man's equality to the Church, of his equality to the State, and of his equality to every other man. It is yet in all men's memory that, a few years ago, the liberal churches complained that the Calvinistic church denied to them the name of Christian. I think the complaint was confession: a religious church would not complain. A religious man, like Behmen, Fox, or Swedenborg is not irritated by wanting the sanction of the Church, but the Church feels the accusation of his presence and belief.

It only needs that a just man should walk in our streets to make it appear how pitiful and inartificial a contrivance is our legislation. The man whose part is taken and who does not wait for society in anything, has a power which society cannot choose but feel. The familiar experiment called the hydrostatic paradox, in which a capillary column of water balances the ocean, is a symbol of the relation of one man to the whole family of men. The wise Dandamis, on hearing the lives of Socrates, Pythagoras and Diogenes read, "judged them to be great men every way, excepting that they were too much subjected to the reverence of the laws, which to second and authorize, true virtue must abate very much of its original vigor."

And as a man is equal to the Church and equal to the State, so he is equal to every other man. The disparities of power in men are superficial; and all frank and searching conversation, in which a man lays himself open to his brother, apprises each of their radical unity. When two persons sit and converse in a thoroughly good understanding, the remark is sure to be made, See how we have disputed about words! Let a clear, apprehensive mind, such as every man knows among his friends, converse with the most commanding poetic genius, I think it would appear that there was no inequality such as men fancy, between them; that a perfect understanding, a like receiving, a like perceiving, abolished differences; and the poet would confess that his creative imagination gave him no deep advantage, but only the superficial one that he could express himself and the other could not; that his advantage was a knack, which might impose on indolent men but could not impose on lovers of truth; for they know the tax of talent, or what a price of greatness the power of expression too often pays. I believe it is the conviction of the purest men that the net amount of man and man does not much vary. Each is incomparably superior to his companion in some faculty. His want of skill in other directions has added to his fitness for his own work. Each seems to have some compensation yielded to him by his infirmity, and every hinderance operates as a concentration of his force.

These and the like experiences intimate that man stands in strict connection with a higher fact never yet manifested. There is power over and behind us, and we are the channels of its communications. We seek to say thus and so, and over our head some spirit sits which contradicts what we say. We would persuade our fellow to this or that; another self within our eyes dissuades him. That which we keep back, this reveals. In vain we compose our faces and our words; it holds uncontrollable communication with the enemy, and he answers civilly to us, but believes the spirit. We exclaim, "There's a traitor in the house!" but at last it appears that he is the true man, and I am the traitor. This open channel to the highest life is the first and last reality, so subtle, so quiet, yet so tenacious, that although I have never expressed the truth, and although I have never heard the expression of it from any other, I know that the whole truth is here for me. What if I cannot answer your questions? I am not pained that I cannot frame a reply to the question, What is the operation we call Providence? There lies the unspoken thing, present, omnipresent. Every time we converse we seek to translate it into speech, but whether we hit or whether we miss, we have the fact. Every discourse is an approximate answer: but it is of small consequence that we do not get it into verbs and nouns, whilst it abides for contemplation forever.

If the auguries of the prophesying heart shall make themselves good in time, the man who shall be born, whose advent men and events prepare and foreshow, is one who shall enjoy his connection with a higher life, with the man within man; shall destroy distrust by his trust, shall use his native but forgotten methods, shall not take counsel of flesh and blood, but shall rely on the Law alive and beautiful which works over our heads and under our feet. Pitiless, it avails itself our our success when we obey it, and of our ruin when we contravene it. Men are all secret believers in it, else the word justice would have no meaning: they believe that the best is the true; that right is done at last; or chaos would come. It rewards actions after their nature, and not after the design of the agent. "Work," it saith to man, "in every hour, paid or unpaid, see only that thou work, and thou canst not escape the reward: whether thy work be fine or coarse, planting corn or writing epics, so only it be honest work, done to thine own approbation, it shall earn a reward to the senses as well as to the thought: no matter how often defeated, you are born to victory. The reward of a thing well done, is to have done it."

As soon as a man is wonted to look beyond surfaces, and to see how this high will prevails without an exception or an interval, he settles himself into serentiy. He can already rely on the laws of gravity, that every stone will fall where it is due; the good globe is faithful, and carries us securely through the celestial spaces, anxious or resigned, we need not interfere to help it on: and he will learn one day the mild lesson they teach, that our own orbit is all our task, and we need not assist the administration of the universe. Do not be so impatient to set the town right concerning the unfounded pretensions and the false reputation of certain men of standing. They are laboring harder to set the town right concerning themselves, and will certainly succeed. Suppress for a few days your criticism on the insufficiency of this or that teacher or experimenter, and he will have demonstrated his insufficiency to all men's eyes. In like manner, let a man fall into the divine circuits, and he is enlarged. Obedience to his genius is the only liberating influence. We wish to escape from subjection and a sense of inferiority, and we make self-denying ordinances, we drink water, we eat grass, we refuse the laws, we go to jail: it is all in vain; only by obedience to his genius, only by the freest activity in the way constitutional to him, does an angel seem to arise before a man and lead him by the hand out of all the wards of the prison.

That which befits us, embosomed in beauty and wonder as we are, is cheerfulness and courage, and the endeavor to realize our aspirations. The life of man is the true romance, which when it is valiantly conducted will yield the imagination a higher joy than any fiction. All around us what powers are wrapped up under the coarse mattings of custom, and all wonder prevented.

It is so wonderful to our neurologists that a man can see without his eyes, that it does not occur to them that it is just as wonderful that he should see with them; and that is ever the difference between the wise and the unwise: the latter wonders at what is unusual, the wise man wonders at the usual. Shall not the heart which has received so much, trust the Power by which it lives? May it not quit other leadings, and listen to the Soul that has guided it so gently and taught it so much, secure that the future will be worthy of the past?

14

Manners and Customs

Alexander Mackay: The Western World*

Alexander Mackay (1806-52) was a journalist, a breed just coming into its own in the 1840's. A Scot who had lived for a time in Canada, Mackay was sent to Washington by the London *Morning Chronicle* to cover the Oregon negotiations, then approaching the crisis stage. His "grand tour" by way of the Ohio and Mississippi rivers was motivated by nothing more profound than a newspaperman's curiosity about people and places and probably the hope that the resulting book would earn a few pounds for its peripatetic author.

Mackay's ability to distinguish the essential from the superficial aspects of life, his complete objectivity, and his literary skill in presenting what he saw raise him high above the general run of European commentators on the American scene. The selection reproduced here is the first portion of a chapter entitled "General View of American Society."

For a more general point of view and broader treatment of American social history in the period, Carl Russell Fish, *The Rise of the Common Man, 1830-1850* (New York: Macmillan, 1927) is still a standard work. Covering a smaller time-span in greater detail is Robert E. Riegel, *Young America, 1830-1840* (Norman, Okla.: U. of Oklahoma Press, 1949). The reader should note (1) what method the author uses to exhibit peculiar characteristics of American society; (2) the extent to which he maintains an objective view of his subject; (3) what he regarded as the fundamental difference in the social development of Europe and of America and the consequences of this difference; (4) what led him to conclude that the rich in America could not dominate the social order; (5) what evidence of social class and of class consciousness he found; and (6) what sectional distinctions he observed.

---

*Alexander Mackay, *The Western World; or Travels in the United States in 1846-1847* (Philadelphia, 1849), I, pp. 125-36.

IF THERE IS MUCH IN THE SOCIAL DEVELOPMENT OF
America that strikes an European as different from
that to which he has been accustomed, he should recollect that
society, in the two hemispheres, rests upon very different bases.
In the old world, where the feudal relations are still permitted
so largely to influence the arrangement of the social system,
society presents an agglomeration of distinct parts, each having
its determinate relation to the rest, and the members of each
having the range of their sympathies confined to their own
particular sphere. European society, in its different manifestations, is constituted, as it were, of a series of different layers,
which, though in close contact, only partially fuse into each
other. The consequence is, that, although a common tie of mutual dependence unites the whole, there is no common feeling
pervading it, each class looking chiefly within itself for its
sources of enjoyment and intellectual gratification, and recog-
nising the others more as political necessities than as social
adjuncts. The sympathies of one order touch, but do not inter-
twine with, those of another, each living within itself, as if it
had no interest in common with the others, and holding little
intercourse with them. This distinctiveness of class is also accompanied with an inequality of position, which exaggerates
the prevailing exclusiveness, and fetters the general relations of
society with a constraint and formalism, which renders one class,
by turns, arrogant and awkward, and the other supercilious and
condescending. Within each the social graces are more or less
cultivated, and the refinements of life more or less displayed;
the constraint is visible at their line of contact, as mutual dislike
is often found to pervade the borders of two civilized and amicable states. In its general aspect, therefore, the internal intercourse of European society is less marked by kindness than by
formality, less regulated by sympathy than by rule.

Very different from this are both the basis and the manifestation of society in America. There social inequality has never
been a recognised principle, moulding the social fabric into arbitrary forms, and tyrannically influencing each person's position in the general scheme. Society in America started from the
point to which society in Europe is only yet tending. The equal-

ity of man is, to this moment, its corner-stone. As often as it has exhibited any tendency to aberration, has it been brought back again to this intelligible and essential principle. American society, therefore, exhibits itself as an indivisible whole, its general characteristics being such as mark each of the different classes into which European society is divided. That which develops itself with us as the sympathy of class, becomes in America the general sentiment of society. There is no man there whose position every other man does not understand; each has in himself the key to the feelings of his neighbour, and he measures his sympathies by his own. The absence of arbitrary inequalities banishes restraint from their mutual intercourse, whilst their mutual appreciation of each other's sentiments imparts a kindness and cordiality to that intercourse, which in Europe are only to be found, and not always there, within the circle of class.

The ease, and sincerity of manner, which spring from this social manifestation, are so marked, as immediately to strike even the most apathetic observer. There is very little in America of what we understand by acquaintanceship. Intercourse leads to friendship, or it leads to nothing, it being contrary to an American's nature to feel indifferent, and yet look cordial. Having none of the sympathies, he has none of the antipathies of class; his circle is his country; and in that circle, admitting of no superiors, he sees none but equals. Not but that there are in America many who are superior, in the share which they possess of all the conventional ingredients of a gentleman, to the great bulk of their countrymen, and to whom cultivated society is more grateful than that which is rude and undisciplined. The distinction of polish and refinement is all the difference that is discernible on the surface of American society, there being no exclusiveness of feeling, or isolation of sympathy concealed beneath a polished exterior. The American is first and essentially an American, and then a gentleman: with him refinement is not the enamel which conceals what is beneath, but the polish which brings out the real grain, exhibiting him in a better light, but ever in the same character. I have often been struck with the readiness with which the ease and frankness characteristic of American intercourse, have led parties to an unreserved interchange of views and sentiments, although they might have come from the most remote parts of the country, and had never seen each other before. How can it be otherwise, when the Georgian can put himself at once into the position of the Missourian, and the resident of Louisiana finds in himself the counterpart of the inhabitant of Maine? It is this ease of manner which so frequently offends the stranger, who does not comprehend its origin: that which is the natural result of the universality of feeling and sympathy in America, is regarded as an impudent liberty with us, when a member of one class dares to address one of another, in those terms of familiarity, which nothing but a community of interest and sentiment can render tolerable. An American can be as reserved as any body else, when he comes in contact with one whom he does not understand, or who will not understand him—and this is the reason why so many travellers in America, who forget to leave their European notions of exclusiveness at home, and traverse the republic wrapped in the cloak of European formalism, find the Americans so cold in their demeanour, and erroneously regard their particular behaviour to themselves as the result of a general moodiness and reserve.

It is obvious, however, that to retain this ease and accessibility of manner, it is very necessary to guard the equality of condition which is at their very foundation. Americans are all equal, not only in the eye of the law, but in social position, there being no rank to which one man is born and from which another is excluded, any more than there is political status, which, instead of being gained by personal effort, is a mere matter of inheritance. In European society, the superior ranks have every advantage in the cultivation of manner; for when not with equals, they are with inferiors, and thus learn ease and acquire self-possession. So it is with all Americans, who have no superiors to put, by their presence, an awkward, constrained, and artificial cast upon their actions. But let this equality of condition be invaded, and let a distinct class arise in America, with distinct interests and views of its own, and let that class take form and obtain an organized footing in the community, and the natural and unaffected manner, which marks the intercourse of society in that country, will give place to the artificial traits which indicate its European manifestations; and against this danger

American society has constantly to struggle. It is difficult, where there are vast accumulations of wealth, to adhere to a horizontal scale in social conditions. In America wealth has great influence, and the circle of its possessors is daily being enlarged, a state of things which would bode no good to the social equilibrium, were it not for the presence of other and counteracting influences. If there is a very wealthy class in America, there is not a very poor class, by whose co-operation the wealthy class might act with effect upon the mass intervening between the two extremes. Indeed, so far as competence involves the absence of poverty, there is in America no class which can strictly be denominated poor; that is to say, there is no class whose condition is incompatible with their independence. It is evident, therefore, that although wealth has undoubtedly its influence, and invests its possessor with a certain share of adventitious consideration; it has, as yet, no power in America to alter the essential characteristic of society—that universal equality which is based on universal independence. In the political equality of the people is also to be found another of the counteracting influences which check the social tendencies of wealth. In the great political lottery which is constantly being drawn in America, no man, however rich, can tell how greatly he may be benefited by another man, however indifferent may be his circumstances: and, indeed, it is not the rich who have there the greatest political influence; it is the busy bustling politician, who plunges into the thick of the fight, and works his way to the influence which he covets, at the expense of his time, his convenience, and often his better feelings. With so many, and frequently such rough competitors, to deal with in the political race, the wealthy, to whom life has other attractions, retire from the scramble, leaving the ring in the possession of the energetic, the needy, and the adventurous. Thus it is, that if the rich man has a political object of his own to subserve, he cannot afford to lose the aid of his less wealthy neighbour, but frequently more influential politician. The consequence is, that between the political footing of the one and the wealth of the other, they meet on neutral ground, where they find themselves restored to that equality which, but for the circumstances in which they are placed, might have been permanently disturbed. If, on the other hand, the rich man has no

selfish object in view, he knows not how soon his poorer neighbour, in the constant fermentation which is going on around
him, may be suddenly thrown into a political position, which
gives him in the eye of wealth fully as much consideration as it
can draw to itself; and this process is of daily occurrence in
America. The political arena is filled with those who plunge into
it from the very depths of society, as affording them a shorter
road to consideration than that which they would have to pursue
in the accumulation of property. Daily accessions being made
to the wealthy class itself, whilst there is no definite section of
society from which it is known that they will spring; and daily
transmutations going on from obscurity to political importance,
whilst political aspirations are limited to no class, and political
aid may be received from an individual, emanating from the
humblest sphere,—render it impossible, without the presence of a
poor and absolutely dependent class, for wealth, at least in its
present development, to over-ride the social order of things
established in America. Keeping this in view, it need surprise no
one to find a free and unreserved intercourse subsisting externally
amongst all the members of the community. The man of leisure,
the professional man, and the merchant, the mechanic, the arti-
san, and the tradesman, meet each other on equal terms, the
only obstacle that can arise between them being, on the part of
any of them, impropriety of behaviour or infamy of character.
So long as the ballot-box is in the hands of those with whom the
suffrage is universal, so long will the poorer classes have it in
their power to check any social aberrations in the more wealthy,
should the latter be inclined to substitute for the general easy
intercourse which prevails, an exclusive social and political
regime.

The reader will scarcely have to be told that all this is applicable only to society in its grander and more comprehensive
sense. It has nothing to do with the arrangements of the parlour,
or the etiquette of the drawing-room. It is not society in its
purely domestic or *in-door* character, to which his attention has
been drawn; but to society in its general and *out-door* sense, to
the great social life of the people considered as a people. When
we leave the national survey for the comparatively insignificant
arena of fashionable life, we find much that will appear excep-

tional to what has been here said; but the exceptions are mere grafts upon the great social trunk which we have been considering, drawing their life and nourishment from it, and partaking of many of its characteristics, instead of being growths emanating from the root, and typical of the very nature of the tree. The picture just considered, if it possesses no very strong lights, is devoid of deep shadows; but that which I am now about to sketch, in connexion with the social habits of the people, in a more limited sense, is more marked with differences, if not replete with contrasts.

It may as well here be premised that, in America, the ladies exercise an undisputed sway over the domestic hearth. Home is their sphere, and to them all the arrangements of home are exclusively left. In many respects, this is the case in every civilized society; but in Europe the family is, in some points, as much under the control of external influences, as the individual, denying to those who manage the household that perfect freedom of action which they enjoy in America. Let no querulous lady, who thinks that she has not enough of her own way, imagine that this implies, on the part of her more fortunate American sister, an absolute immunity from marital control. Wives in America know their place, and keep it, as generally as they do here, although how far that may be, might be difficult to tell. But, whilst in their social relations they are less fettered by existing institutions than European women, there is a more general abdication in their favour, on the part of husbands, in all that concerns the domestic arrangements and external relations of the family, than is, perhaps, to be found anywhere else.

The consequence of this is curious enough. The social position of the husband is not carried, in all its extent, into the social relations of his family. His sphere of action is without, where all are on an equal footing; but in the position of his family, and in their intercourse with those of his neighbours, he finds no such principle very generally recognised. Equality without—exclusiveness within—such seem to be the contrasts of American life. The professional man may be on the very best of terms with the blacksmith, but ten chances to one if the daughters of the professional man know the blacksmith's daughters, or if they would acknowledge it if they did. In-door life in America is fenced round by as many lines as social life in Europe. There is not a community there, any more than here, but has its fashionable quarter and its fashionable circle. This may be all very natural, but it is not in conformity with the general aspect of their national social life, that they carry with them into these coteries all the exclusiveness of feeling which forms so marked a feature in the social fabrics of the old world. In a widely extended country, like the transatlatic republic, and a widely scattered community, like that which peoples it, it is to be expected that these feelings would manifest themselves, in different places, in very different degrees. In some, however, they assume a form quite as inveterate as they do with ourselves; and young ladies will turn up their delicate but saucy noses at the bare idea of an acquaintanceship with those, with whose fathers or brothers their own fathers or brothers may be on terms of the most perfect familiarity. The circle once drawn, it is not very easy for those without to transcend it. The family that introduces a new member, is held responsible for his or her good behaviour and respectability; and it is not always that the countenance of a particular family will suffice to give a party the free range of the favoured circle.

In great communities, where the circle of society is large, and the lines have been long drawn, one need not be surprised at this, the fashionables finding within their own circle sufficient sources of amusement and gratification. But it is singular to witness the speedy development of the feeling in a new community, where inequality of circumstances is scarcely yet known; where all are, side by side, though in different ways, perhaps, equally engaged in the pursuit of the same end. Indeed, it is in these communities that the feeling is generally carried to its most ludicrous extent; society in the older and large cities having assumed a fixed form, in which each family has its appropriate place; but in the new towns, the prize of social pre-eminence being yet to be striven for, those who are uppermost for the time being, assume a very supercilious attitude to those below them. It is in these matters that the men in America take very little part. Whilst they are engaged providing the means, the mother and the daughters are using them in working the family into its true position as regards society.

The exclusive feature of American society is no where brought so broadly out as it is in the city of Philadelphia. It is, of course, readily discernible in Boston, New York, and Baltimore; but the line drawn in these places is not so distinctive or so difficult to transcend as it is in Philadelphia. The fashionables there are more particular in their inquiries, than are their neighbours, before they give admittance to the stranger knocking at their gates. As a general rule, an unexceptionable recommendation is all that is necessary in America to secure the stranger a ready acceptance by those to whom he is presented. The presumptions are all in favour of his fitness for the sphere which he aspires to adorn. To this, however, society in Philadelphia forms the most notable exception; a recommendation there only operating to put the new comer on his probation, and if found wanting, his recommendation goes for no more than it is worth; being estimated more from the proved qualities of the party receiving, than from the standing or authority of the party giving it. Once admitted, however, society in Philadelphia will be found amply to compensate for any delays and uncertainties with which the preliminary ordeal may have been accompanied. It is intellectual without being pedantic, and sprightly without being boisterous. It seems to be a happy blending of the chief characteristics of Boston and New York society. In both society is more accessible than in Philadelphia. In Boston the nucleus on which it turns is the literary circle of the place, which, comprising individuals and families of all grades of wealth, gives to society there a more democratic cast than it possesses either in New York or Philadelphia. It must be confessed, however, that there is a literary affectation about it, which is easier to be accounted for than endured, Bostonians always appearing to best advantage when they are farthest from home. In New York, again, the commercial spirit predominates over every other, and largely infuses itself into the society of the city. There is a permanent class of wealthy residents, who form the centre of it; its great bulk being composed of those who, by themselves or friends, are still actively engaged in the pursuits of commerce. With a few exceptions it is, therefore, in a state of constant fluctuation, in accordance with the fluctuating fortunes of commercial life. Its doors are guarded, but they seem never to be closed, and you have a constant stream flowing in and out. The consequence is, that there is much more heart than refinement about it. It is gay to a degree, sprightly and cordial, but far less conventional than the corresponding circle in Philadelphia. Society in the latter has all the advantages incident to a large community, in which the commercial spirit does not overbear every thing else, and in which literature is cultivated as an ornament, more than pursued as a business. In their habitual intercourse with each other the Philadelphians have an ease of manner which is perfectly charming. They are familiar without being coarse. It is not until the stranger gets upon the footing of being thus treated by them, that he begins to appreciate the real pleasures of Philadelphia life. It is only after he has surmounted the barrier of formalism which encounters him on his first entrance, that he becomes aware of the genial and kindly spirit that pervades the circle to which he is introduced. In many respects, Philadelphia life is the best counterpart which America affords to the social refinements of Europe, whilst it has at bottom a warmth and cordiality, the manifestation of which is not always compatible with the exigencies of European etiquette.

In a social point of view, there is this difference in America between the north and the south; that in the former, society, in its narrower sense, takes its chief development in towns, whereas, in the latter, it is more generally confined to the rural districts. This difference is chiefly attributable to the different systems which obtain in the distribution of property, and to other causes, social and political, which will be presently adverted to. As a general rule, in the north and west there is no such thing as a country society, in the ordinary acceptation of the term. The land is divided into small lots, each man, generally speaking, occupying only as much as he can cultivate. The whole country is thus divided into farms; there are few or no estates. The rural population is almost, without exception, a working population, with little leisure, if they had otherwise the means, to cultivate the graces of life. As you travel through the country you see multitudes of comfortable houses and good farming establishments, but no mansions. There is not, in fact, such a class in existence there as is here known as the country gentry. A more unpromising set of materials from which to construct an elegant social fabric, can scarcely be conceived than these northern and western farmers. The following incident will illustrate the whole class. I was acquainted with a farmer in Western New York, who was lucky enough to stumble upon a piece of land with a good "water privilege," which he soon turned to account, and became the "jolly miller" of the surrounding district. By means of his mill, he amassed what, for one in his condition, was a considerable fortune; and, at the instigation of his wife, who was fonder of show than her husband was, turned some of it to account in building a handsome two-story stone house, in contact with the unpretending wooden one, which they had inhabited for years. It was not, however, until the house had been built that they discovered that they had no use for it. When I knew them, and it had then been built five years, but two rooms in the whole house were furnished,—a parlour for great occasions, and a "spare bed-room;" the family continuing to eat, drink, and sleep in the old wooden building, to which they had been accustomed, and which still remained as a wing to the new house, which was seldom or ever made any use of. And so it is with most of them. Their habits are those of industry and frugality, predisposing them neither for fine houses, fine clothes, nor fine equipages. It is quite true that many of them do move into their "new houses," but they bring all the tastes and habits of the old house with them, and alter their condition but little by the change. Such is the phase which rural life presents in the north and west, with a few slight exceptions, such as are to be found in the upper portion of the Genesee Valley, along that of the Mohawk, and by the shores of the Hudson in New York, where some families have accumulated in their hands large properties, and live in a style which presents a marked contrast to the rural life around them.

In the south, on the other hand, things assume a very different aspect. In the States of Maryland, Virginia, the two Carolinas, Georgia, and Florida, as indeed in all the Southern States, land is possessed, as with us, in larger quantities; the owners, as in England, generally living on their estates. It is thus that, although Baltimore has its social circle, the chief society in Maryland is to be found in the counties; whilst, in the same way, the capital of Virginia affords but a faint type of the society of the State. In the rural life of these two States, and in that of South

Carolina, are to be found many of the habits and predilections
of colonial times, and a nearer approach to English country life
than is discernible in any other portion of the republic. The
country is divided into large plantations, containing, in many instances, many thousands of acres; on which reside the different
families, in large and commodious mansion-houses, surrounded
by multitudes of slaves and by all the appliances of rural luxury.
It is thus that, removed as they are from the necessity of labour,
and being interrupted in their retirement only by the occasional
visits of their friends and neighbours, the opportunity is afforded
them of cultivating all those social qualities which enter into our
estimate of a country gentry. In the society of the Southern Atlantic States, but particularly in that of the three last mentioned,
there is a purity of tone and an elevation of sentiment, together
with an ease of manner and a general social applomb, which are
only to be found united in a truly leisure class. Any general picture of American society would be very incomplete, into which
was not prominently introduced the phase which it exhibits in the
rural life of the South.

In some instances, American society is broken into subsidiary
divisions through the influence of religion. I do not here allude
to the effect which sect has in this respect, and which is in some
places so powerful as virtually to establish a system of mutual
non-intercourse. The division referred to is more into congrega-
tions than sects; the frequenters of particular places of worship
having frequently little or no social intercommunication with
those of others, even when they belong to the same denomination. The *odium theologicum* has nothing to do with this, nor
would, probably, any such social division exist, especially between members of the same denomination, but for the frequency
with which their religious duties bring the members of each
church together. Between Prayer meetings, and Bible Society
meetings, and Dorcas Society meetings, and Sunday School
Teachers' meetings, nearly every night in the week, in addition
to Sunday, sees them brought together,—a constancy of association, which soon induces them to regard all beyond their own
number with a feeling of indifference. The Dorcas Societies, in
particular, are great favourites with the ladies more religiously
inclined, seasoning, as they do, a bit of this world's enjoyment

with the simultaneous performance of the obligations of charity. The ladies of a congregation, married and expectant, the latter generally predominating, meet in rotation at their respective houses at an early hour in the afternoon; sew away industriously by themselves until evening, when the young gentlemen are introduced with the tea and coffee; whereupon work is suspended, and a snug little party is the hebdomadal consequence, characterized by a good deal of flirtation, and closed by prayer: the young men afterwards escorting the young ladies home, and taking leave of them, to meet them again next week under the same happy circumstances.

Bitter as party feeling frequently is in the United States, it is seldom permitted very materially to influence the relations of society. Not that the ladies eschew politics, but they do not refuse to commingle on that account; nor will they permit the political disputes of their male relations to disturb the arrangements which they have made for themselves. Fathers, brothers, and husbands, may tear each other's eyes out at their political tournaments; but wives, sisters, and daughters meet each other in friendly intercourse as before—gathered under the same roof, singing the same songs, and giggling at the same nonsense. Sensible, this, as compared with the ridiculous extent to which party hostility has been carried in the neighbouring province of Canada, where those on opposite sides, and all connected with them, have not only refused to associate but actually even to deal with each other.

There is no feature common to all the departments of American society, which will so soon impress itself upon the stranger as the prominent position occupied in it by the young ladies. In Europe, if they are not kept there, they at least remain somewhat in the back-ground. In America, on the other hand, they are in the foremost rank, and in fact constitute the all in all. Cards of invitation are frequently issued in their names—it being often "The Misses So-and-so" who invite, instead of "Mr. and Mrs. So-and-so." The mother is invariably eclipsed by her daughters. Indeed, I have known instances in which parties were given, at which she never made her appearance; the whole being done with her concurrence and assistance, but she keeping back from a participation in the prevailing gaiety—just because she has no inclination to join in it, prudently judging—wise woman!—that her time for such frivolities is past. The young ladies take the whole burden of the matter upon themselves—receive the guests, and do all the honours of the house. The absent mamma has her health frequently inquired for, but nobody ever thinks of wondering that she is not present. She is perhaps all the time in an adjoining room, superintending the arrangement of the comestibles. She regards the whole as the young ladies' doing, and leaves them to work their way out of it the best way they can. And very well they generally manage to do so—the opportunity which it affords them of cultivating the virtue of self-reliance being by no means thrown away. The young gentlemen, in making visits too, *may* ask at the door for the lady of the house, but such considerateness is a piece of pure supererogation, the young ladies being the parties generally called on, and frequently the only parties seen, if not the only parties asked for. Nor is a long acquaintanceship necessary to establish this footing of pleasant familiarity. You are introduced at a party to a young lady, dance with her, talk a little, and if she is at all pleased with you, the chances are all in favour of your being invited to call upon her— but by the somewhat guarded phraseology that "we" and not "she" will be very happy to see you. It is your own fault if, from that moment, you are not on intimate and friendly terms with her.

Agreeable as all this may be in some respects, it has very serious disadvantages in others. It imparts to society a general air of frivolity with which it could favourably dispense. When pert young misses of sixteen take it all into their own hands, what else could be expected? Not that all young ladies in America remain at sixteen, either in conduct or in years; but the younger portion of them just admitted into society make themselves more or less the pivot on which it turns. A young girl lives a life of great seclusion until she does come out, but, having an occasional peep at the conduct of her elder sisters or friends, her mind is made up as to the part she is to act before she is formally ushered into the arena. With the exception of some of the more refined and intellectual circles of the large towns, it is sometimes painful to witness the frivolous character of an American social assembly. There is no repose, nothing of a subdued tone about it. The few whose refinements and tastes would favourably influence it, if permitted to do so, are overborne by the numbers as well as by the forwardness of those who impress it with their own immaturities. Society in America is thus like a young hoyden that wants taming—like an inexperienced romp, as yet impatient of the fetters of conventional propriety. The difficulty is, that the remedy for this does not seem very near at hand, for the young blood which influences society to-day will be superseded by that of to-morrow. American society is thus deprived of the best of all teachers—experience; for, by the time that a lady learns how to act an easy and more subdued part, there is no prominent place for her in the social circle.

The consequence of this is, that both men and women of intellectual tastes and quiet habits withdraw more or less from society altogether. It is seldom, therefore, that conversation in a social assembly takes a sober, rational turn. Dreary commonplaces, jokes and vapid compliments, form the staple of conversation, all which is attended by a never-ceasing accompaniment of laughter, which is frequently too boisterous for all tastes. Such being its prominent characteristics on the female side, the picture does not improve when we examine the part borne in it by the men. It is seldom that one ever sees the generality of men rise above the level of their female acquaintances, either in intel-lectual culture or social refinement. In all civilized communities, women have, in this resepct, much in their power. It is for them to select their own associates; and such as aspire to their intimacy will be careful to possess themselves of all those qualifications which are made indispensable to its enjoyment. In American society, the really intellectual man holds a position of comparative isolation. To take his part with the rest, or to be tolerable in their sight, he must be-little himself to the social standard adhered to by those around him. The great proportion of the young men who frequent the social circle, if anything, fall within, than exceed this standard. Indeed, it could scarcely be otherwise, when we consider how alien are their common pursuits to the acquisition of those higher qualities which shine so prominently in the social arena elsewhere, and how little is really required of them to come up to the mark in the estimation of those with whom they associate. A good command of common-places, with a large stock of the "small change" of conversation, will do far more for a man in American society, generally considered, than the possession of higher qualifications will accomplish for him. The Americans certainly worship talent, and hold in high esteem the man of great intellectual acquirement; but they generally prefer reverencing him at a distance to coming in close contact with him; at all events, if he takes any share in their *réunions,* he is more acceptable when he leaves his distinctive qualities behind him. I have seen grave senators, who understood this well, cut the most ludicrous figures, in attempting to render themselves agreeable to giggling young misses, who made very little ceremony with them. Some of them succeed well in the process of intellectual descent, particularly those who have no very great distance to descend. But others find their attempts mere caricatures on frivolity, and, after a few awkward endeavours to accord with circumstances, very frequently withdraw altogether from circles, to the requirements of which they cannot conform themselves.

15

California, 1849

Bayard Taylor: Eldorado*

Probably no single event since the Louisiana Purchase so aroused popular imagination nor had so far-reaching an effect upon American life as the discovery of gold in California in 1848. Certainly no event up to that time received more attention from the press and later from writers of fiction. One of the first reporters on the scene, representing Horace Greeley's New York *Tribune*, was Bayard Taylor (1825-78), who at 24 was a veteran traveler and writer. He would go on to achieve enduring literary fame, largely because of his still unrivaled English translation of Goethe's *Faust*.

To save time Taylor took the faster sea route by way of Panama, arriving in San Francisco in mid-August of 1849. His dispatches to the *Tribune* were collected and published in book form the following year under the appropriate title, *Eldorado*. The chapter reproduced here deals not with the gold fields but with Taylor's first impressions of San Francisco, whose boisterous economy was an accurate index of the mounting output of "dust."

For additional reading there is no better book than Taylor's own, which was reprinted by Knopf in 1949. John W. Caughey, *Gold is the Cornerstone* (Berkeley: U. of California Press, 1948) is excellent. George R. Stewart, *The California Trail* (New York: McGraw-Hill, 1962) covers from original sources both the routes and the results of the California migration. To be noted are (1) evidences of the cosmopolitan nature of the town's population; (2) the character of the physical expansion of the community; (3) the nature of the price structure; (4) the contrast in availability of eastern and locally fabricated articles; and (5) evidences of social instability.

---

*Bayard Taylor, *Eldorado* (New York, 1850), I, pp. 54-62.

I LEFT THE PANAMA, IN COMPANY WITH LIEUT. BEALE, in the boat of the U. S. ship Ohio, which brought Lieutenant Ells on board. We first boarded the noble ship, which, even in San Francisco harbor, showed the same admirable order as on our own coast. She had returned from Honolulu a few days previous, after an absence of three months from California. The morning of our arrival, eighteen of her men had contrived to escape, carrying with them one of the boats, under fire from all the Government vessels in the harbor. The officers were eager for news from home, having been two months without a mail, and I was glad that my habit of carrying newspapers in my pockets enabled me to furnish them with a substantial gratification. The Ohio's boat put us ashore at the northern point of the anchorage, at the foot of a steep bank, from which a high pier had been built into the bay. A large vessel lay at the end, discharging her cargo. We scrambled up through piles of luggage, and among the crowd collected to witness our arrival, picked out two Mexicans to carry our trunks to a hotel. The barren side of the hill before us was covered with tents and canvas houses, and nearly in front a large two-story building displayed the sign: "Fremont Family Hotel."

As yet, we were only in the suburbs of the town. Crossing the shoulder of the hill, the view extended around the curve of the bay, and hundreds of tents and houses appeared, scattered all over the heights, and along the shore for more than a mile. A furious wind was blowing down through a gap in the hills, filling the streets with clouds of dust. On every side stood buildings of all kinds, begun or half-finished, and the greater part of them mere canvas sheds, open in front, and covered with all kinds of signs, in all languages. Great quantities of goods were piled up in the open air, for want of a place to store them. The streets were full of people, hurrying to and fro, and of as diverse and bizarre a character as the houses: Yankees of every possible variety, native Californians in *sarapes* and sombreros, Chilians, Sonorians, Kanakas from Hawaii, Chinese with long tails, Malays armed with their everlasting creeses, and others in whose embrowned and bearded visages it was impossible to recognize any especial nationality. We came at last into the plaza, now dignified by the name of Portsmouth Square. It lies on the slant side of the hill, and from a high pole in front of a long one-story adobe building used as the Custom House, the American flag was flying. On the lower side stood the Parker House—an ordinary frame house of about sixty feet front—and towards its entrance we directed our course.

Our luggage was deposited on one of the rear porticos, and we discharged the porters, after paying them two dollars each—a sum so immense in comparison to the service rendered that there was no longer any doubt of our having actually landed in California. There were no lodgings to be had at the Parker House—not even a place to unroll our blankets; but one of the proprietors accompanied us across the plaza to the City Hotel, where we obtained a room with two beds at $25 per week, meals being in addition $20 per week. I asked the landlord whether he could send a porter for our trunks. "There is none belonging to the house," he said he; "every man is his own porter here." I returned to the Parker House, shouldered a heavy trunk, took a valise in my hand and carried them to my quarters, in the teeth of the wind. Our room was in a sort of garret over the only story of the hotel; two cots, evidently of California manufacture, and covered only with a pair of blankets, two chairs, a rough table and a small looking-glass, constituted the furniture. There was not space enough between the bed and the bare rafters overhead, to sit upright, and I gave myself a severe blow in rising the next morning without the proper heed. Through a small roof-window of dim glass, I could see the opposite shore of the bay, then partly hidden by the evening fogs. The wind whistled around the eaves and rattled the tiles with a cold, gusty sound, that would have imparted a dreary character to the place, had I been in a mood to listen.

Many of the passengers began speculation at the moment of landing. The most ingenious and successful operation was made by a gentleman of New York, who took out fifteen hundred copies of The Tribune and other papers, which he disposed of in two hours, at one dollar a-piece! Hearing of this I bethought me of about a dozen papers which I had used to fill up crevices in packing my valise. There was a newspaper merchant at the corner of the City Hotel, and to him I proposed the sale of them, asking him to name a price. "I shall want to make a good profit on the retail price," said he, "and can't give more than ten dollars for the lot." I was satisfied with the wholesale price, which was a gain of just four thousand per cent!

I set out for a walk before dark and climbed a hill back of the town, passing a number of tents pitched in the hollows. The scattered houses spread out below me and the crowded shipping in the harbor, backed by a lofty line of mountains, made an imposing picture. The restless, feverish tide of life in that little spot, and the thought that what I then saw and was yet to see will hereafter fill one of the most marvellous pages of all history, rendered it singularly impressive. The feeling was not decreased on talking that evening with some of the old residents, (that is, of six months' standing,) and hearing their several experiences. Every new-comer in San Francisco is overtaken with a sense of complete bewilderment. The mind, however it may be prepared for an astonishing condition of affairs, cannot immediately push aside its old instincts of value and ideas of business, letting all past experiences go for naught and casting all its faculties for action, intercourse with its fellows or advancement in any path of ambition, into shapes which it never before imagined. As in the turn of the dissolving views, there is a period when it wears neither the old nor the new phase, but the vanishing images of the one and the growing perceptions of the other are blended in painful and misty confusion. One knows not whether he is awake or in some wonderful dream. Never have I had so much difficulty in establishing, satisfactorily to my own senses, the reality of what I saw and heard.

I was forced to believe many things, which in my communications to The Tribune I was almost afraid to write, with any hope of their obtaining credence. It may be interesting to give here a few instances of the enormous and unnatural value put upon property at the time of my arrival. The Parker House rented for $110,000 yearly, at least $60,000 of which was paid by gamblers, who held nearly all the second story. Adjoining it on the right was a canvas-tent fifteen by twenty-five feet, called "El-dorado," and occupied likewise by gamblers, which brought $40,000. On the opposite corner of the plaza, a building called the "Miner's Bank," used by Wright & Co., brokers, about half the size of a fire-engine house in New York, was held at a rent of

$75,000. A mercantile house paid $40,000 rent for a one-story building of twenty feet front; the United States Hotel, $36,000; the Post-Office, $7,000, and so on to the end of the chapter. A friend of mine, who wished to find a place for a law-office, was shown a cellar in the earth, about twelve feet square and six deep, which he could have at $250 a month. One of the common soldiers at the battle of San Pasquale was reputed to be among the millionaires of the place, with an income of $50,000 *monthly*. A citizen of San Francisco died insolvent to the amount of $41,000 the previous Autumn. His administrators were delayed in settling his affairs, and his real estate advanced so rapidly in value meantime, that after his debts were paid his heirs had a yearly income of $40,000. These facts were indubitably attested; every one believed them, yet hearing them talked of daily, as matters of course, one at first could not help feeling as if he had been eating of "the insane root."

The prices paid for labor were in proportion to everything else. The carman of Mellus, Howard & Co. had a salary of $6,000 a year, and many others made from $15 to $20 daily. Servants were paid from $100 to $200 a month, but the wages of the rougher kinds of labor had fallen to about $8. Yet, notwithstanding the number of gold-seekers who were returning enfeebled and disheartened from the mines, it was difficult to obtain as many workmen as the forced growth of the city demanded. A gentleman who arrived in April told me he then found but thirty or forty houses; the population was then so scant that not more than twenty-five persons would be seen in the steets at any one time. Now, there were probably five hundred houses, tents and sheds, with a population, fixed and floating, of six thousand. People who had been absent six weeks came back and could scarcely recognize the place. Streets were regularly laid out, and already there were three piers, at which small vessels could discharge. It was calculated that the town increased daily by from fifteen to thirty houses; its skirts were rapidly approaching the summits of the three hills on which it is located.

A curious result of the extraordinary abundance of gold and the facility with which fortunes were acquired, struck me at the first glance. All business was transacted on so extensive a scale that the ordinary habits of solicitation and compliance on the one hand and stubborn cheapening on the other, seemed to be entirely forgotten. You enter a shop to buy something; the owner eyes you with perfect indifference, waiting for you to state your want; if you object to the price, you are at liberty to leave, for you need not expect to get it cheaper; he evidently cares little whether you buy it or not. One who has been some time in the country will lay down the money, without wasting words. The only exception I found to this rule was that of a sharp-faced Down-Easter just opening his stock, who was much distressed when his clerk charged me seventy-five cents for a coil of rope, instead of one dollar. This disregard for all the petty arts of money-making was really a refreshing feature of society. Another equally agreeable trait was the punctuality with which debts were paid, and the general confidence which men were obliged to place, perforce, in each other's honesty. Perhaps this latter fact was owing, in part, to the impossibility of protecting wealth, and consequent dependence on an honorable regard for the rights of others.

About the hour of twilight the wind fell; the sound of a gong called us to tea, which was served in the largest room of the hotel. The fare was abundant and of much better quality than we expected—better, in fact, than I was able to find there two months later. The fresh milk, butter and excellent beef of the country were real luxuries after our sea-fare. Thus braced against the fog and raw temperature, we sallied out for a night-view of San Francisco, then even more peculiar than its daylight look. Business was over about the usual hour, and then the harvest-time of the gamblers commenced. Every "hell" in the place, and I did not pretend to number them, was crowded, and immense sums were staked at the monte and faro tables. A boy of fifteen, in one place, won about $500, which he coolly pocketed and carried off. One of the gang we brought in the Panama won $1,500 in the course of the evening, and another lost $2,400. A fortunate miner made himself conspicuous by betting large piles of ounces on a single throw. His last stake of 100 oz. was lost, and I saw him the following morning dashing through the streets, trying to break his own neck or that of the magnificent *garañon* he bestrode.

Walking through the town the next day, I was quite amazed

to find a dozen persons busily employed in the street before the United States Hotel, digging up the earth with knives and crumbling it in their hands. They were actual gold-hunters, who obtained in this way about $5 a day. After blowing the fine dirt carefully in their hands, a few specks of gold were left, which they placed in a piece of white paper. A number of children were engaged in the same business, picking out the fine grains by applying to them the head of a pin, moistened in their mouths. I was told of a small boy having taken home $14 as the result of one day's labor. On climbing the hill to the Post Office I observed in places, where the wind had swept away the sand, several glittering dots of the real metal, but, like the Irishman who kicked the dollar out of his way, concluded to wait till I should reach the heap. The presence of gold in the streets was probably occasioned by the leakings from the miners' bags and the sweepings of stores; though it may also be, to a slight extent, native in the earth, particles having been found in the clay thrown up from a deep well.

The arrival of a steamer with a mail ran the usual excitement and activity of the town up to its highest possible notch. The little Post Office, half-way up the hill, was almost hidden from sight by the crowds that clustered around it. Mr. Moore, the new Postmaster, who was my fellow-traveler from New York, barred every door and window from the moment of his entrance, and with his sons and a few clerks, worked steadily for two days and two nights, till the distribution of twenty thousand letters was completed. Among the many persons I met, the day after landing, was Mr. T. Butler King, who had just returned from an expedition to the placers, in company with General Smith. Mr. Edwin Bryant, of Kentucky, and Mr. Durivage, of New Orleans, had arrived a few days previous, the former by way of the Great Salt Lake, and the latter by the northern provinces of Mexico and the Gila. I found the artist Osgood in a studio about eight feet square, with a head of Captain Sutter on his easel. He had given up gold-digging, after three months of successful labor among the mountains.

I could make no thorough acquaintance with San Francisco during this first visit. Lieutenant Beale, who held important Government dispatches for Colonel Fremont, made arrangements to leave for San José on the second morning, and offered me a seat on the back of one of his mules. Our fellow-passenger, Colonel Lyons, of Louisiana, joined us, completing the mystic number which travelers should be careful not to exceed. We made hasty tours through all the shops on Clay, Kearney, Washington and Montgomery streets, on the hunt of the proper equipments. Articles of clothing were cheaper than they had been or were afterwards; tolerable blankets could be had for $6 a pair; coarse flannel shirts, $3; Chilian spurs, with rowels two inches long, $5, and Mexican sarapes, of coarse texture but gay color, $10. We could find no saddle-bags in the town, and were necessitated to pack one of the mules. Among our camping materials were a large hatchet and plenty of rope for making lariats; in addition to which each of us carried a wicker flask slung over one shoulder. We laid aside our civilized attire, stuck long sheath-knives into our belts, put pistols into our pockets and holsters, and buckled on the immense spurs which jingled as they struck the ground at every step. Our "animals" were already in waiting; an *alazan*, the Californian term for a sorrel horse, a beautiful brown mule, two of a cream color and a dwarfish little fellow whose long forelock and shaggy mane gave him altogether an elfish character of cunning and mischief.

16

The Compromise of 1850

Daniel Webster's "Seventh of March" Speech*

By 1850 the slavery question threatened to disrupt the Union. The issue between North and South, postponed for a generation by the Missouri Compromise but aggravated by the long delay, was the extension or containment of slavery. If the territory acquired as a result of the Mexican War were to be carved into free states, the South would have a minority in the Senate as she already had in the House of Representatives, and her "peculiar institution" would be doomed. Aging Henry Clay offered resolutions intended to keep the peace among the states for yet a little longer. The debate that followed was highlighted by the dying Calhoun's embittered demand for a permanent sectional veto; by Webster's urgent plea for compromise; by William H. Seward's appeal to a morality beyond the Constitution; and by the appearance of John Charles Fremont and William M. Gwin with a California charter barring slavery and credentials as senators from a state yet to be acknowledged.

In his "Seventh of March" speech Daniel Webster (1782-1852) made the last great oratorical effort of his matchless career. It cost him much of his popularity in the North, where it was looked upon as a sellout to the "slave power," but it was probably decisive in effecting the compromise of 1850 that postponed the resort to arms for another decade.

The best full-length biography of Webster is Claude M. Fuess, *Daniel Webster* (2 vols.; Boston: Little, Brown, 1930). The best detailed study of the compromise in context is Allan Nevins, *Fruits of Manifest Destiny, 1847-1852* (New York: Scribner, 1947). In the excerpt reproduced here the reader should note (1) characteristics of the style, tone, and mood of Webster's speech; (2) what elements he stressed in his summary of events leading up to the debate; (3) what attitude Webster took toward the Constitution; (4) by what means he sought to balance northern against southern grievances in order to

---

Congressional Globe, 31st Congress, 1st Session, pp. 476-84.

pave the way for compromise; (5) what he thought of the problem
of fugitive slaves; (6) his judgment of the abolitionists and how their
activities affected his belief in the principle of freedom of the press;
and (7) how he received the idea of the possible division of the
United States.

MR. PRESIDENT,—I wish to speak to-day, not as a Massachusetts
man, nor as a Northern man, but as an American, and a member
of the Senate of the United States. It is fortunate that there is a
Senate of the United States; a body not yet moved from its propriety, not lost to a just sense of its own dignity and its own high
responsibilities, and a body to which the country looks, with
confidence, for wise, moderate, patriotic, and healing counsels.
It is not to be denied that we live in the midst of strong agita-
tions, and are surrounded by very considerable dangers to our
institutions and government. The imprisoned winds are let loose.
The East, the North, and the stormy South combine to throw the
whole sea into commotion, to toss its billows to the skies, and
disclose its profoundest depths. I do not affect to regard myself,
Mr. President, as holding, or as fit to hold, the helm in this
combat with the political elements; but I have a duty to perform,
and I mean to perform it with fidelity, not without a sense of
existing dangers, but not without hope. I have a part to act, not
for my own security or safety, for I am looking out for no frag-
ment upon which to float away from the wreck, if wreck there
must be, but for the good of the whole, and the preservation of
all; and there is that which will keep me to my duty during this
struggle, whether the sun and the stars shall appear, or shall not
appear for many days. I speak to-day for the preservation of the
Union. "Hear me for my cause." I speak to-day, out of a solicitous
and anxious heart, for the restoration to the country of that quiet
and that harmony which make the blessings of this Union so rich,
and so dear to us all. These are the topics that I propose to
myself to discuss; these are the motives, and the sole motives,
that influence me in the wish to communicate my oninions to
the Senate and the country; and if I can do any fhing, however
little, for the promotion of these ends, I shall have accomplished
all that I expect.

Mr. President, it may not be amiss to recur very briefly to the events which, equally sudden and extraordinary, have brought the country into its present political condition. In May, 1846, the United States declared war against Mexico. Our armies, then on the frontiers, entered the provinces of that republic, met and defeated all her troops, penetrated her mountain passes, and occupied her capital. The marine force of the United States took possession of her forts and her towns, on the Atlantic and on the Pacific. In less than two years a treaty was negotiated, by which Mexico ceded to the United States a vast territory, extending seven or eight hundred miles along the shores of the Pacific, and reaching back over the mountains, and across the desert, until it joins the frontier of the State of Texas. It so happened, in the distracted and feeble condition of the Mexican government, that, before the declaration of war by the United States against Mexico had become known in California, the people of California, under the lead of American officers, overthrew the existing Mexican provincial government, and raised an independent flag. When the news arrived at San Francisco that war had been declared by the United States against Mexico, this independent flag was pulled down, and the stars and stripes of this Union hoisted in its stead. So, Sir, before the war was over, the forces of the United States, military and naval, had possession of San Francisco and Upper California, and a great rush of emigrants from various parts of the world took place into California in 1846 and 1847. But now behold another wonder.

In January of 1848, a party of Mormons made a discovery of an extraordinarily rich mine of gold, or rather of a great quantity of gold, hardly proper to be called a mine, for it was spread near the surface, on the lower part of the south, or American, branch of the Sacramento. They attempted to conceal their discovery for some time; but soon another discovery of gold, perhaps of greater importance, was made, on another part of the American branch of the Sacramento, near Sutter's Fort, as it is called. The fame of these discoveries spread far and wide. They inflamed more and more the spirit of emigration towards California, which had already been excited; and adventurers crowded into the country by hundreds, and flocked towards the Bay of San Francisco. This, as I have said, took place in the winter and spring of 1848.

The digging commenced in the spring of that year, and from that time to this the work of searching for gold has been prosecuted with a success not heretofore known in the history of this globe. You recollect, Sir, how incredulous at first the American public was at the accounts which reached us of these discoveries; but we all know, now, that these accounts received, and continue to receive, daily confirmation, and down to the present moment I suppose the assurance is as strong, after the experience of these several months, of the existence of deposits of gold apparently inexhaustible in the regions near San Francisco, in California, as it was at any period of the earlier dates of the accounts.

It so happened, Sir, that although, after the return of peace, it became a very important subject for legislative consideration and legislative decision to provide a proper territorial government for California, yet differences of opinion between the two houses of Congress prevented the establishment of any such territorial government at the last session. Under this state of things, the inhabitants of California, already amounting to a considerable number, thought it to be their duty, in the summer of last year, to establish a local government. Under the proclamation of General Riley, the people chose delegates to a convention, and that convention met at Monterey. It formed a constitution for the State of California, which, being referred to the people, was adopted by them in their primary assemblages. Desirous of immediate connection with the United States, its Senators were appointed and representatives chosen, who have come hither, bringing with them the authentic constitution of the State of California; and they now present themselves, asking, in behalf of their constituents, that it may be admitted into this Union as one of the United States. This constitution, Sir, contains an express prohibition of slavery, or involuntary servitude, in the State of California. It is said, and I suppose truly, that, of the members who composed that convention, some sixteen were natives of, and had been residents in, the slave-holding States, about twenty-two were from the non-slave-holding States, and the remaining ten members were either native Californians or old settlers in that country. This prohibition of slavery, it is said, was inserted with entire unanimity.

It is this circumstance, Sir, the prohibition of slavery, which has contributed to raise, I do not say it has wholly raised, the dispute as to the propriety of the admission of California into the Union under this constitution. It is not to be denied, Mr. President, nobody thinks of denying, that, whatever reasons were assigned at the commencement of the late war with Mexico, it was prosecuted for the purpose of the acquisition of territory, and under the alleged argument that the cession of territory was the only form in which proper compensation could be obtained by the United States from Mexico, for the various claims and demands which the people of this country had against that government. At any rate, it will be found that President Polk's message, at the commencement of the session of December, 1847, avowed that the war was to be prosecuted until some acquisition of territory should be made. As the acquisition was to be south of the line of the United States, in warm climates and countries, it was naturally, I suppose, expected by the South, that whatever acquisitions were made in that region would be added to the slave-holding portion of the United States. Very little of accurate information was possessed of the real physical character, either of California or New Mexico, and events have not turned out as was expected. Both California and New Mexico are likely to come in as free States; and therefore some degree of disappointment and surprise has resulted. In other words, it is obvious that the question which has so long harassed the country, and at some times very seriously alarmed the minds of wise and good men, has come upon us for a fresh discussion; the question of slavery in these United States. . . .

Mr. President, in the excited times in which we live, there is found to exist a state of crimination and recrimination between the North and South. There are lists of grievances produced by each; and those grievances, real or supposed, alienate the minds of one portion of the country from the other, exasperate the feelings, and subdue the sense of fraternal affection, patriotic love, and mutual regard. I shall bestow a little attention, Sir, upon these various grievances existing on the one side and on the other. I begin with complaints of the South. I will not answer, further than I have, the general statements of the honorable Senator from South Carolina, that the North has prospered at the expense of the South in consequence of the

manner of administering this government, in the collecting of
its revenues, and so forth. These are disputed topics, and I
have no inclination to enter into them. But I will allude to other
complaints of the South, and especially to one which has in my
opinion just foundation; and that is, that there has been found at
the North, among individuals and among legislators, a disinclina-
tion to perform fully their constitutional duties in regard to the
return of persons bound to service who have escaped into the
free States. In that respect, the South, in my judgment, is right,
and the North is wrong. Every member of every Northern legislature is bound by oath, like every other officer in the country, to
support the Constitution of the United States; and the article of
the Constitution* which says to these States that they shall
deliver up fugitives from service is as binding in honor and
conscience as any other article. No man fulfills his duty in any
legislature who sets himself to find excuses, evasions, escapes
from this constitutional obligation. I have always thought that
the Constitution addressed itself to the legislatures of the States
or to the States themselves. It says that those persons escaping
to other States "shall be delivered up," and I confess I have always been of the opinion that it was an injunction upon the
States themselves. When it is said that a person escaping into
another State, and coming therefore within the jurisdiction of
that State, shall be delivered up, it seems to me the import of the
clause is, that the State itself, in obedience to the Constitution,
shall cause him to be delivered up. That is my judgment. I have
always entertained that opinion, and I entertain it now. But when
the subject, some years ago, was before the Supreme Court of
the United States, the majority of the judges held that the power
to cause fugitives from service to be delivered up was a power to
be exercised under the authority of this government. I do not
know, on the whole, that it may not have been a fortunate
decision. My habit is to respect the result of judicial deliberations
and the solemnity of judicial decisions. As it now stands, the
business of seeing that these fugitives are delivered up resides
in the power of Congress and the national judicature, and my
friend at the head of the Judiciary Committee has a bill on the
subject now before the Senate, which, with some amendments to
it, I propose to support, with all its provisions, to the fullest

extent. And I desire to call the attention of all sober-minded men at the North, of all conscientious men, of all men who are not carried away by some fanatical idea or some false impression, to their constitutional obligations. I put it to all the sober and sound minds at the North as a question of morals and a question of conscience. What right have they, in their legislative capacity or any other capacity, to endeavor to get round this Constitution, or to embarrass the free exercise of the rights secured by the Constitution to the persons whose slaves escape from them? None at all; none at all. Neither in the forum of conscience, nor before the face of the Constitution, are they, in my opinion, justified in such an attempt. Of course it is a matter for their consideration. They probably, in the excitement of the times, have not stopped to consider of this. They have followed what seemed to be the current of thought and of motives, as the occasion arose, and they have neglected to investigate fully the real question, and to consider their constitutional obligations; which, I am sure, if they did consider, they would fulfil with alacrity. I repeat, therefore, Sir, that here is a well-founded ground of complaint against the North, which ought to be removed, which it is now in the power of the different departments of this government to remove; which calls for the enactment of proper laws authorizing the judicature of this government, in the several States, to do all that is necessary for the recapture of fugitive slaves and for their restoration to those who claim them. Wherever I go, and whenever I speak on the subject, and when I speak here I desire to speak to the whole North, I say that the South has been injured in this respect, and has a right to complain; and the North has been too careless of what I think the Constitution peremptorily and emphatically enjoins upon her as a duty.

Complaint has been made against certain resolutions that emanate from legislatures at the North, and are sent here to us, not only on the subject of slavery in this District, but sometimes recommending Congress to consider the means of abolishing slavery in the States. I should be sorry to be called upon to present any resolutions here which could not be referable to any committee or any power in Congress; and therefore I should be unwilling to receive from the legislature of Massachusetts any

instructions to present resolutions expressive of any opinion whatever on the subject of slavery, as it exists at the present moment
in the States, for two reasons: first, because I do not consider
that the legislature of Massachusetts has any thing to do with it;
and next, because I do not consider that I, as her representative
here, have any thing to do with it. It has become, in my opinion,
quite too common; and if the legislatures of the States do not
like that opinion, they have a great deal more power to put it
down than I have to uphold it; it has become, in my opinion,
quite too common a practice for the State legislatures to present
resolutions here on all subjects and to instruct us on all subjects.
There is no public man that requires instruction more than I do,
or who requires information more than I do, or desires it
more heartily; but I do not like to have it in too imperative a shape. I took notice, with pleasure, of some remarks
made upon this subject, the other day, in the Senate of Massachusetts, by a young man of talent and character, of whom the
best hopes may be entertained. I mean Mr. Hillard. He told the
Senate of Massachusetts that he would vote for no instructions
whatever to be forwarded to members of Congress, nor for any
resolutions to be offered expressive of the sense of Massachusetts
as to what her members of Congress ought to do. He said that he
saw no propriety in one set of public servants giving instructions
and reading lectures to another set of public servants. To his own
master each of them must stand or fall, and that master is his
constituents. I wish these sentiments could become more common. I have never entered into the question, and never shall, as
to the binding force of instructions. I will, however, simply say
this: if there be any matter pending in this body, while I am a
member of it, in which Massachusetts has an interest of her own
not adverse to the general interests of the country, I shall pursue
her instructions with gladness of heart and with all the efficiency
which I can bring to the occasion. But if the question be one
which affects her interest, and at the same time equally affects
the interests of all the other States, I shall no more regard her
particular wishes or instructions than I should regard the wishes
of a man who might appoint me an arbitrator or referee to decide
some question of important private right between him and his
neighbor, and then *instruct* me to decide in his favor. If ever

there was a government upon earth it is this government, if ever there was a body upon earth it is this body, which should consider itself as composed by agreement of all, each member appointed by some, but organized by the general consent of all, sitting here, under the solemn obligations of oath and conscience, to do that which they think to be best for the good of the whole.

Then, Sir, there are the Abolition societies of which I am unwilling to speak, but in regard to which I have very clear notions and opinions. I do not think them useful. I think their operations for the last twenty years have produced nothing good or valuable. At the same time, I believe thousands of their members to be honest and good men, perfectly well-meaning men. They have excited feelings; they think they must do something for the cause of liberty; and, in their sphere of action, they do not see what else they can do than to contribute to an Abolition press, or an Abolition society, or to pay an Abolition lecturer. I do not mean to impute gross motives even to the leaders of these societies, but I am not blind to the consequences of their proceedings. I cannot but see what mischiefs their interference with the South has produced. And is it not plain to every man? Let any gentleman who entertains doubts on this point recur to the debates in the Virginia House of Delegates in 1832, and he will see with what freedom a proposition made by Mr. Jefferson Randolph for the gradual abolition of slavery was discussed in that body. Every one spoke of slavery as he thought; very ignominious and disparaging names and epithets were applied to it. The debates in the House of Delegates on that occasion, I believe, were all published. They were read by every colored man who could read, and to those who could not read, those debates were read by others. At that time Virginia was not unwilling or afraid to discuss this question, and to let that part of her population know as much of the discussion as they could learn. That was in 1832. As has been said by the honorable member from South Carolina, these Abolition societies commenced their course of action in 1835. It is is said, I do not know how true it may be, that they sent incendiary publications into the slave States; at any rate, they attempted to arouse, and did arouse, a very strong feeling; in other words, they created great agitation in the North against Southern slavery. Well, what was the result? The bonds of the slaves were bound more firmly than before, their rivets were more strongly fastened. Public opinion, which in Virginia had begun to be exhibited against slavery, and was opening out for the discussion of the question, drew back, and shut itself up in its castle. I wish to know whether any body in Virginia can now talk openly as Mr. Randolph, Governor McDowell, and others talked in 1832, and sent their remarks to the press? We all know the fact, and we all know the cause; and every thing that these agitating people have done has been, not to enlarge, but to restrain, not to set free, but to bind faster, the slave population of the South.

Again, Sir, the violence of the Northern press is complained of. The press violent! Why, Sir, the press is violent everywhere. There are outrageous reproaches in the North against the South, and there are reproaches as vehement in the South against the North. Sir, the extremists of both parts of this country are violent; they mistake loud and violent talk for eloquence and for reason. They think that he who talks loudest reasons best. And this we must expect, when the press is free, as it is here, and I trust always will be; for, with all its licentiousness and all its evil, the entire and absolute freedom of the press is essential to the preservation of government on the basis of a free constitution. Wherever it exists there will be foolish and violent paragraphs in the newspapers, as there are, I am sorry to say, foolish and violent speeches in both houses of Congress. In truth, Sir, I must say that, in my opinion, the vernacular tongue of the country has become greatly vitiated, depraved, and corrupted by the style of our Congressional debates. And if it were possible for those debates to vitiate the principles of the people as much as they have depraved their tastes, I should cry out, "God save the Republic!"

Well, in all this I see no solid grievance, no grievance presented by the South, within the redress of the government, but the single one to which I have referred; and that is, the want of a proper regard to the injunction of the Constitution for the delivery of fugitive slaves.

There are also complaints of the North against the South. I need not go over them particularly. The first and gravest is, that the North adopted the Constitution, recognizing the existence of slavery in the States, and recognizing the right, to a certain extent, of the representation of slaves in Congress, under a state of sentiment and expectation which does not now exist; and that, by events, by circumstances, by the eagerness of the South to acquire territory and extend her slave population, the North finds itself, in regard to the relative influence of the South and the North, of the free States and the slave States, where it never did expect to find itself when they agreed to the compact of the Constitution. They complain, therefore, that, instead of slavery being regarded as an evil, as it was then, an evil which all hoped would be extinguished gradually, it is now regarded by the South as an institution to be cherished, and preserved, and extended; an institution which the South has already extended to the utmost of her power by the acquisition of new territory.

Well, then, passing from that, every body in the North reads; and every body reads whatsoever the newspapers contain; and the newspapers, some of them, especially those presses to which I have alluded, are careful to spread about among the people every reproachful sentiment uttered by any Southern man bearing at all against the North; every thing that is calculated to exasperate and to alienate; and there are many such things, as every body will admit, from the South, or some portion of it, which are disseminated among the reading people; and they do exasperate, and alienate, and produce a most mischievous effect upon the public mind at the North. Sir, I would not notice things of this sort appearing in obscure quarters; but one thing has occurred in this debate which struck me very forcibly. An honorable member from Louisiana addressed us the other day on this subject. I suppose there is not a more amiable and worthy gentleman in this chamber, nor a gentleman who would be more slow to give offence to any body, and he did not mean in his remarks to give offence. But what did he say? Why, Sir, he took pains to run a contrast between the slaves of the South and the laboring people of the North, giving the preference, in all points of condition, and comfort, and happiness, to the slaves of the South. The honorable member, doubtless, did not suppose that he gave any offence, or did any injustice. He was merely expressing his opinion. But does he know how remarks of that sort will be received by the laboring people of the North? Why, who are the laboring people of the North? They are the whole North. They are the people who till their own farms with their own hands; freeholders, educated men, independent men. Let me say, Sir, that five sixths of the whole property of the North is in the hands of the laborers of the North; they cultivate their farms, they educate their children, they provide the means of indpendence. If they are not freeholders, they earn wages; these wages accumulate, are turned into capital, into new freeholds, and small capitalists are created. Such is the case, and such the course of things, among the industrious and frugal. And what can these people think when so respectable and worthy a gentleman as the member from Louisiana undertakes to prove that the absolute ignorance and the abject slavery of the South are more in conformity with the high purposes and destiny of immortal, rational human beings, than the educated, the independent free labor of the North?

There is a more tangible and irritating cause of grievance at the North. Free blacks are constantly employed in the vessels of the North, generally as cooks or stewards. When the vessel arrives at a Southern port, these free colored men are taken on shore, by the police or municipal authority, imprisoned, and kept in prison till the vessel is again ready to sail. This is not only irritating, but exceedingly unjustifiable and oppressive. Mr. Hoar's mission, some time ago, to South Carolina, was a well-intended effort to remove this cause of complaint. The North thinks such imprisonments illegal and unconstitutional; and as the cases occur constantly and frequently, they regard it as a great grievance.

Now, Sir, so far as any of these grievances have their foundation in matters of law, they can be redressed, and ought to be redressed; and so far as they have their foundation in matters of opinion, in sentiment, in mutual crimination and recrimination, all that we can do is to endeavor to allay the agitation, and cultivate a better feeling and more fraternal sentiments between the South and the North.

Mr. President, I should much prefer to have heard from every member on this floor declarations of opinion that this Union could never be dissolved, than the declaration of opinion by any body, that, in any case, under the pressure of any circumstances, such a dissolution was possible. I hear with distress and anguish the word "secession," especially when it falls from the lips of those who are patriotic, and known to the country, and known all over the world, for their political services. Secession! Peaceable secession! Sir, your eyes and mine are never destined to see that miracle. The dismemberment of this vast country without convulsion! The breaking up of the fountains of the great deep without ruffling the surface! Who is so foolish, I beg every body's pardon, as to expect to see any such thing? Sir, he who sees these States, now revolving in harmony around a common centre, and expects to see them quit their places and fly off without convulsion, may look the next hour to see the heavenly bodies rush from their spheres, and jostle against each other in the realms of space, without causing the wreck of the universe. There can be no such thing as a peaceable secession. Peaceable secession is an utter impossibility. Is the great Constitution under which we live, covering this whole country, is it to be thawed and melted away by secession, as the snows on the mountain melt under the influence of a vernal sun, disappear almost unobserved, and run off? No, Sir! No Sir! I will not state what might produce the disruption of the Union; but, Sir, I see as plainly as I see the sun in heaven what that disruption itself must produce; I see that it must produce war, and such a war as I will not describe, *in its twofold character.*

Peaceable secession! Peaceable secession! The concurrent agreement of all the members of this great republic to separate! A voluntary separation, with alimony on one side and on the other. Why, what would be the result? Where is the line to be drawn? What States are to secede? What is to remain American? What am I to be? An American no longer? Am I to become a sectional man, a local man, a separatist, with no country in common with the gentlemen who sit around me here, or who fill the other house of Congress? Heaven forbid! Where is the flag of the republic to remain? Where is the eagle still to tower? or is he to cower, and shrink, and fall to the ground? Why, Sir, our ancestors, our fathers and our grandfathers, those of them that are yet living amongst us with prolonged lives, would rebuke and reproach us; and our children and our grandchildren would cry out shame upon us, if we of this generation should dishonor these ensigns of the power of the government and the harmony of that Union which is every day felt among us with so much joy and gratitude. What is to become of the army? What is to become of the navy? What is to become of the public lands? How is each of the thirty States to defend itself? I know, although the idea has not been stated distinctly, there is to be, or it is supposed possible that there will be, a Southern Confederacy. I do not mean, when I allude to this statement, that any one seriously contemplates such a state of things. I do not mean to say that it is true, but I have heard it suggested elsewhere, that the idea has been entertained, that, after the dissolution of this Union, a Southern Confederacy might be formed. I am sorry, Sir, that it has ever been thought of, talked of, or dreamed of, in the wildest flights of human imagination. But the idea, so far as it exists, must be of a separation, assigning the slave States to one side and the free States to the other. Sir, I may express myself too strongly, perhaps, but there are impossibilities in the natural as well as in the physical world, and I hold the idea of a separation of these States, those that are free to form one government, and those that are slave-holding to form another, as such an impossibility. We could not separate the States by any such line, if we were to draw it. We could not sit down here to-day and draw a line of separation that would satisfy any five men in the country. There are natural causes that would keep and tie us together, and there are social and domestic relations which we could not break if we would, and which we should not if we could.

Sir, nobody can look over the face of this country at the present moment, nobody can see where its population is the most dense and growing, without being ready to admit, and compelled to admit, that ere long the strength of America will be in the Valley of the Mississippi. Well, now, Sir, I beg to inquire what the wildest enthusiast has to say on the possibility of cutting that river in two, and leaving free States at its source and on its branches, and slave States down near its mouth, each forming a separate government? Pray, Sir, let me say to the people of this country, that these things are worthy of their pondering and of their consideration. Here, Sir, are five millions of freemen in the free States north of the river Ohio. Can any body suppose that this population can be severed, by a line that divides them from the territory of a foreign and an alien government, down somewhere, the Lord knows where, upon the lower banks of the Mississippi? What would become of Missouri? Will she join the *arrondissement* of the slave States? Shall the man from the Yellow Stone and the Platte be connected, in the new republic, with the man who lives on the southern extremity of the Cape of Florida? Sir, I am ashamed to pursue this line of remark. I dislike it, I have an utter disgust for it. I would rather hear of natural blasts and mildews, war, pestilence, and famine, than to hear gentlemen talk of secession. To break up this great government! to dismember this glorious country! to astonish Europe with an act of folly such as Europe for two centuries has never beheld in any government or any people! No, Sir! no, Sir! There will be no secession! Gentlemen are not serious when they talk of secession.

Sir, I hear there is to be a convention held at Nashville. I am bound to believe that, if worthy gentlemen meet at Nashville in convention, their object will be to adopt conciliatory counsels; to advise the South to forbearance and moderation, and to advise the North to forbearance and moderation; and to inculcate principles of brotherly love and affection, and attachment to the Constitution of the country as it now is. I believe, if the convention meet at all, it will be for this purpose; for certainly, if they meet for any purpose hostile to the Union, they have been singularly inappropirate in their selection of a place. I remember, Sir, that, when the treaty of Amiens was concluded between France and England, a sturdy Englishman and a distinguished orator, who regarded the conditions of the peace as ignominious to England, said in the House of Commons, that, if King William could know the terms of that treaty, he would turn in his coffin! Let me commend this saying of Mr. Windham, in all its emphasis and in all its force, to any persons who shall meet at Nashville for the purpose of concerting measures for the overthrow of this Union over the bones of Andrew Jackson!

Sir, I wish now to make two remarks, and hasten to a conclusion. I wish to say, in regard to Texas, that if it should be hereafter, at any time, the pleasure of the government of Texas to cede to the United States a portion, larger or smaller, of her territory which lies adjacent to New Mexico, and north of 36°30′ of north latitude, to be formed into free States, for a fair equivalent in money or in the payment of her deubt, I think it an object well worthy the consideration of Congress, and I shall be happy to concur in it myself, if I should have a connection with the government at that time.

I have one other remark to make. In my observations upon slavery as it has existed in this country, and as it now exists, I have expressed no opinion of the mode of its extinguishment or melioration. I will say, however, though I have nothing to propose, because I do not deem myself so competent as other gentlemen to take any lead on this subject, that if any gentleman from the South shall propose a scheme, to be carried on by this government upon a large scale, for the transportation of free colored people to any colony or any place in the world, I should be quite disposed to incur almost any degree of expense to accomplish that object. Nay, Sir, following an example set more than twenty years ago by a great man, then a Senator from New York, I would return to Virginia, and through her to the whole South, the money received from the lands and territories ceded by her to this government, for any such purpose as to remove, in whole or in part, or in any way to diminish or deal beneficially with, the free colored population of the Southern States. I have said that I honor Virginia for her cession of this territory. There have been received into the treasury of the United States eighty millions of dollars, the proceeds of the sales of the public lands ceded by her. If the residue should be sold at the same rate, the whole aggregate will exceed two hundred millions of dollars. If Virginia and the South see fit to adopt any proposition to relieve themselves from the free people of color among them, or such as may be made free, they have my full consent that the government sall pay them any sum of money out of the proceeds of that cession which may be adequate to the purpose.

And now, Mr. President, I draw these observations to a close. I have spoken freely, and I meant to do so. I have sought to

make no display. I have sought to enliven the occasion by no
animated discussion, nor have I attempted any train of elaborate
argument. I have wished only to speak my sentiments, fully and
at length, being desirous, once and for all, to let the Senate
know, and to let the country know, the opinions and sentiments
which I entertain on all these subjects. These opinions are not
likely to be suddenly changed. If there be any future service
that I can render to the country, consistently with these sentiments and opinions, I shall cheerfully render it. If there be not,
I shall still be glad to have had an opportunity to disburden
myself from the bottom of my heart, and to make known every
political sentiment that therein exists.

And now, Mr. President, instead of speaking of the possibility
or utility of secession, instead of dwelling in those caverns of
darkness, instead of groping with those ideas so full of all that
is horrid and horrible, let us come out into the light of day; let
us enjoy the fresh air of Liberty and Union; let us cherish those
hopes which belong to us; let us devote ourselves to those great
objects that are fit for our consideration and our action; let us
raise our conceptions to the magnitude and the importance of
the duties that devolve upon us; let our comprehension be as
broad as the country for which we act, our aspirations as high as
its certain destiny; let us not be pigmies in a case that calls for
men. Never did there devolve on any generation of men higher
trusts than now devolve upon us, for the preservation of this
Constitution and the harmony and peace of all who are destined
to live under it. Let us make our generation one of the strongest
and brightest links in that golden chain which is destined, I
fondly believe, to grapple the people of all the States to this
Constitution for ages to come. We have a great, popular, constitutional government, guarded by law and by judicature, and
defended by the affections of the whole people. No monarchical
throne presses these States together, no iron chain of military
power encircles them; they live and stand under a government
popular in its form, representative in its character, founded upon
principles of equality, and so constructed, we hope, as to last for
ever. In all its history it has been beneficent; it has trodden
down no man's liberty; it has crushed no State. Its daily respiration is liberty and patriotism; its yet youthful veins are full of

enterprise, courage, and honorable love of glory and renown. Large before, the country has now, by recent events, become vastly larger. This republic now extends, with a vast breadth, across the whole continent. The two great seas of the world wash the one and the other shore. We realize, on a mighty scale, the beautiful description of the ornamental border of the buckler of Achilles:—

> Now, the broad shield complete, the artist crowned
> With his last hand, and poured the ocean round;
> In living silver seemed the waves to roll,
> And beat the buckler's verge, and bound the whole.